ADORNO *en* AMÉRICA

ADORNO *in* AMERICA

DAVID JENEMANN

 University of Minnesota Press
Minneapolis
London

The University of Minnesota Press is grateful for permission to include
materials from the following sources in this book: in chapters 1 and 2, from
Central Files, 1891–1971, box 549/7–8, University Archives and
Columbiana Library, Columbia University (including materials from Paul F.
Lazarsfeld Papers); in chapters 1 and 2, American Jewish Committee
Archives; in chapters 1, 2, and 3, from Rockefeller Archive Center; and
in chapters 2 and 3 and the Coda, from the Theodor W. Adorno Archiv and
the Horkheimer/Pollock Archiv, Frankfurt am Main, Germany.

B
3199
.A34
J46
2007

Published by the University of Minnesota Press
111 Third Avenue South, Suite 290
Minneapolis, MN 55401-2520
http://www.upress.umn.edu

Library of Congress Cataloging-in-Publication Data

Jenemann, David, 1971–
    Adorno in America / David Jenemann.
        p. cm.
    Includes bibliographical references and index.
    ISBN 978-0-8166-4808-5 (hc : alk. paper) — ISBN 978-0-8166-4809-2
(pb : alk. paper)
    1. Adorno, Theodor W., 1903–1969. 2. Popular culture—United
States. 3. Germany—Intellectual life—20th century. I. Title.
    B3199.A34J46 2007
    193—dc22

                                            2006034691

Printed in the United States of America on acid-free paper

The University of Minnesota is an equal-opportunity educator and
employer.

12 11 10 09 08 07   10 9 8 7 6 5 4 3 2 1

CONTENTS

ACKNOWLEDGMENTS

In *Minima Moralia*, Adorno writes, "To say 'we' and mean 'I' is one of the most recondite insults." Elsewhere in the book he also claims, "In many people it is already an impertinence to say 'I.'" It strikes me that an author is uncomfortably situated between these two statements. While it feels presumptuous, and perhaps even underhanded, to implicate others in the possible failings of a work, it is no less hubristic and ungracious to suggest that one did it alone. I would like to express my deepest thanks to all those who lent their advice and support to the production of this manuscript without unduly besmirching their otherwise impeccable reputations.

Since so much of this project involved ferreting out little-seen archival sources, I should first say thank you to all the librarians and archivists who helped me hunt for the material cited in this book. The Interlibrary Loan staffs at the University of Minnesota and the University of Vermont were indefatigable in pursuing textual clues and rare documents, and I was often astonished by their ability to obtain even the most obscure book or pamphlet. The staffs of the various archives I visited and telephoned were also unfailingly helpful and kind; in particular, I mention Gunnar Berg and Fruma Morer at YIVO and Charlotte Bonnelli at the American Jewish Committee. Jochen Stollberg at the Max Horkheimer-Archiv in Frankfurt was a marvelous host, and I will always be grateful for his afternoon coffees and endless patience with my requests. Henri Lonitz of the Theodor W. Adorno Archiv sent me some encouraging words and graciously allowed me to read an advance copy of the final volume of Adorno's and Horkheimer's letters. One final librarian deserves special thanks: my sister, Laura Jenemann, helped me negotiate the wheres and hows of archival research, and her counsel and moral support are lovingly acknowledged.

Adorno in America began as my Ph.D. dissertation at the University of Minnesota, where I was a student in the Comparative Studies in Discourse and Society Program. The interdisciplinary methods I absorbed in the program inform this book, as does the rigorous and kind training I received from such scholars as Paula Rabinowitz, Jochen Schulte-Sasse, John Mowitt, Tom Pepper, Cesare Casarino, and Robin Brown. I can only hope that this book stands as evidence of the time and care they extended to my education—and my deep gratitude for their efforts. Likewise, numerous peers and friends at Minnesota helped me shepherd this book into existence; among these, Malcolm Potek, Gauti Sigthorsson, Cecily Marcus, and Brynnar Swenson deserve special thanks.

At the University of Vermont, my colleagues in the English Department and the Program in Film and Television Studies have been extremely supportive. Sarah Nilsen, Hilary Neroni, and Todd McGowan each read chapters of the manuscript, and their criticisms and suggestions—as well as their friendship—have much enhanced the final product. Val Rohy and Greg Bottoms have likewise been good friends and exceptionally sage about the process of writing, and their ideas have found their way into the book. Also at the University of Vermont, I had the good fortune to have Elizabeth Waysek for a research assistant. Elizabeth was a great sport and a diligent aid in tidying up permissions and tracking down sources, and her knowledge of German was an added—and much appreciated— boon. The director of the Humanities Center, Robyn Warhol, also deserves thanks for sending me to the 2005 English Institute at Harvard University, where one of the themes was Adorno. There were many and varied productive discussions at the English Institute, and not a few of them have informed this book.

Robert Hullot-Kentor's advice and encouragement have been invaluable; further, his generosity with the manuscript of Adorno's *Current of Music* was an unforeseen and immeasurable boon. I feel quite lucky to have had the pleasure of getting to know him during the writing of this book.

I have also been fortunate to receive the comments of Max Pensky, who read the manuscript twice, each time offering ideas that helped me develop this project in exciting and unanticipated ways. One of Professor Pensky's wiser counsels was that choosing a book title is like dressing one's children. Books squirm and fidget as you try to slip a title over their heads, and if an author chooses a title poorly, the book winds up looking mismatched and sloppy. As I allude in the introduction, this book tried on a number of titles, including "Transmissions," "Where Anything Could Be Possible," and even "Snug, New-Fangled, Sky-Rocket," but while none of those looked quite right, they all shared the subtitle "Adorno in America, 1938–1953." By the time my editors and I had decided to drop the dates in favor of the simplicity of "Adorno in America," I had lazily forgotten that I was dressing my child in borrowed clothes. "Adorno in America" is the title of an essay by Martin Jay. I have never met Professor Jay, but he is the reason why I—and many Americans—can and do read Adorno today. I hope, therefore, that he not only can forgive my larceny but will also accept this book as a gesture of respect for the profound influence he has had on its creation.

My editors at the University of Minnesota Press deserve thanks, first for championing the book's publication, and second for the expert development and aid they have provided. Richard Morrison, Heather Burns, Adam Brunner, and Laura Westlund made the thorny process of bringing a book to print almost painless, and it has been a treat to work with such a thoughtful, thorough team. Likewise, the book's copy editor, Kathy Delfosse, was both rigorous and graceful, and each of her queries and suggested changes has markedly improved this text.

No worthwhile idea develops without cultivation from one's friends, and two friends in particular have seen this book grow from the germ of an idea to what it is now. Without their aid, guidance, and sometimes goading, this book would be severely impoverished. My teacher and mentor Richard Leppert first taught me Adorno, and he continues to teach me what it means to be a responsible scholar and writer. At each stage of this book's development, he has been its—and my—most steadfast supporter, and I am extraordinarily fortunate to have had him in my corner. Likewise, my friend Andrew Knighton was a sounding board for most of the ideas contained here, and I count on him to deflate my wildest pretensions while at the same time encouraging me to strive for something exceptional. To the extent that this book succeeds, much of the credit lies with Richard and Andrew, and I can scarcely express how much I value their friendship.

I would be especially remiss if I didn't acknowledge how much I value the love and support of my parents, Michael and Donna Jenemann.

Finally, *Adorno in America* would not be possible in any way without the support of my wife, Lisa Brighenti, and our children, Isaac, Anna, and Luke. I dedicate this book to them, with all my love.

INTRODUCTION: DREAMS IN AMERICA

As Martin Jay wrote, now more than two decades ago, "The exemplary anecdotes are known to us all":

> [Theodor] Adorno arrives in America in 1938 to work on Paul Lazarsfeld's Princeton Radio Research Project. . . . A decade later, the *Institut für Sozialforschung* is invited back to Frankfurt, and Adorno, with no hesitation, joins Max Horkheimer and Friedrich Pollock in its reconstruction. . . . he leaves his exile home for good in 1953 and never looks back.[1]

The years since those lines were written have done little to alter those anecdotes or their inevitable outcome; the narrative of emigration, alienation, and return is ineluctable and irrefutable. The tale of Adorno's disorientation in the United States, his dismay at his reception, and his disgust with the products of American culture is so often cited that it has become a litany—and sometimes a dirge—for the embattled existence of the European intellectual in America. Still, a curious episode from that exiled time might yet help us to better understand the import of those years.

In April 1941, Max Horkheimer and his wife, Maidon, drove through the American Southwest on their way to their new home in Southern California.

Horkheimer, then director of the Institute of Social Research, the exiled Frankfurt scholars who had found a wartime home at Columbia University, was relocating to the West because of his poor health. Day-to-day administration of the Institute's New York office and its various research projects had been left in the hands of Horkheimer's assistant director, Friedrich Pollock. In Carlsbad, New Mexico, Horkheimer stopped his gray 1941 Buick Century and sent a telegram to Pollock, which read:

> AGREE NEUMANN IF NO HARM TO PROJECT THROUGH ACKNOWLEDGMENT OF MY
> ABSENCE. INSTRUCTION—FAVEZ SHOULD BE WORDED VERY CAREFULLY TO AVOID
> MISUNDERSTANDING BY BERN OFFICES. SUGGEST CABLE ASKING WHETHER FAVEZ
> PROCURED MEDICAL CERTIFICATE AND WHETHER REGARDING SITUATION SHE
> THINKS APPLICATION ADVISABLE. PLEASE TELL ME LOWENTHALLS PROPOSITION.
> SEND LETTERS AND SILVERPERLS TO LASZLO. CONSULT TEDDIE AND OTHERS WHAT
> CAN POSSIBLY BE DONE TO BACK PROJECT FURTHER. DID YOU GIVE MEMORANDUM
> TO UACIVER SHALL WIRE NEXT TELEGRAM ADDRESS TOMORROW.
>   ALRIGHT[2]

The telegram is mundane and innocuous. It deals with the nascent Studies in Prejudice project, which was to occupy the Institute's time and resources for many of its American years, and result, most famously, in the influential book on conformity and domination *The Authoritarian Personality*. The message also hints at the business of visa applications, a nigglesome bureaucratic headache that was nonetheless part of the exile community's daily existence as friends and colleagues tried to make their way out of war-torn Europe.[3]

Indeed, Horkheimer's telegram would merit no special mention were it not for the fact that someone, perhaps the Western Union clerk, found Horkheimer's activity and demeanor—or maybe just his German accent—suspicious and forwarded the telegram to the FBI. There, it joined hundreds of other documents concerning Horkheimer, his colleagues, and the Institute as part of the FBI's ongoing and pervasive investigations into potentially "subversive" activities on the part of "enemy aliens." The telegram was subjected to cryptographic analysis in an attempt to piece together any possible code it might contain. Horkheimer, who closed many of his correspondences to Pollock with the affirmative "Alright," was given that name as an alias, as well as the name "Harkheimer," a misspelling courtesy of Western Union. FBI agents tracked the Horkheimers across the country, interviewing hotel clerks along their route. Horkheimer's driver was followed. The car registration was traced to Pollock. The proceedings of the investigation and all subsequent correspondence were filed under the heading "Internal Security."

Altogether, the investigative activities spurred by Horkheimer's telegram lasted three months, until J. Edgar Hoover himself sent a letter to the special agent in charge of the case in El Paso, Texas. From what we now know about the FBI director, it is perhaps not surprising that he was so intimately familiar with the field office's ongoing investigations. What is surprising, however, is Hoover's knowledge of the Institute. His letter provides a detailed and well-informed description of Horkheimer (with correct spelling), the Institute and its members, and their history, sources of funding, and projects. In a regal passive voice, Hoover concludes the letter with a summary evaluation of the case:

> The telegram forwarded by your office contains several words that could possibly be code. However, it is suggested that these words in most instances at least are the names of other German Jewish refugees. . . . It is believed that the telegram in its entirety referred to legitimate transactions of the above Institute, or projects in which the Institute is interested, and accordingly it is not desired that any additional investigation be conducted.[4]

Despite Hoover's recommendation, this was not to be the last time that a telegram—either from or regarding Horkheimer—set off a flurry of activity regarding the Institute.[5] Nor, as their voluminous FBI files attest, were members of the Institute ever free from a certain degree of surveillance during their stay in the United States. But while the extensive investigation into the activities of the so-called Frankfurt School forms a fascinating part of their years in the United States,[6] another element of the telegram episode merits attention. The garbling and misreading of the telegram represents in microcosm one of the fundamental interests of the Institute while in America: the problems posed by new and burgeoning communications technologies, and the way their mutilated messages were used in administered society.

What the FBI's obsession with the trivial elements of Horkheimer's message illustrates is how the electronic transmission of information can, at the hands of state interests, transform subjects and deprive them of their identity and specificity, Hoover's admonition to cease operations notwithstanding. This transformation potentially takes place at every level of the communication. From sender to transmitter to receiver, the electronic message is fundamentally malleable. The formal constraints of transmission itself, as in the specified, economized language of telegrams, are often to blame; but this mutability conveys with it the notion that the subject communicated over the wires and through the ether might also be a source of misinformation, a potential saboteur. Through the telegram, Horkheimer goes from being a "professor" to a "spy," the Western Union official changes from "clerk" to "informant," and Pollock is no longer a "colleague" but an "accomplice." All these identities are ultimately arbitrated by the state in the form of the FBI and the person of J. Edgar Hoover. As the investigation into "Alright's" activities tacitly acknowledges, the meanings of electronic messages were often determined outside the purview of the sender and recipient. The capacity to "read" messages was not, as it were, *lost* in transmission, but regulated. Hoover's letter reveals that such oversight and interpretation was not part of a grand conspiracy but was, rather, the day-to-day life of refugees and citizens alike in 1940s America. Hoover and his agents would decide what a message meant, or perhaps decide when a meaning was impenetrable. Even when a message was innocuous, it still might be code.

Horkheimer's telegram episode, while all too characteristic of the FBI's tactics during the period (and perhaps today), is an isolated incident. One sender and one (intended) receiver are involved, and an administrative authority intervenes in the process. Writ large across systems of mass communication, however, this incident illustrates the problems of how meaning is transmitted, who determines those meanings, how and why those meanings were organized, and, ultimately, what meanings survived transmission—problems that were of primary concern for Horkheimer and his colleagues. Anxiety over these issues was particularly acute in America, where the various mass-communications media were cataclysmically and irrevocably transforming the subject's capacity to send and receive information. Older forms of expression such as the symphony and the novel were, at the hands of the radio, movies, and television, being altered at a formal level. For a European exile, forced to "pass through" America and gamely attempt to maintain his identity, there was no doubt an uncomfortable resonance between his own situation and that of European artworks rearranged for radio broadcasts or adapted for the movies. Not coincidentally, the exile for whom these issues were to be perhaps the most pressing appears as one of the "coded" names in Horkheimer's telegram: "Teddie"—Theodor Wiesengrund Adorno.

This book is a study of the collision between German intellectual history, as embodied by Adorno, and the American popular culture he wrote about, analyzed, and wrestled with during his exile years in the United States (1938–1953).[7] As my quotation from Jay indicates, this topic might seem surprisingly dated. In the wake of Adorno's centenary,[8] there is a veritable cottage industry of Adorno scholarship. Not only have three separate biographies recently appeared, timed to coincide with Adorno's hundredth birthday, but Suhrkamp, Adorno's publisher, is also rapidly releasing Adorno's *Nachgelassene Schriften*, which will run to thirty-five printed volumes. There is clearly much that Adorno scholars have yet to chew on, but there is so much that has already been digested. Despite how relatively unknown Adorno was in the United States when he died in 1969, since the early 1970s, when two books, Fredric Jameson's *Marxism and Form* and Jay's *The Dialectical Imagination*, reintroduced Adorno to America, Adorno's star has been on the rise.[9] Today, there are literally thousands of essays and hundreds of books about Adorno on subjects ranging from Adorno's critique of jazz to his value to Foucault scholars to his usefulness as a *proponent* of fundamentalist Christian radio practices.[10] And for every one of those texts, there is probably at least one revisitation of the so-called Adorno–Benjamin debates. Indeed, the fortunes of the two men, Adorno and Walter Benjamin, seem perpetually intertwined, and the interest spurred by the recently completed publication of Benjamin's collected works has likewise helped generate a demand for more Adorno scholarship and revised translations of long-available texts.

As could be expected, much of the scholarship concerning Adorno deals with his encounter with what he famously called "the culture industry." Whether pro- or contra-Adorno, these efforts tend to confirm the horror Adorno felt when faced with the products of the mass media and of America in general. However, what nearly all these texts fail to consider is that for nearly fifteen years, Adorno lived in America, and became, for very nearly a decade, an American citizen.[11] During this period Adorno immersed himself fully in American culture, while at the same time struggling to maintain his German identity, both by continuing to write in German and through his commitment to dialectical thought.[12]

The first part of the preceding sentence deserves some attention. Although scholars are increasingly reassessing Adorno's relationship to America and popular culture, for a long time the overriding impression of Adorno has been that of the anti-American intellectual elitist. This opinion dates back almost to the American exile period itself, when a number of defenders of the mass media singled out the Frankfurt School as representatives of a dangerous Marxist-influenced effort to undermine U.S. culture.

As the sociologist Edward Shils wrote of the Institute of Social Research members in an essay typical of the criticism heaped on Adorno as well as of a certain scholarly red-baiting, elitism and anti-Americanism were essentially one and the same. "Their anti-capitalistic and, by multiplication, anti-American attitude," he claimed, "found a traumatic and seemingly ineluctable confirmation in the popular culture of the United States."[13] Shils may represent an extreme case, but his arguments reflect the views of generations of scholars who, citing Adorno's negative pronouncements on jazz, Donald Duck, and Mickey Rooney, willingly accept the notion that Adorno had little sensitivity for his exile home.

To be fair, Adorno himself doesn't help matters much. There are no end of authors who cite the radio speech in which Adorno claimed, in pointed reference to Martin Heidegger (who stayed in Germany as a member of the Nazi Party), that "it is hardly an exaggeration to claim that every consciousness today that has not appropriated the American experience, even if with resistance, has something reactionary to it."[14] This statement, perhaps more than any other, seems to confirm the widely held suspicions regarding Adorno's intellectual and political anti-Americanism. But very few of those who deploy this statement do so as Adorno himself would—dialectically. Most scholars tend to read Adorno as valorizing what he calls "reactionary consciousness." The argument runs like this: In the face of the administration of life at every level, the only recourse for the individual is to stand firm against identification with the social system and the colonization of the intellect. The only righteous position would hence be disengagement from that system. Even for Adorno's defenders, therefore, the resulting picture of Adorno tends to be that of the aloof, intellectual purist, scornful of the detritus of kitsch and nostalgic for a utopian community of aesthetic "experts" that never existed in the first place. This image of Adorno derives, in part, from those same authors who helped resurrect him in the 1970s, Jay and Jameson. In Jay's description, Adorno was a "mandarin cultural conservative" who displayed a "visceral distaste for mass culture" and who "found no successful way to link his theory with the politics of the proletariat or any other radical social force."[15] Jay's argument, not surprisingly, depends on a reading of Adorno's later essays, such as "Commitment" and "Resignation," as well as on Adorno's consideration of art's place in society in *Aesthetic Theory*. In "Commitment," for example, Adorno famously writes that "art is not a matter of pointing up alternatives, but rather of resisting, solely through artistic form, the course of the world which continues to hold a pistol to the heads of human beings."[16] While such statements reflect Adorno's ongoing debate with such "committed" artists as Bertolt Brecht and Jean-Paul Sartre, as well as his suspicions regarding any political praxis that would require of the individual identification with a system—any system—no matter how seemingly progressive, the intimation that art's job was to hold the world at bay also tends to render Adorno liable to charges of "intellectual narcissism and self-indulgence."[17]

For Jameson's part, it is Adorno's language, notoriously difficult and off-putting, that sets him apart from the masses. Anyone who wants to appreciate Adorno must rise to his level in order to read him; one cannot expect Adorno to condescend to one's tastes:

> In the language of Adorno—perhaps the finest dialectical intelligence, the finest stylist, of them all—density is itself a conduct of intransigence: the bristling mass of abstractions and cross-references is precisely intended to be read in situation, against the cheap facility of what surrounds it, as a warning to the reader of the price he has to pay for genuine thinking.[18]

Taken at face value, Jameson's and—especially—Jay's statements merit some reconsideration. At the level of politics, Adorno's well-known dedication to the powers of resignation and autonomy today suggest an unlikely intellectual affinity with the radical reenvisioning of the proletariat by the followers of the Italian *autonomia* movement (whose intellectual heirs include Antonio Negri, Paolo Virno, and Giorgio Agamben). Both camps offer dedicated refusals of the subject's identification with systems and concepts, and both powerfully invoke "negation" as the only legitimate form of identity. This shared interest hints at a reading of Adorno that may yet indeed have something to contribute to the idea of a "radical social force."[19] But to simply accept the image of Adorno as an intellectual loner, no matter how noble or romantic the portrayal of that elitism (and I do not necessarily want to suggest that on the whole Jay and Jameson are guilty of this), is to miss the ways Adorno also sees "reactionary consciousness" as a deficient mode of experience. To dismiss Adorno as politically and socially detached is also to misunderstand how thoroughly he immersed himself in America's myriad forms of entertainment and communication. Despite Adorno's genuine horror at many elements of the culture industry, during his stay in the United States he nonetheless dedicated himself to its study from top to bottom, learning the principles of broadcasting, production, and transmission as well as the economic and technological conditions under which mass-culture texts were consumed.

While a number of recent books have attempted to bring Adorno to bear on contemporary popular culture, thus arguing for his relevance to readers today,[20] this book makes the case that it is in rediscovering Adorno's actual encounter with American cultural practices during his exile that one can best understand his continuing importance. Contrary to the widely held belief, even among his defenders, that Adorno was disconnected from America and disdained its culture, I argue that Adorno comes by his criticism—no matter how biting—honestly and with sensitivity for its material conditions. No ivory-tower aesthete, Adorno was thoroughly engrossed by the day-to-day life of radio networks and studio filmmaking. For example, one of the central theoretical innovations Adorno expressed in his analysis of the radio broadcast for Paul Lazarsfeld's Rockefeller Foundation–funded Princeton Radio Research Project (PRRP) was his notion that the medium operated as a "physiognomy."[21] That is, that thing that audiences designated as "radio" was, in fact, the contradictory unity of a multifaceted cultural-industrial form that simultaneously encompassed the sites of production, performance, distribution, and reception, as well as the technical and economic preconditions of a given broadcast's transmission. The radio therefore was a chimerical body that must be understood as a complex dialectical process. Asked to do "administrative" social research on the likes and dislikes of radio listeners, Adorno argued instead that audience responses cannot be objectively distinguished from the realities of industrial capital, marketing, song plugging, and the star system; nor can the sound engineering of a symphony be considered apart from the development of the radio mechanism, the evolution of small, private listening spaces, and the demands of broadcast advertising. These factors, which mediate and transform the listening experience, render the question of liking or disliking a given piece of music over the radio overly simplistic at best, dangerously shortsighted at worst. Such a holistic approach as the one Adorno took to this and other forms of the mass media is hardly a simply reactionary one. Rather, it is an intellectual strategy that delves deeply into the real preconditions and practices of the culture industry. But the thorniness of Adorno's intellectual methodology was precisely not what many of Adorno's new colleagues, committed to the fact-oriented, empirical methodologies of sociological research, had in mind. What good was a dialectically mutating radio physiognomy to a researcher—and a radio network—interested in the most basic answer to the question "Who listens to what programs, and why?" If anything, Adorno's interest in and knowledge of America, by virtue of his hunger to understand all the intricate inner workings of the mass media, often outstripped those of the native "experts" with whom he was unfavorably compared.

Part of what this book attempts to recover, then, is a sense of just how catholic and penetrating Adorno's interests were, and how extensive his encounter with mass culture was, at every stage of production and consumption. Until recently, much of Adorno's research into the intricate material practices of the culture industry has remained unknown, unpublished, or simply ignored. While Adorno's published output during the exile years was impressive, there are perhaps an equal number of projects that were consigned to obscurity. Some were scrapped for financial reasons, as in the case of the dense, intricate, and monumental *Current of Music: Elements of the Radio Theory;* some work was done in obscurity, under a necessary sentence of anonymity, as was the case with Adorno's collaboration with Thomas Mann on the musical elements of *Doctor Faustus;* and finally, some undertakings simply disappeared, as did an abortive film project Adorno and Horkheimer developed for the Studies in Prejudice project. The "exemplary anecdotes" of Adorno's American exile may be well known, but for the most part, the multiform and far-reaching implications of his intellectual activities in America have remained almost completely unexplored. It is the central premise of this book that by rescuing those less "exemplary" activities from obscurity, one can begin to reformulate the questions about just what America meant to Adorno and how important his exile experience was to a material, even sensuous, theory of modernity and mass culture.[22]

Hence, I make use of a wide range of archival materials in my effort to portray Adorno's intellectual concerns during the exile. Among these materials are numerous memos, letters, and unpublished documents that help flesh out the impetus behind Adorno's unorthodox Marxian critique of what he famously called the "culture industry."[23] Further, by virtue of his contacts with Paul Lazarsfeld and his Bureau of Applied Social Research, Adorno often had unfettered access to the internal documents of entertainment and advertising firms and hence a unique insight into the day-to-day machinations of the culture industry's administrators. Nearly all this material, so crucial to understanding Adorno's virulent response to the corporate control of the arts, has remained unexamined, not only by Adorno scholars but also by those interested in the history of the mass media. Through source leads provided in Adorno's work, I have tracked down a rich body of resources, including NBC- and CBS-produced adult-oriented "children's" books, designed to attract potential advertisers, and "educational" manuals, intended for general audiences, that tout the value of radio, television, and the movies. From these little-studied materials, one gains a deeper understanding of the stakes of Adorno's cautionary essays as well as a richer appreciation for the genuine concern he had for citizens caught in the networks' grasps. Just as the episode with Horkheimer's telegram reveals the extent to which the exiles were subjected to FBI surveillance, the network documents illustrate a concerted effort by media corporations to monitor and influence every aspect of individuals' lives. These marketing materials suggest that the manipulation of audiences by media agencies was far more calculating than even Adorno claims. As the midcentury poet and novelist Kenneth Fearing describes publishing industry attitudes in his thriller *The Big Clock,* the functionaries of a *Time* magazine–like enterprise were well aware of the control they exercised and were equally well aware of the rules of the culture industry:

> What we decided in this room, more than a million of our fellow-citizens would read three months from now, and what they read they would accept as final. They might not know they were doing so, they might even briefly dispute our decisions, but still they would follow the reasoning we presented, remember the phrases, the tone of authority, and in the end their crystallized judgments would be ours.[24]

Fearing's assessment of the New York publishing world rings true with Adorno's observations of the culture industry at the ground level and corresponds with the overall tone of "authority" and manipulation one sees in the publicity material that helped mold Adorno's opinions.

It is not coincidental that the rapidly increasing degree of marketing surveillance in the period mirrors the extensive government monitoring that Adorno and his fellow "enemy aliens" endured. Like Horkheimer and many of the other exiled Jewish intellectuals, Adorno also attracted the attention of the FBI and the State Department. Through the Freedom of Information Privacy Act, I have obtained Adorno's files as well as those of his colleagues, and I incorporate their contents into my study. These documents provide an invaluable record of the political landscape and the aura of suspicion under which émigré scholars had to work, and they also suggest a burgeoning culture of surveillance in which the networks, studios, and publishers also participated. Considered together, these various unpublished materials provide the crucial historical context not only for the formation of Adorno's aesthetic theories and political consciousness but also for the history of the American mass media and their effect on post-war consciousness generally.

As the mass of newly published and soon-to-be published material illustrates, despite the disruptions of exile—indeed, perhaps because of them—the years Adorno spent in New York and California were particularly fertile ones, and ones that had marked effects on his postexile years. As he insisted years after his repatriation to Germany, "I believe 90 percent of all that I've published in Germany was written in America."[25] And, *pace* Jameson, the influence of America reaches down into Adorno's language itself; his later works are peppered with English words and Americanisms, and it is clear from Adorno's letters that he was fascinated by this language that he nonetheless found utterly discomfiting. In Horkheimer's papers, for example, there appears a long list of English words and phrases that Adorno was assiduously compiling that included such entries as "new-fangled," "sky-rocket," "snug," and "a check to which there were no strings attached."[26] Further, Adorno was hardly as removed from culture-industry productions as we might suspect. Not only did he learn the technological and economic procedures of radios, movies, and television from the ground up, but he also indulged in a bit of media stardom himself. As Stefan Müller-Doohm writes in his recent biography of Adorno, in February 1940, "he made his debut on American radio. When Eduard Steuermann and the Kollisch Quartet presented works by Schoenberg, Zemlinsky, Eisler and Krenek, Adorno took part by delivering an introductory talk."[27] And after Adorno returned to Germany, he became even more of a media figure, appearing on televised interview programs and delivering frequent radio lectures, some of which, including "On the Question: What Is German?" and "Scientific Experiences of a European Scholar in America," have been published in the collection *Critical Models: Interventions and Catchwords*. That Adorno essentially enjoyed and capitalized on his influence as a media celebrity in Germany during the years following his exile is the focus of a massive work by Alex Demirovic.[28] This revised impression of Adorno's relationship to media practices is slowly percolating among Adorno scholars both in Europe and in America, but until recently few readers of Adorno acknowledged the influence of exile on Adorno's thought or focused directly on the intellectual and cultural milieu into which Adorno was thrust during the 1930s and '40s. Still fewer considered the fact that the techniques and technologies of mass culture were as important to Adorno's work as were the cultural products themselves.[29] Instead of addressing how the American entertainment industry influenced Adorno's critique of modernity and the rise of a global "pseudo-American" culture, given the forcefulness of his reaction to those industries, many scholars instead consign him to a retrogressive position that Adorno himself disdained.

In "Dedication" in *Minima Moralia*, Adorno writes that "he who wishes to know the truth about life in its immediacy must scrutinize its estranged form, the objective powers that determine individual existence even in its most hidden recesses."[30] This evocation of "estranged" life resonates in a number of registers, each of which is explored with dialectical rigor in *Minima Moralia*. Estrangement certainly corresponds to the historical conditions of exile and the increasing marginalization of intellectual labor and the "melancholy science" of philosophy that Adorno identified as part of his own alienation. But so too does estrangement characterize the life of subjects for whom, through various reproducible media, "life has become appearance." Nearly twenty years before Guy Debord and Marshall McLuhan would each in his own way argue that the relationship between subjects was that of spectacular and illusory mediation, Adorno would, by virtue of his own exile experiences, arrive at the same inevitable conclusion. Starting with his own wartime predicament, "that of the intellectual in emigration," Adorno proceeds in *Minima Moralia* to paint the portrait of subjects who, in the face of objective historical conditions, have ceased to be subjects at all. "What the philosophers once knew as life," Adorno laments, referring at once to his own existence and to the classical notion of the bourgeois subject, "has become the sphere of private existence and now of mere consumption, dragged along as an appendage of the process of material production, without autonomy or substance of its own. . . . Our perspective of life has passed into an ideology which conceals the fact that there is life no longer."[31]

While it would seem that such statements are leveled primarily at events in Europe, what *Minima Moralia* makes abundantly clear is that the mass-media transformations of bourgeois aesthetics are as much to blame for the liquidation of the individual as are the mass murders committed in the camps. In America, those aesthetic forms that previously spoke of an (inwardly) free individual are submitted to a type of aesthetic Taylorism that renders them efficient market tools. The result is that, translated and transmitted in the American idiom, the autonomous artwork is reduced to a function of commerce, and subjects to mere consumers. "Illuminated in the neon-light," Adorno says in the aphorism "English Spoken," "culture displays its character as advertising."[32]

Hence, this book is both about what happened to Adorno while in

America and what happens to art forms when they submit to the technological and economic demands of the culture industry. And the places Adorno
called home during his exile years, New York and Los Angeles, were not in-
cidental to his understanding of these transformations in art and the challenges facing the subject. While each of these cities had a rightful claim to
being called the capital of the twentieth century, they made this claim for
different reasons. When Adorno arrived in New York in 1938, the city was
the center of radio production, advertising, and publishing, and for him
the alienation embodied by mass broadcasts that carried multiple members of a giant audience along a single, relentless path was, in many ways,
mirrored in the landscape of sky-arching buildings full of busy workers and
subways trundling underground passengers to their destinations. And yet
while New York was a city of gleaming towers, it also was one of seething streets, very much a "mass" city, full of life. When, in the "Music in
Radio" memorandum produced for the PRRP, Adorno describes the sensation of walking out of his building and hearing the same piece of music
following him down the street from each open window, the experience is at
once dehumanizing and yet evocative of the crush of humanity. For all its
overwhelming elements, the ebb and flow of the New York populace would
have been at least recognizable to an émigré from a European metropolis.
The codes of the flaneur could still apply as one walked the streets. But in
1941, Adorno followed Horkheimer to Los Angeles, and there things were
decidedly different. For Adorno, the car culture of Los Angeles represented
an advance in alienation over the Old World and even over the island of
skyscrapers and subway tunnels in New York. A sense of isolation and
atomization is accentuated in Los Angeles by the diffusion of the population throughout the ever-expanding landscape: one car for every 1.6 Los
Angelenos in 1925—the rest of the country wouldn't reach that level of
saturation for another quarter century. Further, by 1930, 94 percent of all
dwellings were single-family homes.[33] The topos of Los Angeles cannot
be understood apart from the integration of human beings, their private,
isolated dwellings, and their mechanical means of transportation, already
reaching critical mass a decade before the majority of exiles arrive. As if
feeling this alienating union of human and machine seep into his own bones
as he tooled through the Southern California streets in a 1936 Plymouth,
in *Minima Moralia* Adorno writes, "Which driver is not tempted, merely by
the power of his engine, to wipe out the vermin of the street, pedestrians,
children and cyclists? The movements machines demand of their users
already have the violent, hard-hitting jerkiness of Fascist maltreatment."[34]

Whereas in New York Adorno had the experience of neighborhoods and bustling apartment buildings to counteract the isolation of skyscraper, in Los Angeles the division of labor in the workforce was replicated by the enclosed box on four tires and further attenuated by the loneliness of the one- or two-bedroom bungalow.

It was in just such a low-rent bungalow in Santa Monica that Adorno found himself for the better part of a decade. And while Adorno languished there, "Los Angeles (and its alter-ego, Hollywood)," as Mike Davis explains in *City of Quartz*, "becomes the archetypal site of massive and unprotesting subordination of industrialized intelligentsias to the program of capital."[35] The mechanism for this subordination was, undoubtedly, in part the movies and, ultimately, television. Hollywood gathers and scatters, consolidating the world in its visual narratives and sending those altered images back out into the world. In so doing, cinema enables capital to expand, diffusing itself to every cranny of the planet so that by the end of the twentieth century, "Los Angeles" was everywhere. This monopolization of "culture" and its subsequent redistribution to emerging global markets was to have profound effects on how subjects come into consciousness worldwide. As in New York, where he had unique access to radio stations and advertising firms, in the well-connected California exile community, Adorno was able to gain entrée to the world of Hollywood glitterati. Contrary to the accepted portrait, Adorno wasn't simply reading his horoscope and riding in his car; rather, he was witness to the developments of the motion pictures firsthand.

It is by virtue of Adorno's intense contact with the mass media that one can understand how he does resist what Davis calls the "unprotesting subordination of industrialized intelligentsias to the program of capital." And this resistance, this unwillingness to capitulate to the seductions of the culture industry, is what continues to make Adorno worth studying in an age when the seductions seem less like seductions and more like what has always been so. For the late Edward Said, it was this unwillingness to give in to America while at the same time embracing it that made Adorno one of his intellectual heroes. In his well-known essay "Reflections on Exile," Said holds up Adorno as the model of intellectual rigor in the face of the various pressures the exile feels to conform and "just go along":

> Necessarily, then, I speak of exile not as a privilege, but as an alternative to the mass institutions that dominate modern life. Exile is not, after all, a matter of choice: you are born into it, or it happens to you. But provided that the exile refuses to sit on the sidelines nursing a wound, there are

things to be learned: he or she must cultivate a scrupulous (not indulgent
or sulky) subjectivity. Perhaps the most rigorous example of such
subjectivity is to be found in the writings of Theodor Adorno. . . .
Ruthlessly opposed to what he called the "administered" world, Adorno
saw all life as pressed into ready-made forms, prefabricated "homes."
He argued that everything that one says or thinks, as well as every object
one possesses, is ultimately a mere commodity. Language is jargon,
objects are for sale. To refuse this state of affairs is the exile's intellectual
mission. Adorno's reflections are informed by the belief that the only
home truly available now, though fragile and vulnerable, is in writing.
Elsewhere, "the house is the past. . . ." In short, Adorno says with
grave irony, "it is part of morality not to be at home in one's home."
To follow Adorno is to stand away from "home" in order to look at it with
the exile's detachment. For there is considerable merit in the practice of
noting the discrepancies between various concepts and ideas and what
they actually produce. We take home and language for granted; they
become nature, and the underlying assumptions recede into dogma
and orthodoxy.[36]

Following Said's line of reasoning, "not to be at home in one's home" becomes, for Adorno, not merely the unfortunate fact of an exile's historical
circumstances but also an ethical imperative to be carried along even should
a return from exile be offered. Thus, Adorno both embraces America *and*
holds it at arm's length. To be an American while criticizing America and
to be a European while exiled from Europe, that was the lot Adorno drew
for himself when coming to this country.

The combined sense of ambivalence and foreboding that Adorno felt
about embattled European experience and the way America threatened to
take over everything that makes that intellectual experience unique is palpable in a curious text Adorno sent to Horkheimer at some point in 1942.
Entitled "Träume in Amerika: Drei Protokole" (Dreams in America: Three
Protocols), this three-page manuscript contained Adorno's recollections of
three dreams from his first few years in the United States and was ultimately published in *Aufbau,* a journal of writings by exiled Germans. The
horror that links each of the dreams is the sense that some recognizable
European icon is being tainted, transformed by its contact with America.
Thus, in one dream, the title character of Charles Baudelaire's "Don Juan
in Hell" becomes a mixture of ham actor and demagogue, and instead of
silently floating into the afterworld, he mouths platitudes about freedom
and individuality while sailing on a riverboat at an American folk festival.
In another dream, Hamburg has been transformed into a secret base for

Franklin D. Roosevelt, and the grand port city, traditional center of German commerce, threatens to become a staging ground for the pro-Hitler president of General Motors, William S. Knudsen. In the third, the paths near Amorbach, where Adorno spent his holidays as a boy, morph into a road on the West Coast. In each instance, the chimerical offspring of Europe and America is something monstrous, but that monstrosity is the price exiles pay for their contact with the America to which they have fled. They are saved by America and yet destroyed by its entertainment, its commodities, its "snug, new-fangled, sky-rockets." Perhaps Adorno's fear of this hybridity is most clearly allegorized by the dream set in Hamburg, which ends with Adorno trapped in the basement of Roosevelt's headquarters, unable to make it back to the ground floor, and surrounded by crocodiles that "had the heads of extraordinarily beautiful women." What one of the crocodile women tells Adorno could stand as a motto for the whole exile experience, the seductions of American culture and the threat of total incorporation: "She told me that it didn't hurt to be devoured. To make it easier for me she promised me first the most wonderful things."[37] It is perhaps no wonder that these were the dream protocols that Adorno decided to send to Horkheimer for publication in an exile journal. In Adorno's dreams, as in America itself, there wasn't a check for which there were no strings attached.

The assimilation and possible subordination of the European experience to its American counterpart clearly weighed upon Adorno and informed much of his exile work. His analysis of Aldous Huxley's *Brave New World*, for example, becomes a meditation on the challenges faced by the intellectual in emigration. Written in America, yet not published until after Adorno's return to Germany, the essay "Aldous Huxley and Utopia" finds Adorno looking to his fellow exile for a fading glimmer of hope that there is some escape from the type of capitulation American mass culture demands:

> In place of the wilderness which the pioneer intended to open up
> spiritually as well as materially and through which he was to accomplish
> his spiritual regeneration, there has arisen a civilization which absorbs all
> of life in its system, without allowing the unregimented mind even those
> loopholes which European laxness left open into the epoch of the great
> business concerns. It is made unmistakably clear to the intellectual from
> abroad that he will have to eradicate himself as an autonomous being if he
> hopes to achieve anything or be accepted as an employee of the super-trust
> into which life has condensed.[38]

For an American reader, particularly one who has had the luxury of not feeling the sting of exile, this inability to "stand away from 'home'" often makes Adorno very difficult to read and tends to result in the charges of elitism when it comes to American culture. Nonetheless, I would suggest that it is precisely the challenge Adorno lays out in his alienating prose that holds up exile as an—perhaps *the*—ethical position from which to approach American life, and it is this challenge that American readers of Adorno might productively embrace. Adorno points toward a possibility of recognizing the way the culture of movies, radio, magazines, television, newspapers, billboards, fast food—the culture of illusions and fantasy and dreams that for Americans so resolutely and comfortably feels like home— is also that which alienates us, severs us from our intellectual existence, threatens to devour us. What we consider "home" is really no home at all, and that is the very definition of the *Unheimlich*, the uncanny. This is why Adorno's American dreams are so resonant, because they suggest the dread that the increasing homogenization of the world undertaken by American mass culture results in a situation whereby everywhere feels just like home, but none of those places is home itself.

It could well be said that Adorno's project, far from being an elitist one, points toward a future where each person shares in a form of subjective exile. By saying this, though, I by no means want to diminish or ignore the objective political and economic circumstances that led Adorno and his colleagues to seek refuge in this country in the 1930s. Rather, I would offer that what Adorno brought—and still brings—to this country is a deep commitment to addressing the ways each of us share in the dislocations of the modern world. His is therefore a fundamentally generous critique that seeks to return to each person some sense of what is lost in commodity culture.

As Said writes, in yet another paean, Adorno extends readers the courtesy of gesturing toward a future where everyone is brought together by their alienation. What binds them is not some program for political praxis; it is the ethics of being away from home:

> It might be possible to say that the aim of some forms of criticism is to exemplify, do, embody a certain kind of activity without in the least attempting to produce effects of disciplehood or doctrine in the reader. Quite clearly, Adorno's work is the most extreme form of this combination of distance and performance that we have; like Proust he points to things, but he does so in the modes afforded him by negative dialectics, obsessively and, it seems, untiringly. Yet he cannot be paraphrased nor,

in a sense, can he be transmitted: the notion of an Adorno *fils* is quite laughable.[39]

I take very seriously Said's claim that Adorno cannot be followed, as though his writing were a script or Holy Writ, but I differ from Said over the issue of whether Adorno can be transmitted to future generations and would suggest that what is transmitted is precisely what Said himself so clearly valorized: the "morality not to be at home in one's home." As Adorno famously writes in *Minima Moralia,* "In his text, the writer sets up house. . . . For a man who no longer has a homeland, writing becomes a place to live." But writing, like a radio broadcast or a filmed story, suggests a mediation of experience, a transfer between poles that threatens to alter the fundamental essence of the subject. In this regard, writing is very much like exile, and so, Adorno claims that in writing, the writer must perforce also experience homelessness:

> The demand that one harden oneself against self-pity implies the technical
> necessity to counter any slackening of intellectual tension with the utmost
> alertness, and to eliminate anything that has begun to encrust the work
> or to drift along idly, which may at an earlier stage have served, as gossip,
> to generate the warm atmosphere conducive to growth, but is now left
> behind, flat and stale. In the end, the writer is not even allowed to live
> in his writing.[40]

This book strives to give readers a sense of that homelessness in Adorno's writing and of just how alienating Adorno found his exile host, America, in the 1930s and '40s by rediscovering the intricate and multifaceted practices of the culture industry he faced and ultimately resisted. In so doing, I also hope to convey why Adorno's "message in a bottle" can and must be transmitted to generations who have gotten comfortable with the world of appearance and who have forgotten just how uncomfortable and precarious their own situation actually is. Since one of Adorno's primary interests in America is in how the mass media transform their objects, the book takes as one of its overarching questions the issue of how the various mechanisms of the culture industry operate as forms of mediation.

As many of the archival materials from the radio and television networks illustrate, there is a conscious and concerted effort on the part of the culture industry to convince audiences that broadcasts are, in fact, unmediated and therefore provide transparent access to the truth. Everything from the tabernacle-like construction of the old radio box to the networks' rhetorical descriptions of the better world just behind the radio dial functions to obscure the mechanism itself in favor of the "truth" the mass media regulate and reveal. Adorno is finely attuned to these techniques, nowhere more so than in his descriptions of what mass-media transmissions do—physically and philosophically—to older aesthetic forms like the novel or the symphony. As his friend and former teacher Siegfried Kracauer puts it, "the transmitting apparatus overwhelms the contents transmitted."[41] But the culture industry Adorno faced tried to foster the illusion that the autonomous artwork (and its correlate, subjectivity) is unmutilated in transit. This is the seductive illusion that Adorno strives to shatter.

I should caution, however, that for Adorno, perhaps the dialectical tradition's most sensitive heir, the solution to the problem of the artwork's mediation is not so simple. Mediation may be an established fact of the post-Hegelian conditions of modernity, but that mediation is also its own form of immediacy. In his Hegel studies, Adorno writes of this intractable dialectic that "one can no more speak of mediation without something immediate than, conversely, one can find something immediate that is not mediated."[42] The challenge, therefore, is to determine not only how mass-culture transmissions deprive the subject of their immediacy but also how some vestige of immediacy is transformed and preserved. Hegel, Adorno writes, "criticizes immediacy in principle and not merely as being atomistic and mechanical; immediacy always already contains something other than itself—subjectivity—without which it would not be 'given' at all, and by that token it is not objectivity."[43] This statement suggests the radical nature of Adorno's encounter with the culture industry. If mediation is itself the precondition for the immediate, subjective, and nonidentical, it is not enough to consider how mass-media transmissions betoken alienation and reification; one must also consider how they preserve the subject, if only through its destruction. The tortuous manipulations that the culture industry inflicts on its aesthetic wares may indicate the end of the subjective experience of (and in) art, but for Adorno, even the mournful memory of what was once alive in artworks offers the promise of a better world.

This talk of writing and exile, mediation and longed-for transformations leads inevitably to the question of translation. I initially wanted to call this book "Transmissions," in hopes of both conveying something of its focus on the culture-industry broadcasts that Adorno encountered and alluding to one of the central pitfalls for those who read Adorno in English: Something is inevitably lost in translation. This situation is nowhere more acute than in *Negative Dialectics,* translated by E. B. Ashton, where "transmission" itself becomes the problematic term. In the book, the German word for "mediation" (*Vermittlung*) is routinely mistranslated as "transmission." Hence, in Adorno's analysis of the bad faith displayed by Heideggerian ontology, the English translation reads:

> Heidegger's realism turns a somersault: his aim is to philosophize formlessly, so to speak, purely on the ground of things, with the result that things evaporate for him. Weary of the subjective jail of cognition, he becomes convinced that what is transcendent to subjectivity is immediate for subjectivity, without being conceptually stained by subjectivity. . . . Since the *transmissions* of our subjectivity cannot be thought out of the world, we want to return to stages of consciousness that lie before the reflection upon subjectivity and *transmission*. This effort fails.[44]

Since mediation/transmission is inescapable, Adorno continues, Heidegger has to collapse the distinction between mediation and Being. In this case, Adorno claims, Heidegger offers us an impossible tautology, whereby, in the English translation, "Transmission is transmitted by what it transmits."[45]

Despite the problematic transformation of "mediation" into "transmission," the idea to title this book "Transmissions" sought to embrace the term and Adorno's English translations generally because they reinforce this notion that seems so crucial to understanding Adorno's relationship to America: If the text is an uneasy home for the homeless, the translated text is a doubly exiled space, where, because of unfamiliarity, any number of things can get lost, misplaced, bumped, and scratched.

Anyone who studies Adorno will have faced the near-mandatory caveat that the English translations of Adorno are imperfect at best, mutilating at worst. Since I first began reading Adorno as a student, I have always felt that these warnings were both daunting and discouraging, as though I was being told that unless I could read Adorno in German, my understanding would always be second-rate. These dire warnings smacked of their own type of elitism, in part because they seemed to deny that an American reader could possibly find something powerful and resonant in Adorno's writings, even though so many of them were written in this country and, at some fundamental level, about the American experience.

I reject that idea. What's more, I believe that the insistence on what an English speaker *cannot* understand threatens to undermine what an American reader *can* take from Adorno as a critic and as a vital intellectual force. It is true: Perhaps more than any other writer, Adorno can probably only be fully understood in German; the very structure of his sentences, and the way the German syntax aids in those sentences' ability to negate their own meanings, help convey those meanings. But the Adorno I'm interested in is the American Adorno: not just the Adorno who wrote some of his most important critiques of the mass media in English, but the Adorno whom Americans get to know through his translated works. The choice not to make too much of translation difficulties reflects my commitment not to derail or demean the reader, but it also represents a tacit acknowledgment that this book is about Adorno in America, the Adorno we're stuck with, both the long-neglected day-to-day existence of the actual, historical figure and also his texts, the ones that that we in this country get to read. Thus the word "transmission," as it appears in *Negative Dialectics*, is still a useful one when thinking about mass-media broadcasts as forms of mediation that nonetheless attempt to appear ontological, to appear comfortably in their place. And so, with a few exceptions, where I have had to make brief translations of letters or archival documents, I have decided to use preexisting translations rather than to try to bring the English closer to its German home. They might be flawed and messy, but they are also powerful, and funny, and sad, and destabilizing, and like Adorno, even in their "damaged" American form, they still are still very much alive.

The structure of my book takes its cue from a 1945 lecture delivered in America entitled "What National Socialism Has Done to the Arts." In his speech, Adorno claims that his fear is not that fascism will survive in Europe through direct adherence to the principles of National Socialism but, rather, that "the arts . . . as far as they have contact with the broad masses, above all moving pictures, radio, and popular literature, will indulge in a kind of streamlining in order to please the customer, a sort of pseudo-Americanization."[46] In an effort to trace this "pseudo-Americanization" of the arts, its implications for contemporary subjects, and its link to totalitarian ideals, I have organized my book into four chapters. The first, "The Monster under the Stone," situates Adorno's exile in America in its cultural and academic context, discussing the rise of mass-media research and the use of empirical surveys and sociological studies to capture audiences and sell products to consumers. Further, this chapter introduces the various academic projects to which Adorno was attached (among them the PRRP and Studies in Prejudice) and his growing reservations about the so-called benevolence or objectivity of the types of research he was being asked to conduct. To Adorno's mind, Paul Lazarsfeld's vision of administrative research was itself a particularly pernicious form of mediation. Using the raw data of questionnaires to determine listening patterns and subjective interests, positivist research did violence to the human subject by reducing it to a series of objective categories. These categories could in turn be used as the culture industry's raw material for its ongoing manipulation of the audience's eyes, ears, and minds. As Adorno wrote in the "The Experiential Content of Hegel's Philosophy," "In order to be able to operate with the clean, clear concepts it brags about, science establishes such concepts and makes its judgments without regard for the fact that the life of the subject matter for which the concept is intended does not exhaust itself in conceptual specification."[47] Nevertheless, as Adorno discovered during his work with Lazarsfeld, the pose of objectivity and transparency was in fact the mark of science's conceptual mediation of the facts and the mechanism of subjective domination.

When put in the hands of radio networks, movie studios, and television stations, this type of research lends itself to the dehumanization of audiences and the reduction of artworks to their streamlined, surface elements. The examination of the rise of administrative research provides the springboard for the following three chapters, which take as case studies those forms of aesthetic transmission that Adorno felt "above all" constituted the Americanization of the arts in the wake of fascism: radio, motion pictures, and literature. Adorno's writings on each of these means of mass communication paint a picture of the arts as increasingly turning their backs on a notion of the free-willed creative individual in favor of a heavily administered network of consumption and control under the guise of a supposedly democratic popular entertainment.

Therefore, in chapter 2, on radio, "Adorno in Sponsor-Land," I look at the ways the stated mission of the Columbia Broadcasting System (CBS) and the National Broadcasting Company (NBC) to "broadcast in the public interest" runs contrary to the actual economic and aesthetic machinations undertaken in an effort to capture the largest audience. Using the concept of "radio physiognomics" taken from *Current of Music*, as well as Adorno's discussion of NBC's *Music Appreciation Hour*,[48] I consider the various techniques the radio used to subject listeners to its authoritarian unity. At the same time, I discuss Adorno's analysis of the technologically mutilated radio symphony as the counterpoint to illusory social coherence. By virtue of the technical constraints of midcentury radio, Adorno claims the listener is treated to a sonic reproduction that, although evoking the formal properties of the symphony, is really no symphony at all. This destruction of the symphonic form reduces the individual musical elements into interchangeable units that echo the listener's own atomized position as alienated laborers. In this view, the educational aspect of broadcasting, so heavily touted in the early days of radio, takes on the aspect of a mass job-training program. Listeners are transformed into laborers, whose unpaid work is sold to the advertising agencies. To illustrate this point, the chapter concludes with a number of "children's" books developed by the networks for the benefit of the advertisers. In these texts, the administrative authority of the networks is made plain and is illustrated with chilling good humor.

In chapter 3, "*Below the Surface:* Frankfurt Goes to Hollywood," I consider how Adorno dealt with subjects' inability to see the destructive effects of transmission in visual media. Adorno's discussion of the illusory "transparency" of movies and television leads to an in-depth analysis of the abortive film project that he and Horkheimer developed as part of their work with the American Jewish Committee (AJC). The episode is fascinating, not only because it illustrates many of the theoretical problems identified with narrative cinema, but also because it suggests that Adorno's relationship with Hollywood and the filmmaking community was much closer and more complicated than has previously been acknowledged. The failures of *Below the Surface*, as the film was called, as well as Adorno's suggestions regarding other films, offer insights into Adorno's subsequent writings on cinema and television and hint at the way narrative cinema might itself transmit the nonidentical.

With the problem of the diminished subject of the artwork in the forefront, I turn finally, in chapter 4, "If There Should Be a Posterity," to the problems posed by literature in Adorno's period, and the relationship between putatively high and low literary forms. In both the hard-boiled American fictions of the era and the "montage" technique of Thomas Mann, the novelistic form reveals itself to be increasingly inadequate to what it had once promised: the notion of the free-willed interior subject. Adorno's contributions to Mann's *Doctor Faustus* and his insistence on the novel's "hope beyond hopelessness" illustrate the ways the subject might survive its own death and how the novel, surpassed by newer forms of mass media, might hold the best promise for the future of the subject. After considering a number of texts that deal, at one level or another, with the problem of literacy in the late 1940s and the 1950s, texts ranging from David Riesman's classic *The Lonely Crowd* to Chrylser-Plymouth's less-than-classic ad campaign featuring the ridiculously heroic cartoon character Chuck Carson, I conclude the chapter with a discussion of the ways Adorno consigned himself to Mann's text, thereby willing himself to a posterity he would never witness. This act of generosity, in which Adorno finds a home in the perpetuity of homelessness, represents, I contend, a salient example of the way immediacy can survive its mediation, history can speak to the present, and the subject can be actualized in a time beyond itself. Despite Mann's best efforts to obscure Adorno in *Faustus*, Adorno blasts from the page, and he brings with him the entire history of exile.

On the opening page of Adorno's first project in America, the memorandum "Music in Radio" prepared for PRRP, he tries to describe his cross between empiricism and critical theory by admitting, "In a way it is neither 'fish nor flesh.'"[49] His modest assessment could well serve as a motto for this book. Neither a history nor a theoretical critique, neither a biography nor a sociological analysis, this is a hybrid book that seeks to provide a sense of the texture of Adorno's American experience without hewing to any one particular methodology. To a large extent, I believe that the historical context of his exile helps illuminate Adorno's theories, while at the same time his critique can help readers today make sense of America in the period. At the same time I have tried to avoid using biographical details to offer any sort of psychological explanation for Adorno's writings and actions and instead hope that those details merely add shade and color to the picture of a dialectical relationship between an exile and his wartime refuge. To the extent that there are these multiple methodologies at play, I would perhaps do well to adopt a second motto for my efforts, the one Adorno's mentor Kracauer uses when opening his *Theory of Film:* "It would be fair to advise the reader at the outset that this book does not include all of the things he may be looking for."[50] To those readers of Adorno looking for an intricate reworking of the collected mass of Adorno scholarship or for erudite twists and turns as I go trundling down every theoretical rabbit hole, I am afraid I must say that this is not that book. The reasons I made this choice have to do with my desire to make the book clear and coherent, coupled with my firm belief that what has precluded many American readers from truly appreciating the importance and power of Adorno's thought has been the tendency among some Adorno scholars to portray him as obtuse, convoluted, and aloof from the America he criticized, even while they are defending him against charges of being obtuse, convoluted, and aloof.

Thus, I have tried to avoid getting caught up in the thorny, dialectically intricate arguments of both Adorno and his devotees in favor of rediscovering the America that made Adorno so profoundly suspicious and that, at the same time, he nevertheless genuinely admired. As I have indicated, there are countless sources on Adorno, as there are ample writings on the Frankfurt School, exile, the mass media, and so on. Many of these texts are valuable and enlightening, and where a scholar's intervention has been particularly helpful, or where an argument has been made that I find especially trenchant, I have done my best to include those references. I hope that it is obvious how deeply I am influenced by and indebted to the breadth and depth of the entire range of Adorno scholarship, but I am also aware that my decision not to survey the full corpus of Adorno literature may lead to a number of omissions and violate some of the accepted protocols of academic writing. My only defenses for this tactic are that I tend to prefer legibility to pyrotechnic displays of erudition, and that giving every writer who has expressed an opinion on Adorno his or her due would mean a much longer, more cumbersome book. This text is meant to be a social history in which Adorno is the main but by no means the only character, and what follows attempts to reevaluate the exile years as something paradoxically like a proper home for Adorno. If I fail in that task, I have no defense at all.

1 THE MONSTER UNDER THE STONE
ADORNO AND THE RISE OF ADMINISTRATIVE RESEARCH

Against that positivism which stops before phenomena, saying, "there are only facts," I should say: no, it is precisely facts that do not exist, only interpretations.

—Friedrich Nietzsche

In Adorno's original typescript manuscript of *Minima Moralia*, there is an aphorism, titled "Procrustes," one of several subsequently excised from the final, published text of the book. In the aphorism, Adorno baldly and witheringly attacks "the sneering empiricist sabotage" that he fears is destined to take over the academy. Defending autonomous thought against its "throttling" by "book-keeping, administration, annual reports and balance sheets," Adorno laments the collusion between scholarly sociological research and the corporate world. "The procedure of the official social sciences," he continues, "is little more now than a parody of the businesses that keep such sciences afloat while really needing it only as an advertisement."[1]

Written in 1945, "Procrustes" diagnoses the increasing tendency of universities to collaborate with corporations as though knowledge were an industrial product to be bought and sold, a situation that Adorno finds especially egregious when research turns its calculating gaze toward an aesthetic object. Adorno's ire derives both from the selling of academic research and from the fact that what the empirical research on art tends to measure is not so much artistic merit as the likes and dislikes of an audience that has lost the capacity to truly enjoy anything but what they have been told to enjoy. What get recorded by those social scientists committed to "the facts" are the patterns of consumption in a society in which consumption has replaced a substantive experience of modern life. Adorno goes on to claim that the very impossibility of experience, and hence of its measurement, is precisely what sociological research can't admit, especially if it is to sell its empirical results to a corporate patron. "The regression of hearing," he claims, using his common phrase, "can only be deduced from the social tendency towards the consumption process as such, and identified in certain traits. It cannot be inferred from arbitrarily isolated and then quantified acts of consumption."[2]

For the Adorno who types this excised aphorism, the place to look for answers can never be only in the consumers of art. An aesthetic theory cannot and should not blame the victim for the sins of the system of production and consumption, as certain strains of empirical research do, by focusing on what people buy without questioning the system that makes that purchase possible. Instead, Adorno explains, theory must examine the entire network of constraints and expectations that form and re-form the individual within society. A thoroughgoing theory of art would take into account not only culture's consumers but also its producers and—perhaps especially—an artwork's means of distribution. Social scientific research proves itself inadequate to the "truth" of society by virtue of its failure to do more than measure responses to cultural stimuli. The symptoms of society stand in for their underlying causes. "That music cannot be really experienced over the radio is, to be sure, a modest theoretical idea," Adorno claims in "Procrustes," "but as translated into research, for instance by the proof that the enthusiastic listeners to certain serious music programmes cannot even recall the titles of the pieces they have consumed, [that idea] yields the mere husk of the theory it claims to verify."[3]

However, only a few years after "Procrustes" was written, while Adorno was visiting Frankfurt, helping Horkheimer rebuild the Institute of Social Research and paving the way for his eventual full-time return to Germany, a representative from the Rockefeller Foundation made the following observations about Adorno's methodological interests and ambitions:

> L[ouis] W[irth] telephoned from the S[ocial] S[cience] R[esearch] C[ouncil] to emphasize his warnings . . . about Horkheimer, Adorno & Company. He says these two are carrying on a tremendous campaign to get support from UN, UNESCO, the German Government, American occupying forces, foundations, and everybody else, and that they are representing themselves as the last word in the latest thing in American social science. LW points out that this goes far beyond the facts and that their chief strength lies in their energy and promotional propensities. . . . while Horkheimer and

Adorno fall far short of representing the best in American social science, they nevertheless do know something about empirical research methods and are perhaps one of the very few potential avenues for developing interest and effort along these lines in the German social science scene.[4]

Between "Procrustes" and the Rockefeller Foundation memo, we therefore see two seemingly very different Adornos regarding the subject of social science research. On the one hand, Adorno condemns the type of sociological research that reduces every subject to a collection of facts and instrumentalizes those facts as an end to some other purpose—selling something. On the other hand, there is the postexile Adorno, touting himself as the next big thing in social science research and offering the possibility of a renaissance in the social sciences in Germany. How is one to reconcile these two figures? Historically, the seeming change of heart could perhaps be attributed to Adorno's sociological work with the American Jewish Committee (AJC) on its Studies in Prejudice book series, work that most famously resulted in the seminal text on the psychology of fascism, *The Authoritarian Personality* (1950), coauthored by Adorno and other exile and American social scientists. However, rather than seeing the positions Adorno takes regarding the methods of social science research as contradictory or as mitigated by the success of his work with the Berkeley Group, as the *Authoritarian Personality* researchers were called, it might be worthwhile to consider how these positions can be understood as complementary and part of a broader, more nuanced approach to the culture industry and its consumers than Adorno is usually credited with having. Indeed, it is Adorno's insistence on a holistic approach to the mass media, their audiences, their technologies, and their producers that causes him to belittle the narrow focus of American sociological research. At the same time, it is Adorno's more wide-ranging and "democratic" methodology that might indeed mark Adorno as "representing the best in American social science," and although it was probably only a convenience, it is perhaps also a measure of the weight Adorno attached to these issues that when filling out his U.S. passport application forms in 1949, of all the professions Adorno could have chosen for himself, on the line for occupation he wrote "sociologist."

It may seem like an odd and arid way to begin a book that proposes to make that case for a more approachable and down-to-earth Adorno to begin with questions about specialized scholarly practices and Adorno's discomfort with them. Indeed, much of the reason readers of Adorno find him so prickly has to do with the "singularly difficult personality and unfortunate torturous style of writing" he displayed when initially attached to American social science research projects.[5] And there is no denying that, particularly in his early days in the United States, Adorno was decidedly cantankerous and intemperate regarding the fact-based "measuring" of culture he was asked to perform. However, since so much of Adorno's exile is spent coming to grips with the mass media and the means by which one could intellectually account for them, and since so much of the criticism of Adorno as an elitist stems from his abortive and often cantankerous first attempts at mass-media research during his early years in America, it is all but inescapable that I begin my examination of Adorno's exile years with his uneasy relationship to the intellectual and methodological principles that he was asked to adopt upon arriving in the United States.

Adorno's disdain for empirically minded social science research and the eruption of this disdain in "Procrustes," as well as his vexed embrace of certain types of social science, can be traced to his contributions to Paul Felix Lazarsfeld's Princeton Radio Research Project (PRRP), the first substantial work Adorno performed upon arriving in New York in 1938. Adorno's treatment of the type of studies being done by those scholars engaged in what Lazarsfeld called "administrative research" is often unselfreflexively harsh, especially given Adorno's subsequent efforts to use empirical methods, albeit dialectically. But "Procrustes," however caustic, has a certain prophetic value. In the years since the aphorism was edited out of *Minima Moralia*, many of the trends Adorno identified have become commonplace methodologies, just as the relationship between the arts, the academy, and private interests have become increasingly intertwined. It is worthwhile, therefore, to revisit the relationship between, on the one hand, Adorno and the Institute of Social Research and, on the one other, Lazarsfeld and the Bureau of Applied Social Research and to consider the social history of audience research. Not only does Adorno's encounter with a developing administrative research shed light on Adorno's reaction to the culture industry, marking, as it did, his first real introduction to America, but it also marks a period when a fundamental change in the methods of knowledge production were taking hold of the academy—with crucial implications for the notions of free will and individuality.

Even in his first days in America, Adorno's unease with a type of research that sought to streamline audience responses was palpable. His dismay is registered as early as 1938 in "The Fetish-Character in Music and the Regression of Listening," an essay written just after his first taste of "applied" social research. On the first page he writes, "If one seeks to find out who 'likes' a commercial piece, one cannot avoid the suspicion that liking and disliking are inappropriate to the situation, even if the person questioned clothes his reaction in those words. . . . An approach in terms of value judgments has become a fiction for the person who finds himself hemmed in by standardized musical goods."[6] The "Fetish-Character" essay has a (perhaps deserved) reputation as one of Adorno's harshest broadsides against the perceived simplicity of American commodity culture. But it is clear from his opening remarks that Adorno reserves as much fire for the means of measuring—and thereby justifying—audience responses to cultural products as he does for the products themselves. Implicit in his critique of the regression of listening is thus always a condemnation of the type of market research that covers for that regression by citing facts to claim that audiences "like" something and, at the same time, truly know what they like.

If the embrace of market research by intellectuals could be associated with one figure, it would have to be Lazarsfeld. An Austrian émigré to the United States in the early 1930s, Lazarsfeld was, as a young scholar, an associate of the positivist Vienna Circle.[7] In America, he founded the Bureau of Applied Social Research, which operated out of Newark, New Jersey, and, eventually, Columbia University. By virtue of his relationship with CBS's Frank Stanton, as well as through a grant from the Rockefeller Foundation, Lazarsfeld was ultimately offered the directorship of the PRRP and Columbia's Office of Radio Research. It was in that capacity that he came into direct contact with Adorno.

Lazarsfeld's relationship to the Institute of Social Research, however, dates at least to his publication of the essay "Some Remarks on the Typological Procedures in Social Research" in volume 6 of the Institute's *Zeitschrift für Sozialforschung* in 1937. The article, which attempts to illustrate the methodological problems of charting a multidimensional object that can only be understood in relation to other multidimensional objects, highlights what will become a central disagreement between Adorno and empirical social scientists. In the essay, Lazarsfeld proposes the reduction of "multi-dimensional attribute space . . . to a one-dimensional order."[8] To paraphrase Lazarsfeld's argument, if the goal of the social sciences is to affirm concepts through the use of empirical facts, in order to be of any use to the social sciences, volatile and fickle subjects must be stabilized and serialized as consistent and coherent objects along standardized axes.

Even when multiple variables exist in a given sample, "reduction" to a standard is still possible. Thus, according to Lazarsfeld:

Where women were distributed according to size, education and beauty, beauty as a serial could be standardized. This means, for instance, that only a limited number of degrees of beauty would be distinguished. The ten percent most beautiful, for instance, would have beauty grade-A; all the combinations of beauty, size and education which differ only in regard to their rank number on the beauty axis in the range of the first ten percent would, therefore fall into one class.[9]

Lazarsfeld's example is disturbing on a number of levels, not least of which being the calculating misogyny inherent in ranking women based on beauty (with size and education factored as variables). For Adorno, it would be no doubt equally troubling to see the aesthetic sense schematized in such a way, and to his mind, this willingness of the social sciences to "liquidate"[10] its subjects, deriving "fixed" elements to graph, was tantamount to a type of subject-murder. If the truth of subjects—what makes us alive and capable of having opinions—is mutability, the oscillation between subjective desires and objective societal conditions, each constantly in flux, then the lifeless "facts" of empirical social science research are inevitably false. This volatility of the subject is at the heart of modernism and the high modernist texts Adorno embraced and celebrated. From Marcel Proust's impossible effort to capture the entirety of his narrator's past in À la recherche du temps perdu, to James Joyce's "I am a stride at a time," and the "ineluctable modality of the visible" that characterize the perambulations of *Ulysses*, the modernist subject utterly resists the logic of a social science that reduces human qualities to data points. Thus, well before experiencing Lazarsfeld's methods firsthand, Adorno registers his dismay with "Some Remarks on the Typological Procedures in Social Research" in a letter to Walter Benjamin dated April 25, 1937, but at the time he indicates a reluctance to tell Horkheimer his concerns lest that "encourag[e] him to number me amongst the grumblers and cavilers."[11]

Not only does this unwillingness to alienate Horkheimer reflect the young Adorno's attempt to curry favor with the Institute's director,[12] but it also shows that Adorno was aware of Horkheimer's desire to bring the demands of critical theory into line with the methods of empirical research. Thus, while evidence of intellectual differences between Adorno and Lazarsfeld date to 1937, the real debate between Lazarsfeld's brand of statistical research and the critical theory of the Frankfurt School takes shape in the first two essays of the exile-renamed *Studies in Philosophy and Social Science*, volume 9 (1941).[13] In hindsight, one can see that the volume, the last the Institute would publish, announces the themes that will energize much of the Institute's subsequent work in the United States. "This present publication," Horkheimer writes in the "Preface," "deals with problems of mass communication." However, Horkheimer's next statements do not develop directly out of the first. Instead, he continues, "It [the publication] is the outcome of collaboration between the Institute of Social Research and Columbia University's Office of Radio Research. As a result of frequent exchanges of views between members of the two institutions, many specific questions have arisen concerning the relationship between critical theory and empirical research."[14] It would seem that Horkheimer's first and third sentences are unconnected; the "problems" of mass communication are not necessarily analogous with the "questions" of the relationship between critical theory and empirical research. Yet Horkheimer's non sequitur is, in retrospect, prophetic for the ways that the exile years would be characterized by the debate between critical theory and administrative research fought over the terrain of mass communication. As indicated by his reference to the Office of Radio Research, radio would be the initial site of dispute, but elements of the critique of radio would extend not only to Adorno's theorization of other mass media but ultimately into *Negative Dialectics* and *Aesthetic Theory* as crucial problematics in Adorno's assessment of modern art and philosophy. The importance of mass communication, and specifically the centrality of radio, to Adorno's thought must be stressed. But while Adorno was still wrestling with the "problems" posed by mass communication, even in his later work it is another matter as to whether he could fully embrace Horkheimer's claim that it was possible "to present examples of an approach especially aware of the necessity to integrate theoretical thinking with empirical analysis."[15] Nevertheless, as if to emphasize this possibility as part of the agenda of the Institute, the first issue of volume 9 concludes with the outline for the Research Project on Anti-Semitism, which was, as evidenced by the *Authoritarian Personality*, perhaps the most successful subordination of the dialectical rigors of critical theory to the demands of empiricism.

At many points before, during, and after the years in America, Institute members—Horkheimer especially—were willing to embrace the methods of empirical sociological research for the ends of critical theory. Perhaps the most salient early example of this tendency is *Autorität und Familie* (*Authority and the Family*), a massive treatment of the relationship between sexuality, labor, and family life in Germany, which relied on the findings of an exhaustive, seven-page questionnaire, whose creation was aided by Lazarsfeld and whose English-language translation was sponsored by the Works Progress Administration. Among the wide-ranging questions asked were "Has your wife a bodily ailment?" "Of what does your daily nourishment chiefly consist?" and, perhaps due to Adorno's influence, "Do you like jazz?"[16]

But to return to the problems that introduce volume 9, one should remember that the issue of mass communication is as central as the question of competing methodologies. No essay makes a greater effort to synthesize these two issues than that which starts the volume: Lazarsfeld's "Remarks on Administrative and Critical Communications Research."

Although, as is the case with Adorno, Lazarsfeld is hardly a household name today, it would be hard to overstate his importance to the development of the then-adolescent mass media and particularly the radio industry. In the interests of his research agenda, during the 1930s and '40s Lazarsfeld developed—or helped develop—many of the audience-measurement techniques still in use today. Moreover, by offering these techniques to media companies, Lazarsfeld paved the way for a more imbricated relationship between the social sciences and the economic world. The British communications scholar David Morrison, who has made Lazarsfeld something of an ongoing project, claims that Lazarsfeld helped pioneer the focus group and was one of the first scholars to forge links between the academy and the business community. Further, Morrison writes that Lazarsfeld rescued the extensive research done in the interest of radio advertisers from its one-dimensional focus:

> The radio industry in the late 1930s was more or less exclusively
> concerned with the listener as a prospective purchaser. The research
> divisions of the radio companies, almost without exception, were organized
> to promote the sale of time, and engaged in little direct research
> themselves. Most of their energy was devoted to the interpretation of data
> obtained from outside agencies such as the Co-operative Analysis of
> Broadcasting (CAB) or Crossley Survey, or Clark-Hooper Survey. Such
> commercial agencies served not only the radio industry itself, but the
> advertising agencies as well; consequently their studies were concerned
> mainly with identifying which members of the radio audience were likely
> to buy the products advertised on the radio.[17]

What Lazarsfeld introduced to the concept of audience research was a university home for these studies and an effort to deduce sociological theory from the results. But this shift from the firm to the faculty was tantamount to a Faustian bargain between the academy and private donors, whether they were corporate, philanthropic, or both. Forced to follow the lead—and the cash—of commercial interests, Lazarsfeld helped inaugurate the shift from knowledge as an end in itself to the instrumentalization of thought in the service of business. While there were certainly many private corporations dedicated to providing research to networks, studios, and publishers, increasingly during the period various elements of the academy transformed their disciplinary and methodological concerns to complement the entertainment industry's desire to track down data and use that data to sell their audiences to advertisers. In the 1930s and '40s, this mutual interest in audiences as sets of empirical data that could explain trends—sociological, political, consumerist—led media corporations and academics to pool their intellectual and financial resources in pursuit of the reading, listening, and viewing habits of the American public. As Lazarsfeld himself writes in the 1941 introduction to a special issue of the *Journal of Applied Psychology* dedicated to progress in radio research, the development of mass-communications research followed directly from the commercial interests of radio networks:

> Studies on the effect of radio are moving into the foreground; material collected for commercial purposes is ever more frequently available for scientific analysis; and related areas such as reading research are developing so fast that the discipline of general communications research seems in the making. . . . So far, because of the ownership structure of American radio, commercial effects are given most attention.[18]

One could argue that, in the long term, this relationship between the academy and the commercial interests of broadcasters and publishers would come to have an irrevocable effect on the production of knowledge and the globalization of intellectual capital. The research projects that are most likely to receive funding are, naturally, those with the most immediate commercial or military applications, and thus with the most foreseeable global appeal. At the time when Adorno was noting this shift in methodological focus in the social sciences, the willingness of certain scholars to take funds from private corporations to pay for research would have more local effects on the dispute between those sociologists involved in "positivist" research and those engaged in critical theory. One could argue that whereas in the early years of the twentieth century, the academy was relatively distinct from the corporate world and gave pride of place to more abstract, theoretical thinking in the social sciences (à la Max Weber and Emile Durkheim), eventually the poles reverse, raising the profile of the dedicated empiricists and transforming them into the visible (and profitable) face of the social sciences.

While Lazarsfeld was not solely responsible for the transformation of the ivory tower into the knowledge factory, he is, because of his influence on administrative market research, emblematic of a shift in the academy away from traditional theoretical modes of thought and toward the rising fortunes of positivism and empirical research. The notion of empirical evidence as the gold standard of knowledge owes its near hegemony to a number of factors, not least of which is the influence of the pragmatists (Charles Peirce, Margaret Mead, John Dewey, and William James) and their homegrown appeal to the American academy. But an equally important factor is the way Lazarsfeld's model of the research institute opened the door to outside funds, making possible any number of heretofore impossible projects. While today associations between universities and the private sector are commonplace, when Lazarsfeld arrived in the United States, outside of military research, the opportunities and the resources for large-scale empirical projects were all but nonexistent. Lazarsfeld's particular genius was his ability to make contacts with a variety of influential industry figures and convince them of the necessity of his research projects. Although eager to defend the purity of Lazarsfeld's research methods against charges that he capitulated to his sponsor's interests, Morrison nonetheless implicates him in erasing the borders between the university and the corporation by claiming that Lazarsfeld "was constantly acting like a businessman in looking for new sources of revenue to support the Bureau and his research operations."[19]

As Kathy Newman relates in the opening chapter of her book on the development of radio advertising and its reception, one of Lazarsfeld's first impacts on U.S. radio was a 1934 study commissioned by Lever Brothers, the makers of Lux soap, to test the effectiveness of their radio advertisements.[20] This study, Newman suggests, helped inaugurate a new era in the production and study of radio programming, and with the dawning of that era came a new, not altogether coherent community of radio experts:

> In the 1930s a new caste of professionals, "the audience intellectuals," played a unique role in producing, appealing to, and studying audiences for radio broadcasting. They helped to shape the audiences for radio programs through advertising, marketing, program selection, and product distribution. Audience intellectuals were made up of two sub-groups of

professionals who often worked together: advertisers/marketers, including copywriters, who worked at advertising agencies and academics who worked as professors of advertising and economics at universities; and university affiliated sociologists, who specialized in quantitative and psychological interview techniques.[21]

Lazarsfeld, Newman insists, was "especially important" to the development of this caste of "audience intellectuals," and so too, she reminds us, was Adorno, by virtue of his first work in the American academy as the "music director" of Lazarsfeld's PRRP. The idea that Lazarsfeld and the Institute of Social Research would collaborate on a special issue of the Institute's journal given over to the idea of synthesizing critical theory and empirical social sciences therefore seems a natural outgrowth of the development of this loosely affiliated group of audience intellectuals.

Whatever the reasons for the collaboration, it is clear that there was a great deal of quid pro quo between the Institute and Lazarsfeld and his colleagues. Morrison implies that Adorno's presence on PRRP came as the result of a fair measure of mutual back-scratching between Lazarsfeld and Horkheimer, a fact to which the table of contents of volume 9 of *Studies in Philosophy and Social Science* only partially testifies.[22] In addition to whatever intellectual prestige the Institute was able to confer on Lazarsfeld at this time, Horkheimer was also providing financial assistance while Lazarsfeld was still in New Jersey. As Morrison puts it, Lazarsfeld's offer to Adorno of the "directorship" of the music division of the PRRP had two purposes; the first was gratitude for this financial support: "He wanted to repay Horkheimer's kindness in providing much needed funds for a small institute he had run in Newark, New Jersey." But, according to Morrison, Lazarsfeld also wanted to lend to the PRRP's music section a certain measure of cultural and intellectual credibility, and "Adorno was just the type of scholar Lazarsfeld was looking for: a sophisticated European theoretical thinker with a knowledge of musical structure."[23] Lazarsfeld, in his memoir, confirms this account, making at the same time specific reference to the hoped-for collaboration of his own research methodology and critical theory: "I was aware of [the] controversial features of Adorno's work, but was intrigued by his writings on the 'contradictory' role of music in our society. I considered it a challenge to see whether I could induce Adorno to try to link his ideas with empirical research."[24]

In addition to what the Institute or Horkheimer could provide financially or Adorno could offer intellectually, Lazarsfeld in turn was able to offer something valuable by hiring Adorno. Together with Horkheimer,

Lazarsfeld (with the influence of Rockefeller Foundation support not too far in the background) was able to present a compelling reason for Adorno to be granted a visa to the United States, which he received in 1938. In a memo dated April 27, 1938, Lazarsfeld explains this plan to his colleagues: "I wrote my initial invitation for him to come to work with us in the name of the Research Center and on Research Center letterhead so that my letter, together with the letter of invitation from the Institute for Social Research, could be a well-coordinated basis for him getting a visa."[25]

By most accounts, Adorno's tenure was rocky, and the recent émigré was described as an elitist dilettante in Lazarsfeld's memoir and elsewhere. In his reflections on his own, much later dealings with the "Frankfurters," Donald MacRae caustically writes, "I thought Adorno, on our first meeting, the most arrogant, self indulgent (intellectually and culturally) man I have ever met. Some 20 years later, I can think of additional claimants for that position, but I doubt if they are serious rivals."[26] Lazarsfeld himself, in an undated memo, expresses the exasperation of his PRRP colleagues by calling Adorno "insulting," "outrageous," and "impossible" and claiming, with regard to Adorno's primary output for PRRP, "Memorandum: Music in Radio," that it contains "grave mistakes of presentation which I would not let any of my graduate students get by with."[27] In the pages of the "Memorandum" found in the Columbia archives, one can trace Lazarsfeld's mounting impatience with Adorno, as his marginal comments, alternating between English and German, often culminate with an angry "Cultur Fetisch!" when Adorno uses a Latin phrase.[28] The third chapter, "Reception," causes Lazarsfeld the most apoplexy, perhaps because it suggests that empirical research and sampling techniques can ultimately at best do no more than confirm theoretical suspicions and would at worst obscure social complexes. Adorno writes:

> The merely qualitative [personal] differences given by this leveling type of tabulation serve, in reality, to hide rather than to emphasize these differences. Without neglecting the "quantitative" material, according to our method it is used primarily for the sake of interpreting the data in terms of our theory rather than being regarded as a result in itself. . . . Perhaps what matters most in radio is not so much what influence it exercises upon people as it is how the general mechanism of society which affects people everywhere shows itself in a new tool in a very distinct and definite way. It seems sound to start our theoretical approach from this point.

In short, for Adorno, theoretical interpretations of society take precedence over facts, because the facts only exist owing to their mediation through that society. Given these statements, perhaps it is the force with which Adorno bites Lazarsfeld's hand that renders much of Lazarsfeld's marginalia illegible except for the increasingly frequent repetition of the word "problem."

For his part, Adorno professes to be a victim of misunderstanding—both his own and that of his colleagues. Adorno's jazz-playing assistant—a "Mennonite," according to Adorno—objected to the foreign methods of his new boss. Adorno claims that

> he had hardly grasped what I was after. A certain resentment in him was unmistakable: the type of culture I brought with me and about which I was genuinely unconceited, critical of society as I already was, appeared to him to be unjustifiable arrogance. He cherished a mistrust of Europeans such as the bourgeoisie of the eighteenth century must have entertained toward the émigré French aristocrats. However little I, destitute of all influence, had to do with social privilege, I appeared to him to be a kind of usurper.[29]

In retrospect, one can certainly grasp Lazarsfeld's exasperation, while at the same time one can understand Adorno's defensive posture and alienation. Whatever Adorno's demeanor, whether ivory-tower aesthete or misunderstood foreigner, his work on PRRP was roundly criticized by his colleagues, and ultimately, when funding to extend Adorno's appointment was withdrawn by the Rockefeller Foundation, he was let go. His output—consisting of the long "Memorandum" (161 pages); a study of an NBC musical-education program, "Analytical Study of NBC's *Music Appreciation Hour*"; and the massive book *Current of Music*—went unpublished. The projected PRRP book on music in radio was reduced to one essay printed in *Radio Research, 1941* ("The Radio Symphony"), and only two other articles, "A Social Critique of Radio Music" (published in *Kenyon Review*) and "On Popular Music" (written with George Simpson), the essay that immediately follows Lazarsfeld's own in volume 9 of *Studies in Philosophy and Social Science,* saw print while Adorno was in the United States. Despite their rocky relationship and the decision (ultimately made by John Marshall of the Rockefeller Foundation) not to renew the funds for the music section, Lazarsfeld displays a remarkable level of generosity toward Adorno and his methods. Even in the angry, sloppily typed reprimand to Adorno written when Lazarsfeld was clearly at the end of his patience, there is the insistence that he respects his colleague. "You and I agree on some parts of your intellectual work," Lazarsfeld claims, and he assures Adorno, "I have an unchanging respect for your ideas and . . . I am sure that our project will in the end profit greatly by your cooperation."[30] Lazarsfeld was also conscientious about Adorno's ego, and as it became evident that Adorno wasn't getting along with his colleagues, he took great care to mitigate whatever administrative blows were about to fall. Thus, in his April 27, 1938, memo to Frank Stanton and Hadley Cantril, he cautions his associate directors, saying, "I request specifically that any final discussion with Wiesengrund [Adorno][31] be reserved for me and that none of the associate directors takes up the matter with him without preliminary consultation with me. I shall, of course, at any time convey to him a decision that the directors' meeting will reach finally. As long as I know such decision to the contrary [that is, to terminate Adorno's funding] is made, the psychological handling of a matter which I consider important will have to be left to me."[32]

This concern for Adorno and respect for his methods—and those of the Institute—can be seen reflected in "Remarks on Administrative and Critical Communications Research," which functions as an attempt to reconcile administrative research in general with what Adorno represented in the specific case of PRRP—critical theory. "All communications research," Lazarsfeld claims in an essentializing gesture, centers on a standard set of problems: "Who are the people exposed to different media? What are their specific preferences? What are the effects of different methods of presentation?" Given this defining catechism, Lazarsfeld presents a "fable" through which he hopes to illustrate the "social and political implications of social research."[33]

The fable—perhaps an oblique reference to the Orson Welles *War of the Worlds* broadcast but also eerily prescient about the treatment of Japanese Americans after Pearl Harbor and Arab Americans after 9/11—describes a hypothetical situation in which, during a state of heightened awareness of the possible "dangers of subversive activities on the part of aliens," a radio broadcaster produces a program that highlights the possibility of said subversive activities. Although the policy of the network and of the government (in this case the same) is that "popular antipathy toward aliens in general should be minimized, and, above all, outbreaks of anti-alien sentiment should be avoided," the inevitable, of course, happens, and following the putatively public-minded original broadcast, "news dispatches . . . bring reports from various parts of the country of outbreaks of feeling against alien groups." What these "outbreaks of feeling" might be remains ominously—and provocatively—vague, but the situation gets worse (at least for the network) when the Federal Communications Commission requests the transcript of the broadcast. As a result of these events, Lazarsfeld continues, the broadcaster mobilizes an army of pollsters, statisticians, and interviewers to get to the bottom of what went wrong and to insulate the network from the resulting fallout. The fruits of this research determine, "to the surprise of the speaker, his sponsors, and the network, [that] what seemed innocent references to the few aliens believed to be engaged in subversive activities were taken by the listener to apply both to aliens generally and to hyphenates from countries thought hostile to American interests and traditions."[34]

The fable's researchers discover, not surprisingly, a seething undercurrent of xenophobia and racism, which the supposedly innocent broadcast catalyzed. Lazarsfeld doesn't make clear who has been damaged—whether the network, its listeners, or the hyphenates suffering through "outbreaks of feeling"—or how the damage is to be repaired, although he does suggest that the reputation of the celebrity announcer is in vital need of recuperation, because much of the repair effort centers on removing the identification between the speaker and the listeners' violent views on "hyphenates." To answer the question "What is to be done?" another phalanx of researchers and social scientists is dispatched. First, of course, social psychologists exonerate the network and blame the listeners. "Strong pro-Ally feeling in this country," the fable explains, "supported by the growing predisposition to fear and feel hostility toward minority groups, led to the overgeneralization of the remarks made in the broadcast address." Following this resituation of blame, with the aid of still more social scientists an onslaught of materials is prepared, taking into account the relative education and income of the target audience; those materials function to ameliorate the now-expunged hypothetical guilt of the original broadcast. To the objection that such a public relations effort might fail—and might present an inordinate expense—the fable responds, "All materials prepared are pre-tested as had been suggested and at a relatively slight expense—indeed, far less expense, proportionately, than merchandisers ordinarily incur in testing the market for new products."[35]

Lazarsfeld's fable thus concludes with a "happy ending" that "can probably take the form of a series of charts which subsequently ease the conscience of all concerned by showing, as their campaign proceeds, a consistent decline in all indices of overt hostility toward the groups against which outbreaks of feeling were directed." But if the happy ending consists in a bevy of charts that ease one's conscience, the fable suggests that through such research, one need never have a crisis of conscience at all. Had the broadcasters made use of these empirical tools originally, the entire episode could have been avoided. "If similar research had made them warier at the outset, need all of this happened?" Lazarsfeld asks. "Perhaps, they conclude, in media like radio where 'instant rejoinder' is often difficult, more trouble should be taken to avoid mistakes like this."[36]

This highly elaborate fable, as recorded in Lazarsfeld's essay and supposedly taken from "a series of discussions from 1939–40," illustrates a research methodology characteristic of Lazarsfeld's contributions to the social sciences. "Research of the kind described so far could well be called *administrative research,*" Lazarsfeld explains. "It is carried through in the service of some administrative agency of public or private character."[37] The remainder of "Remarks on Administrative and Critical Communications Research" is dedicated to demonstrating critical research's potential as a methodology that at once blazes the trail for and tempers administrative research. Critical research is, he says, "to be distinguished from administrative research in two respects: it develops a theory of the prevailing social trends of our times, general trends which yet require consideration in any concrete research problem; and it seems to imply ideas of basic human values according to which all actual or desired effects should be appraised."[38] In making this argument Lazarsfeld cites Horkheimer's essays "Traditional and Critical Theory" and "Philosophy and Critical Theory" as central texts and also notes that the examples of critical research that follow are taken "from studies by T. W. Adorno." On the whole, these examples are fairly faithful to the themes that would come to be associated with the Frankfurt School in general and Adorno in particular:

> The theory of a trend toward promotional culture leads to the conclusion that certain tendencies of our time jeopardize basic human values because people are kept from developing their own potentialities to the full. To be fit for the daily competition, we do not spend our leisure time developing a rich range of interests and abilities, but we use it, willingly or unwillingly, to reproduce our working capacity. Thus, not having acquired any criteria of our own, we succumb to and support a system of promotion in all areas of life, which in turn, puts us in ever-increasing dependence upon such a system; it gives us more and more technical devices and takes away from us any valuable purposes for which they could be used.[39]

It is noteworthy how many of the elements that will come to characterize Adorno's attack on the culture industry percolate within Lazarsfeld's essay. Within the span of three sentences, the notions of free time and pseudo-individuality are introduced, and in the last sentence Adorno's and Horkheimer's famous assertion from *Dialectic of Enlightenment* that "something is provided for everyone so that no one can escape"[40] is given an early dress rehearsal. The individual examples Lazarsfeld provides— for example, of a beer company that cynically uses antiwar slogans to sell its product, thus converting ends to means—illustrate how much he has absorbed some of Adorno's wry dismay. But humor notwithstanding, what is problematic about "Remarks on Administrative and Critical Communications Research" is the way its formal structure is at once internally contradictory and diametrically opposed to the Frankfurt School's critique of the total social process. Just as in the beer ad he criticizes, which uses peace to sell products, the formal logic of Lazarsfeld's essay requires that critical theory become a means to an end. According to Lazarsfeld, administrative research mobilizes "a theory about the prevailing trends toward a 'promotional' culture" as merely the first element in an "operation" that leads to "special" studies and ultimately to "remedial possibilities." For Lazarsfeld, the question of critical theory is what "value . . . such an approach [has] for the specific field of communications research," as though "a theory about the prevailing trends toward a 'promotional' culture" were not an end in itself.[41]

Further, communications research as an "operation" exists to serve as the tool of dominant interests:

> Behind the idea of such research is the notion that modern media of
> communication are tools handled by people or agencies for given purposes.
> The purpose may be to sell goods, or to raise the intellectual standards of
> the population, or to secure an understanding of governmental policies, but
> in all cases, to someone who uses a medium for something, it is the task of
> research to make the tool better known, and thus to facilitate its use.[42]

It is this variability of research's utility that underlines the second major contradiction in "Remarks on Administrative and Critical Communications Research." In one of the calmer sentences of Lazarsfeld's reprimand of Adorno's "Memorandum: Music in Radio," he insists that "before we show your memorandum to other people, it will be necessary that you spend much time on a more concrete presentation. You might think that these are negative in detail. But quite the contrary, only after you translate a research suggestion into operational terms will you be able to decide whether it holds water."[43] Here again appears the notion that critical theory is required to participate in an operational structure, coupled with an insistence on the "concrete" that characterizes much of Lazarsfeld's substantive criticism of Adorno's memo. Adorno is simply too theoretical, too ungrounded in positive data. Even when Adorno's tone is "insulting," Lazarsfeld insists that it be clean and "orderly," that is, empirically grounded:

> On pages 107 and 109 you express a theory that the broadcasting officials who decide on programs pick out so low-grade programs because they are as bad taste as the broad markets have [sic]. Could it not be that those officials are not morons but scoundrels who corrupt the masses against their better knowledge? . . . You see at this point of my argument I don't try to keep you from being insulting, I just try to show you how illogical and without foundation you are when you select one insult rather than another. And if insults are necessary in critical study—I don't want to argue about that now—don't you think that they should be based on an orderly procedure?[44]

Lazarsfeld, to his credit, seems to have a much better grasp of the confines and politics of the system in which he works than does Adorno. But the argument about the orderliness of Adorno's insults so thoroughly misses his point about the shared unfreedom of producers and consumers and the subjective resistance that rigid order would hopefully inspire—but everywhere failed to—as to render Lazarsfeld's suggestions absurd. However, Lazarsfeld's insistence that even one's insults have to be grounded in the facts is completely consistent with the logic of "Remarks on Administrative and Critical Communications Research": Even a critique of the system has to be systematic. Further, by downplaying the potentialities of the fortuitous guesses—and it must be noted that Lazarsfeld dismisses Adorno's most speculative theories by calling them "hunches"—he stakes administrative research's claim to the "right" answer, while consigning theory, critical or otherwise, to the realm of speculation and giving it the aura of something made respectable only through sampling and fact checking. "Although speculation is indispensable for guidance in any kind of empirical work," he declares, "if honestly carried through it will usually lead to a number of alternative conclusions which cannot all be true at the same time. Which one corresponds to the real situation can be decided only by empirical studies."[45]

What is telling about this assertion regarding empirical reality is that, since it denies the possibility of more than one "right" answer, it also denies any truth to dialectical thought, thereby eviscerating critical theory. Critical theory can only be made palatable to administrative research if it is forced to renounce that which makes it powerful, namely, its commitment to the oscillating dialectic between subjects and their objective social conditions. At the same time, however, Lazarsfeld's insistence on the "value" of administrative research for a variety of ends, whether commercial or educational, public or private—as though it were coin good for all debts—undermines the authenticity of his own results by rendering them contingent to the predominant logic of their own utility. In "Remarks on Administrative and Critical Communications Research," Lazarsfeld makes a place for critical theory, but only as a function of empirically grounded administrative research. Lazarsfeld's fable, which purports to explain how radio can be made more democratic, in fact suggests that empirical research can just as easily serve democracy's opposite.

This effort to reduce research, whether critical or administrative, to a utilitarian function is precisely what Adorno laments in "Procrustes," and he sees in this pragmatic use of knowledge a threat to the freedoms that Lazarsfeld claims to uphold. "People do science as long as something pays for it," he claims, and he writes as a man who has witnessed the perversion of both biology and the social sciences in the interest of the eugenics programs of the Reich:

> But they have faith in neither its relevance nor the bindingness of its
> results. They would discard the whole consignment as junk, if changes
> in the social form of organization made redundant, for example, the
> ascertaining of statistical averages, in admiration of which formal
> democracy is mirrored as the mere superstition of the research bureau. . . .
> The whole apparatus of book-keeping, administration, annual reports and
> balance sheets, important sessions and business trips, is set in motion to
> confer on commercial interests the semblance of a general necessity
> elicited from the depths. The self-induced motion of such office work
> is called research only because it has no serious influence on material
> production, still less goes beyond its critique.[46]

Adorno, clearly burned by his association with PRRP, is no doubt being harsh and perhaps needlessly critical of dedicated scientists who, like Lazarsfeld, believed themselves committed to social justice. But to simply think that Adorno was blinkered and elitist would be to deny the palpable dismay Adorno feels at the threat to democracy posed by a commercial system all too willing to use statistical research to reduce individuals to numbers. It would also be to miss the historical context from which Adorno was writing: Not only could he draw on his experience of the perversion of radio as a mass-media form by the German Ministry of Information, but also the preponderance of American material Adorno encountered suggested that radio networks were putting their research to ultimately antidemocratic ends. To understand the extent to which Adorno found it necessary to defend theory against administrative research, and why he believed that battle might also be at one with the struggle for democratic freedoms, one needs to consider the development of audience research and the uses to which Lazarsfeld and others were putting it when Adorno arrived in New York in the late 1930s.

It may be an index of the importance of these "audience intellectuals" and their place within the national consciousness that by the 1940s, the techniques Lazarsfeld and his colleagues pioneered had become so ubiquitous and publicly familiar that they could function as a crucial thematic element of a best-selling novel. In *The Hucksters*, Frederic Wakeman's satire of the radio industry, Vic Norman—echoing Lazarsfeld's work with Lux—is a jaded radio advertising man responsible for the Beautee Soap show and its lackluster star, Figaro Perkins. In one passage, Vic explains to his girlfriend how networks determine who is listening—and to what:

> "Nothing matters in commercial radio but a Hooper, or Crossley rating, whichever one you happen to read. All success is measured by them; most jobs are lost on account of them. The ratings are figured like this. Research people in all the big cities call telephone numbers, picked at random out of the local phone book. When somebody answers, they say 'Is your radio tuned in?' They ask what station and what program and what product is advertised."
>
> "Nobody ever called me," Jean said. "I think it's a fake."
>
> "They only have to call a few thousand people to get a fairly accurate percentage of the whole country, just like a presidential poll. Anyway, if eleven percent of the people answering the phones say they're turned on to the local station, that's broadcasting the Beautee Soap show, starring Figaro Perkins, that means we get an eleven Hooperating."
>
> "Is that all?" Jean was brushing up her lips and admiring herself in a pocket mirror. "Sounds like a lot of fuss over nothing."
>
> "Well, if the research people who figure things out are correct, then an eleven rating means eleven million people are listening to your show—a million people for each Hooper point. On some shows, like *Fibber McGee*

and Molly, as many as forty million people listen. That's why radio can never be an adult art form—too many damn people to please."[47]

The Hucksters, a *New York Times* number-one best seller at the time of its release, is now mainly forgotten. But like his contemporaries Nathanael West and Budd Schulberg, who, in *The Day of the Locust* and *What Makes Sammy Run*, respectively, describe the venality of the movie industry, Wakeman deserves to be rediscovered for his acid portrayal of radio advertising. What Wakeman illustrates, particularly in his portrayal of Jean's skepticism, was precisely what Adorno was encountering in the Bureau of Applied Social Research as it turned its statistical gaze on the artwork.

One of the ironies of Adorno's exile years was that by virtue of his critique of the American mass media and the statistical research that bolstered them, he was derided as anti-American by proponents of the mass media.[48] In *The Hucksters*, however, Wakeman portrays a radio industry every bit as manipulative as the "culture industry" described in Adorno's and Horkheimer's contemporaneous *Dialectic of Enlightenment*. Listeners are reduced to their statistically preordained likes and dislikes and then extrapolated by a factor of 1,000. Individual expression is circumscribed by the demands of pleasing the lowest common denominator. Every artist is hired with a calculating eye toward the Hooper or Crossley rating. Jean's suspicions that the measurement of audiences is a fake is a lament illustrating the mystifying but potent force of data gathering. In a sense, the rating *is* a fake. Since no one has called her, and her individual opinions haven't been registered, Jean rightly sees no direct relationship between her concrete likes and dislikes and what's on the air. Nevertheless, Vic's response, defending the "science" behind polling, precisely illustrates the paradox of the cultural commodity in a mass-mediated society. What is amorphous and intangible (so-called public opinion) supersedes the concrete desires of individuals. These mysterious, subjective "opinions," when schematized by Vic and his research team, become real and have concrete effects on the lives of the listening public, limiting their choices and dictating their preferences. At the same time, the objective reality of Jean's desires disappears like a rumor, a datum that doesn't compute on the spreadsheets at the New York office. In a reversal not unlike the one ultimately diagnosed by Adorno's student Jürgen Habermas, the public sphere mutates into the sphere of publicity, whereby what once was the product of the enlightened bourgeois subject (individual opinion) becomes a standardized commodity for a captive market to buy.[49] For his part, Wakeman, in an almost Adornian mode, claims that this transformation, a capitulation to the lowest common denominator, spells the death of authentic "adult" art. Jean's objection that she thinks it's a fake sounds like the last cry of the disappearing subject in the face of its inexorable liquidation. *The Hucksters* provides a bracing if somewhat breezy account of the relationship between data gathering and broadcast content. Nonetheless, it is worth noting that the techniques described in 1946—cold calls and standardized questionnaires—are among those that Lazarsfeld pioneered in the 1930s, techniques about which Adorno was decidedly suspicious. Further, many of those methods and technologies of audience research are still in use today, perhaps in more sophisticated forms but for essentially the same ends. Much of the dismay Adorno registers in "Procrustes" stems from his belief that the methodology of audience analysis inevitably transforms its objects. To Adorno's way of thinking, Lazarsfeld's embrace of those data-gathering techniques in the interests of the human sciences often served an opposing, dehumanizing end. To understand how the dispute between Adorno and Lazarsfeld still colors the study of audiences, two recent examples from the popular media may help illustrate what Adorno felt was at stake in the media research of the 1930s and '40s and why he believed that "audience intellectuals" tended to serve economic—rather than intellectual—interests.

In April 2002, the National Public Radio (NPR) program *On the Media* broadcast a segment titled "Music Testing." In the teaser for the story, *On the Media*'s host, Brooke Gladstone, explained the historical and technological progress that "Music Testing" traces:

> In the early days of Top 40 radio, some fifty years ago, programmers used rather crude and unscientific methods to determine their playlists—record store sales—phone requests—the number of plays on the local juke box— and of course some programmers and deejays took pride in their gut ability to pick the hits. . . . *Today*, most commercial music stations test each and every song in the laboratory of public opinion research. [For] listeners hoping these tests will mean longer play lists and less repetition, the news isn't so good.[50]

As reported by Paul Ingles, "Music Testing" tells of the various methods radio research firms use to measure the popularity of songs and thereby determine the playlists of contemporary music stations. The two most common of these methods, the auditorium test and the "call out" telephone test, subject participants to hundreds of song "hooks" in ten-second bursts. Either by using a scannable test sheet and the inevitable number-two pencil or by using telephone buttons, participants can rank the hooks from 1 to 5. As Ingles puts it, "1 meaning you'd switch stations, you hate the song so much—5 meaning, 'It rocks, dude!'" Despite the sometimes glib and bemused tone of the report, the implications of audience testing are a narrowed radio playlist and a greater standardization of hits. "To maximize audiences," Ingles claims,

> Many programmers say they must minimize low testing and unfamiliar tunes that give listeners a reason to punch out. The result is active title lists of just a few hundred songs. . . . Testing shows that eighteen- to thirty-five-year-old classic rock fans have had their music tastes completely defined by stations that have played, for example, only Steve Miller's biggest hits.[51]

Not surprisingly, the putatively public NPR implies that these innovative technologies of radio-audience measurement are yet further evidence that commercial radio is interested only in capturing the largest audience share possible rather than in the comparative subtlety and majesty of—at least according to the internal logic and soundtrack of "Music Testing"— deep cuts from Miller's *Sailor* album or David Bowie's *Low*.

The same week that "Music Testing" aired on NPR, NBC's *Today* show ran a segment on the divergent opinions on the Israeli–Palestinian conflict. At that point, in the wake of the so-called Passover massacre, the subsequent occupation of the refugee camp at Jenin and Yasser Arafat's headquarters in Ramallah, and the prolonged holdout of armed Palestinians in the Church of the Nativity at Bethlehem, tensions were at their height and all-out war appeared inevitable. Rhetoric on both sides of the dispute was particularly, if predictably, voluble. In an effort to measure the depths of feeling concerning the issue, *Today* assembled an audience panel consisting of an equal number of pro-Palestine and pro-Israel viewers. The panel was asked to listen to a speech by a representative from the Palestinian Authority, followed by a speech from a member of the Israeli government. While listening, the audience could record their reactions to the speeches, positive or negative, by means of two buttons. The responses were then digitally tabulated and mapped on a computer display, positive responses at the top of the screen, negative at the bottom. The results, of course, depending on the speaker, were two widely divergent V shapes pointing toward the top and bottom of the screen and indicating the magnitude of the divide between the two sides. The segment concluded with both groups interviewed about their likes and dislikes, each claiming that the other side told lies while the representatives of their cause told the truth.

What is worth noting about both the *On the Media* report and the *Today* show's poll is not the patently obvious conclusions reached (people like what's familiar; Israelis and Palestinians can't agree); rather, it is the gee-whiz attitude with which both of these programs treat audience research (radio stations statistically measure the appeal of their playlists; computers can measure people's reaction to broadcasts). There is something both disheartening and disingenuous about the way these broadcasts proclaim their so-called innovations in audience measurement. "Music Testing," for example, outlines an evolutionary narrative from primitivism to enlightenment: Fifty years ago, programming was "crude"; today it is sophisticated, technologically savvy, and ubiquitous. However, despite the "isn't that something" breathlessness that introduces these segments, the techniques and—for the most part—technologies for these tests have been in place since well before Adorno lamented the "sneering empiricist sabotage" of social research in 1945, and many of those techniques were pioneered by Adorno's colleagues on the PRRP.

There is a certain consistency to the selective amnesia the culture industry suffers when it comes to the subject of measuring audiences. As long ago as 1978, in a *Film Comment* essay, Thomas Simonet wryly remarked on the tendency of entertainment corporations (in this case, motion picture companies) to forget the history of audience measurement as part of their own history. "Audience research has been growing from humble beginnings to more grandiose beginnings. But it always seems to be making beginnings."[52] As evidence for this amnesia, Simonet outlines the work of a number of organizations whose job was to deliver to the motion picture studios the greatest number of moviegoers through the use of statistical analysis. The first of the figures Simonet describes is George Gallup Sr., whose Audience Research Institute (ARI) from 1935 to 1952 measured audience reactions to everything from the stars' names to a film's advertising campaign to the film itself. In addition to questionnaires and interviews, Gallup used a machine called a Hopkins Electric Televoting Machine, "through which test audiences, minute by minute, could register how much they liked or disliked a film," not unlike the panelists on the *Today* show asked to record their responses to the Middle Eastern dispute.[53] After Gallup's ARI ceased operations, Simonet continues, Leo Handel and his Motion Picture Research Bureau tried to provide the statistical go-ahead for Hollywood studios. Among the machines Handel employed was the Cirlin Reactograph, a machine comparable to a contemporary polygraph, which recorded the physiological responses of audience members to different scenes, thereby giving a supposedly more authentic description of an audience's actual response to a film.

Simonet suggests that after the 1950s, audience research, at least as far as the motion picture industry is concerned, has gone through a cycle of disappearances and reemergences, with each new appearance of research touted as innovative and revolutionary. IBM punch cards replaced penciled-in forms and in turn were replaced by digital questionnaires. We can see something of this "innovation" in the hyperbole that accompanies the supposedly new research techniques reported by *On the Media* and the *Today* show. Nevertheless, as Simonet wrote in 1978, "Amid the new beginnings, the pioneers keep polling along."[54] The Gallup and Nielsen corporations have been measuring audience opinions and ratings since the 1930s and '40s, respectively. The use of test screenings—and the subsequent reediting of films—is common practice in the film industry, and it is the rare commercial or entertainment-oriented Web site that doesn't allow its surfers to rate something, whether it be a film, a product, or the "helpfulness" of a news article.

Although Simonet's primary interest is motion picture research, he fails to mention that the technologies researchers employed were preceded, in the service of radio research, by the program analyzer developed by Lazarsfeld and Stanton, then director of research and eventually president of CBS. The program analyzer, which *Time* magazine called a "dingus" and Adorno, when forced to use one to measure audience reactions to popular music, derisively referred to as "that machine,"[55] operated on a relatively simple principle. In a sense, it was the manual forerunner to the digital opinion tester used by *Today* or the touch-tone phone used in "Music Testing": Initially, test subjects would listen to a piece of music or a news report and, when hearing something they liked, would press a button that engaged a pen hovering over a spooling line of paper. As Mark Levy describes the apparatus in a 1982 article from the *Journal of Communication,* later models of the analyzer solved the problem of having only a single button, which would often stick in the "on" position, causing ink to spew onto the paper: "Instead of a single 'like' button . . . all later models of the Lazarsfeld-Stanton Program Analyzer gave subjects two controls: a green button held in the right hand to indicate 'like' and a red button for the left hand to show 'dislike.'"[56]

Levy's description of the limits and deficiencies of Lazarsfeld's and

Stanton's program analyzer serves as a critique of the assumptions made by contemporary broadcasts such as "Music Testing" and the *Today* show segment:

> The research assumed, first, that measurements of like–dislike could serve as meaningful indicators of the entire range of subjective reactions to the stimulus; second, that the judgments of liking–disliking were made more or less constantly throughout exposure; third, that experimental subjects evaluated "parts" of the stimulus, rather than reaching holistic judgments about it; and fourth, that the stimulus itself, and not other factors such as the setting of exposure, was the major influence conditioning the audience experience.[57]

Levy's reaction to the analyzer is astute, and it makes understandable Adorno's dismay at having to use Lazarsfeld's and Stanton's machine. The measurement of audience reactions to a cultural product in terms of either positive or negative response relegates those cultural products to the status of commodities. Using the program analyzer is a "crude" technique to the extent that what the analyzer and its more or less sophisticated successors provide is the answer to the baseline question of commerce: Will someone buy this? The subtlety and range of emotions evoked by a news report or an artwork are completely obviated by the binary like/dislike. Even in the case of the 1-to-5 music rankings, the songs suffer by virtue of their reduction to a finite system of assessment, a system that fails to consider musical complexity, style, genre, or, indeed, any criteria other than the catchiness of a ten-second hook or a calculated political sound-bite. The use of an opinion analyzer to assess the Palestinian question seems particularly egregious in this regard. Finally—and this was what was especially troubling to Adorno—when applied to music, the analyzer necessitated and ultimately legitimated atomized and regressive listening, in which the listener is all but required to listen for the hook. That this type of listening was forced upon the audiences at every level of the radio experience was the primary charge Adorno leveled against popular music and broadcasting, and to be required to affirm that type of listening through the very act of diagnosing it had to be, for him, especially irksome.

Returning to the 1930s and '40s, there is ample evidence that these audience-testing and audience-measurement techniques were already an inescapable part of the economic and intellectual fabric of the mass media in the 1930s and '40s. Indeed, for media corporations obsessed with producing the ever-new, the idea of a technological advance in research techniques could itself be used as a marketing ploy. In 1946, the same year Wakeman described the telephone radio techniques of Hooper and Crossley, the A. C. Nielsen company distributed what can only be considered a manifesto that would revolutionize the audience research industry and make Hooper and Crossley obsolete. "The existence of three radio program–rating services has created annoying confusion and wasteful duplication of expense," explains the foreword to *How You Can Get the Ideal Radio Research Service*. Then, using a hydraulic, sexual metaphor that would make Sigmund Freud blush, Nielsen claims, "With rapidly rising intensity, the radio industry is demanding relief." Of course, relief will come in the form of the Nielsen Radio Index Service, and *How You Can Get the Ideal Radio Research Service* makes a bald effort to monopolize the ratings-measurement industry, offering to Hooper and Crossley clients "an opportunity to acquire Nielsen RADIO INDEX on an *especially favorable basis*." Finally, in case the businessman reading the manual wasn't aware of the significance of the Nielsen report, the foreword concludes by insisting that "every executive who has a stake in radio will find it both interesting and profitable to read this material with care."[58]

Reading the material with care reveals something far more insidious than cutthroat business practices, however. *How You Can Get the Ideal Radio Research Service* introduces executives to the Nielsen Audimeter, "the graphic recording instrument installed in a radio receiver in a scientifically selected radio home." While Crossley and Hooper's calling system depended on the arbitrary nature of cold-calling at set times to capture a snapshot of the audience—a technique rendered all the more unreliable by virtue of the fact that it only captured those homes with telephones and had no way of gauging any but the most rudimentary sociological details about the person called—the Nielsen Audimeter tracked listening habits continuously throughout the day. Furthermore, the audimeter was distributed to provide a supposedly accurate cross-section of the population, taking into account city size, family size, type of dwelling, number of rooms, education, occupation, income, and number of radio receivers. While the thoroughness of its coverage was no doubt appealing to the business executive, the voyeurism inherent in the Nielsen Radio Index—voyeurism no less startling because the listener willingly submits to being monitored—has decidedly unsavory implications.

As a means of reinforcing the "scientific" aspects of the audimeter and of emphasizing how that science can aid the business aims of the advertiser, throughout *How You Can Get the Ideal Radio Research Service*, photographs of scientists, equipment, and statisticians are juxtaposed with images of "typical NRI homes" (Figure 1). In one photo, a well-dressed woman cases an apartment. In the next, she towers over a potential audimeter user. The tiny older woman in a housecoat appears to cringe into the corner when menaced by the "carefully trained, full-time" representative of the Statistical Department. On the next page, another elderly woman sits quietly knitting in her parlor, but, the caption explains, "installed in a typical radio receiver—the Audimeter operates silently and unseen" (Figure 2).[59] This electronic spy in the house predates George Orwell's *1984* and confirms Michel Foucault's worst suspicions about the nature of surveillance and discipline in society. What Nielsen listener would tune into "subversive" broadcasts in the era of the House Un-American Activities Committee (HUAC) hearings, which began in 1947?

But in a Nielsen house, Big Brother had a more directly material presence. Not only is every turn of the dial recorded, but so too is each of the family's purchases. Another pair of photos shows a very serious-looking man rifling through the contents of first a kitchen pantry and then a bathroom medicine chest. The purpose of this cabinet voyeurism is not prurience but productivity: "Inventories of radio-advertised commodities are taken in kitchens, pantries, bathrooms and boudoirs. Even basements and garages are included. These home inventories, combined with listening records, produce ratings of sales effectiveness. They also help in selecting the most effective program for advertising each product" (Figure 3).[60] *How You Can Get the Ideal Radio Research Service* represents the forward

Figure 1. From Arthur C. Nielsen, *How You Can Get the Ideal Radio Research Service* (A. C. Nielsen Company, 1946), 32.

Figure 2.
From *How You Can
Get the Ideal Radio
Research Service,* 33.

Figure 3. From *How You Can Get the Ideal Radio Research Service,* 35.

limit of a certain type of audience measurement, dedicated to learning what people listen to so as to better market products to them. As a document, it represents a moment in the history of capitalism when leisure time is transformed into a time of maximum productivity and efficiency. Even when engaged in such innocuous activities as knitting, the audience member is on the clock, creating surplus value for the sponsor. The resemblance between the IBM card that records audience data and the factory time card is clearly not accidental, nor is the name of one of the audimeter models— the "Hunter."

The audimeter and its successors that were used for television did indeed overwhelm the Hooper and Crossley ratings system: Nielsen's integrated technique of surveillance, sociological interviews, and consumption measurement together represent tendencies in audience research as a whole, confirmed not least by the surfeit of photos in *How You Can Get the Ideal Radio Research Service*. The Nielsen manual visually diagnoses the rage to pin down the audience and get a picture of an invisible consumer. In the American broadcasting context, with no radio license or subscriptions to buy and no visible means to confirm consumption, the problems of convincing potential sponsors to advertise and buy shows were magnified for radio. The appeal of an approach to audience measurement like Nielsen's was obvious: Networks and sponsors could correlate what listeners consumed sonically to what they consumed materially. Despite Nielsen's thoroughness, this information in no way answered the question of why audiences liked what they liked and bought what they bought. Thus, from a very early stage, networks, through the use of administrative research, attempted to address these questions. As early as 1929, both NBC and CBS, then two and three years old respectively, released extensive advertising manuals designed to introduce the concept of radio advertising to potential sponsors. Given the hyperbole one generally associates with the mass media—particularly that medium from which the old expression "bigger than radio" derived—the tone of the NBC volume is almost touchingly modest. "Broadcast advertising is that comparatively new medium through which advertisers may 'reach the ear' of the buying public," explains the first sentence of *Broadcast Advertising: A Study of the Radio Medium—the Fourth Dimension of Advertising*. "This book, then, is as brief as it can be; as exhaustive as it must be. Its function is not to sell Broadcast advertising but to explain it; to give its story."[61] On the other hand, the first lines of CBS's *Broadcast Advertising: The Sales Voice of America* are a study in bombast: "Broadcasting holds more romance, more fascination, and is more widely discussed than any other science, art, profession or business in the United States today."[62]

Although the tones of NBC's and CBS's *Broadcast Advertising* manuals, one of humble educational service and the other of ineluctable domination, will be reproduced throughout much of the marketing material published by the radio networks in the next two decades, there are a number of other salient features to these documents. First, although each network and the medium itself is relatively young (broadcasting, so-called, began in Pittsburgh with KDKA's airing of the results of the 1920 presidential election), both CBS and NBC use the statistics in their *Broadcast Advertising* manuals to trace their eventual dominance in the industry (a dominance so thorough that NBC will eventually be ordered by the courts to break up into two networks, Red and Blue). These statistics, primarily tracing the sales figures for advertising from 1927 to 1929, show a steep upward arc commensurate with the rise in the number of radio sets sold and, presumably, the number of advertisers.[63]

What is perhaps more interesting than the sales figures, however, is the evidence that statistics on audience members, their interests, and their buying habits were collected very early on by both networks for the benefit of their sponsors. One of CBS's selling points to its advertisers was its integrated "Research and Merchandising Departments" which were "coordinated to furnish advertisers and their agencies with broadcasting data and ideas for the adequate planning and the merchandising of the radio campaign."[64] Among the duties of the Research and Marketing Departments was the recording and collating of the 3 million letters received by CBS and its sponsors each year to gauge the "influence and following" of each program. For its part, NBC also collated its letters, but it went further and correlated those letters and its listeners to actual and potential buying habits. NBC did not simply deliver listeners; it delivered what its *Broadcast Advertising* terms "quality" listeners:

> It is therefore reasonable to assume that a large percentage of the Radio Audience is made up of people who are capable of buying, and who *do* buy the multitudinous commodities that contribute to the building and maintenance of the American home, and appreciate high-class entertainment. They are capable of and willing to express their interest in most tangible results; namely, purchase of products. . . . The radio audience are [*sic*] for the most part home-owners. They are prospects for every conceivable commodity. Unquestionably the radio audience forms the basis of a market so rich that alert advertisers will not want to neglect

it; a market so large that its very size far outweighs any comparison of its actual cost with other media.[65]

Although NBC claimed that the function of its manual was not to sell broadcast advertising, the soft sell is sophisticated and pervasive, and it counteracts any objection from potential advertisers that radio would attract a disproportionate number of freeloading nonconsumers. Radio owners, *Broadcast Advertising* insists, are home owners and car owners, and, since radio receivers at this time cost "between $100 and $150 complete with accessories," the manual claims that "these members of the Radio Audience are not averse to buying luxuries."[66] The "alert" sponsor, attuned to this "rich" market of "quality," propertied listeners who are only too willing to repay their "interest" in "high-class" entertainment with the purchase of products, will no doubt understand the insinuations. The logic of *Broadcast Advertising* is that consumption is not only smart, it is the foundation of the American home itself. The rhetorical gesture of the manual is to transform every radio listener into a member of the wealthy; in the months before the stock-market collapse, NBC reframes the middle class as a likely candidate for conspicuous consumption. While this consistently proved to be the case in the years following the Depression,[67] in this instance the transformation is effected through *Broadcast Advertising*'s somewhat suspect sleight of hand with its statistics. The manual never actually directly links the number of car owners, home owners, and radio sets, but by delivering the ownership figures of each in close proximity, NBC creates the illusion that there is a necessary relation between these discrete data sets.

If, through the use of audience research, NBC suggested that the rabble are reasonably wealthy, the aim of CBS's *The Very Rich: An Unsentimental Journey into Homes We Often Read About but So Seldom See (Their Gates Are Too High)* (1937) is to make the case that, as far as radio listening goes, the wealthy are just like the rabble—only more so. While the 1929 publications suggest that everyone involved with radio is high-class, the intervention of the Great Depression clearly necessitated a winking us-versus-them populist tone, which is evident in *The Very Rich*'s subtitle. The subsequent text maintains this everyman patter while outlining the challenges posed when advertising across class lines.

> Look at it this way: Here is a group of people (the Very Rich) sometimes suspected of an indifference to radio. They seem, nevertheless, to insist on having a set in every room of their many-roomed houses. (Like the house

in Delaware you may have heard about, with forty bedrooms . . . and forty
radios!)

What is *done* with all these radios? . . .

It was time, we felt, that someone went after *specific* information on
the radio habits of the Very Rich. How much does it cost to catch a
millionaire—when you are using nothing more for bait than is good enough
for the rest of the country? When you are using *one* campaign in *one*
medium for everybody.[68]

In order to solve this puzzle, the book explains, CBS enlisted the help
of the "Bureau of Research Statistics at Boston University." The bureau's
mission was to interview families of the Boston Brahmin community to
measure their listening habits. "None of us knew if we could get into
Boston's Very Rich homes," the manual states, although the very fact of
the book's publication guarantees that entry is a fait accompli. Here again,
the populist tone of *The Very Rich* appears, only to immediately give way
to chumminess and mutual respect between the haves and the have-somes.
"It was too easy to picture butlers, second-men and third-men springing
to arms to keep the rabble out. But we rather underestimated Boston's
good manners. Before the study was done, these members of the faculty
of Boston University obtained personal interviews with principals in 250
carefully selected families in the Metropolitan Boston area."[69]

The results, while not unexpected, are symptomatic of the standardiz-
ing effects of mass communication even at an early stage in its development. The book notes that although the Very Rich own a greater number
of radio sets, their listening tastes are essentially exactly the same as those
of the general population. *Major Bowes Amateur Hour* and Rudy Vallee are
among the favorites of rich and poor alike. As *The Very Rich* reports, "In
one of the commonest of America's activities—listening to the radio—
the Very Rich are not remarkably different from just folks. They respond
to programs in the same way. And they are exposed to the sales-message
in the same way." For the advertiser, the message to be taken from *The
Very Rich* is that "it costs nothing to catch the interest and attention of a
millionaire—by radio. You get him with the same program, at the same
time you get everybody else."[70]

The theoretical and methodological implications of *The Very Rich* help
explain both Adorno's reaction to the mass media and the trends in empirical research that he was forced to countenance while exiled in the United
States. CBS would have its sponsors believe that the comparable listening
habits of rich and rabble reflect the democratizing force of the airwaves.

"Most advertisers can safely afford to ignore the rich," the manual claims. "The manufacturer of a toothpaste, a cereal, or a soap-powder draws little class distinction in the merchandising of his goods. Indeed, to his democratic eyes milady ranks no higher than the milliner. And often, not as high!"[71] However, the logic behind such a sentiment is easily refuted. The equatability of subjects by virtue of what they consume, whether on the radio or at the market, at once betokens the reification of individuals as interchangeable units on a profit-and-loss spreadsheet, while at the same time masking the real class divisions that exist in this country—class divisions that depend, in part, on the provisional elevation of poorer citizens to the same consumer status as the rich. Furthermore, the notion that rich, poor, and middle class alike listen to Rudy Vallee confirms Adorno's deeply held suspicions that kitsch and culture have become one and the same.

But while that line of critique is crucial when Adorno's attention turns specifically to the radio transmission, there is another element in *The Very Rich* that must be noted. On the title page is the legend that the study contained in the manual was "conducted for, but not by, the Columbia Broadcasting System." Whether this line is included in the interests of modesty, honesty, or a desire to not appear unseemly when rifling through the cabinets of the upper crust, the citation signals a shift in the provenance of radio research, one that would ultimately influence Adorno's reception in the American academic community. Whereas in the *Broadcast Advertising* manual from 1929, CBS is proud to list the duties and accomplishments of its Research and Merchandising Departments, here the company readily acknowledge that an outside agency performed the research for the study—specifically, the Boston University Bureau of Research Statistics.

As Hanno Hardt writes in his encyclopedic overview of the history of mass-communications research, "The rise of communications research as a major social-scientific concern was aided by the demands of the marketplace and supported by the tradition of the American functionalism."[72] But while those engaged in this methodological approach, indebted to the traditions of pragmatism and tainted in no small way by Taylorist principles, might claim that their research was devoid of interest, there was and remains an ideological bent to the instrumentalization of data. Hardt continues:

> It was a perspective imbued with optimism reminiscent of American Pragmatism, based on the belief in the perpetuity of the social system and the capacity to overcome instabilities and disorders. Communication as a social process could play a major role in the maintenance of the social

system, and communication research, with its potential for generating knowledge about the relationship between people and political or economic structures in society, rose in importance, politically and academically.[73]

Hardt implicitly suggests that part of the burgeoning success of communications research was a modernist faith in the benefits of technological progress. In the 1940s, the notion that science, particularly statistical science, could and did have an important role in the preservation of societal values was not only a firmly held belief of Lazarsfeld and his colleagues at PRRP but also a recurring theme in popular literary texts, in which scientists were responsible for preserving the historical memory of a people. Perhaps the fantastic trust in the power of a functionalist methodology to maintain the social order is best captured in Isaac Asimov's *Foundation* series of science fiction books, the first stories of which were written in 1941, at the very moment when administrative research was in its ascendancy. *Foundation* introduces the discipline of "psychohistory," a field whose practitioners assemble the sociological data of the galaxy and predict with uncanny accuracy the trends that will lead to the fall of the Galactic Empire. In the series, psychohistorians take responsibility for assembling the galaxy's knowledge into a massive encyclopedia, thereby preserving culture and directing the galactic civilization to its next stage with as little chaos and violence as possible. "The sum of human knowing is beyond any one man; any thousand men," explains psychohistory's founder, Hari Seldon, in the type of portentous expository speech that gives science fiction its charm. The loss of knowledge—particularly "scientific" knowledge—goes hand in hand with the breakdown of the social order. This trend, Seldon explains, is precisely what psychohistorians strive to prevent:

> With the destruction of our social fabric, science will be broken into a million pieces. Individuals will know much of exceedingly tiny facets of what there is to know. They will be helpless and useless by themselves. The bits of lore, meaningless, will not be passed on. They will be lost through the generations. *But,* if we now prepare a giant summary of *all* knowledge, it will never be lost. Coming generations will build on it, and will not have to rediscover it for themselves.[74]

Asimov portrays the fantastic culmination of what Hardt claims is the operating assumption of the prevalent research trends of the period: History is at once both inevitable and knowable, and with the right methodological principles, research can instrumentalize its findings to guarantee the smooth operations of society. The vision of the scientist, who, by virtue of his collection of facts, can literally hold the world together, is clearly part of the appeal for the pioneers of communications research that Hardt describes. But the flip side of this figure of the statistical superhero is the insidious ontological presumption inherent in this brand of knowledge production.[75] What is—*is*, and empirically collected facts inexorably and irreproachably confirm that tautology. But since things are always what they are, and since the social system is supposedly eternal, the actual mechanism of the system becomes opaque. What really makes the system work takes a back seat to the statistical evidence that confirms that system.

Accordingly, the relationship between communications research and the economic structure of mass-communications production and distribution presents an insurmountable paradox. The "mass" media's function is to maintain a system of standardization and exploitation rationalized as natural by virtue of its correspondence to data that media research itself makes sensible. As such, Adorno writes in the postexile essay "The Schema of Mass Culture," what audience research participates in is a vicious circle that arrests historical and aesthetic development. "Inasmuch as any and every product refers back to what has already been preformed, the mechanism of adjustment towards which business interests drives it anyway is imposed upon it once again. Whatever is to pass muster must already have been handled, manipulated and approved by hundreds and thousands of people before anyone can enjoy it."[76] The result, Adorno predicts, is the preservation of history, but not as in *Foundation*, where noble social scientists use statistical data to save civilization; instead, preservation takes the form of ossification—the end of history. With the leveling down of all events into statistical data points, the historical and social specificity of artworks and events is liquidated. Since this system is perpetual and unchanging, guaranteed by the critical mass of statistical evidence, material historical development is impossible. "The consumer," Adorno insists, "is thus reduced to the abstract present."[77] The logic that presumes that historical progression has narrative teleology is confronted by the fact that, by virtue of the real demands of global capital that everything be simultaneously exchangeable, history becomes an evacuated category.

Consider Simonet's position that the culture industry has continually forgotten that the techniques and technologies of audience measurement have essentially always existed. The cyclical reappearance of audience research raises the question of the mass media's relationship to history. By claiming that superannuated technologies and ideas are new and innovative, the contemporary NPR and NBC broadcasts reaffirm the selective amnesia that characterizes the logic of reification and subsumption. Entertainment corporations—not to mention fashion designers and interior decorators—take history and technology as the raw material for each season's product line. As a result, all historical moments and all scientific methodologies can and are plugged into a seamless narrative of exchange.

That the social sciences are themselves implicated in the liquidation of history is a proposition with which many social scientists would no doubt disagree. However, in the book *Culture for the Millions?*—the record of a 1959 symposium assessing the relative merits of mass-communications research and the mass media (with an introduction by Lazarsfeld)—fellow exile Hannah Arendt sounds a cautionary note about the large-scale transmission of entertainment goods and about those whose intellectual labor makes it possible. Although Arendt and Adorno were frequently at odds throughout their careers, both because of their intellectual differences and also because of their vexed respective relationships with Benjamin and Heidegger, here, Arendt's suspicions about scholars whose research buttresses the mass media mirror Adorno's. "The entertainment industry," she writes, "is confronted with gargantuan appetites, and since its wares disappear in consumption, it must constantly offer new commodities. In this predicament, those who produce for the mass media ransack the entire range of past and present culture in the hope of finding suitable material."[78] The implications of this statement are twofold: First, since all time and all space are interchangeable, time and space become continuous and ever present in the dissemination of mass-media texts. There can be no memory because there is no past that is actually "past." The raw materials of history have to be transformed into the contemporary in order to make them consumable. As Arendt goes on to say, the material proffered by the entertainment industry "cannot be offered as it is; it must be prepared and altered in order to become entertaining; it cannot be consumed as it is."[79] Furthermore, with each succeeding generation of consumers, history has to be retooled, as in boot camp, so that a new cohort may be introduced to the same old new things, such as audience research. Second, empirical research, especially as it is used by the entertainment industry to measure and collect audience data for the benefit of this ransacking of history, is both victim and cause of this planification of time and space. When everything is reduced to a system of fungible coordinates or data sets, every situation or methodology can be plugged in anywhere without regard to context or perspective. Although Arendt and Adorno were often at loggerheads, this line of argument is essentially that of "Procrustes," where administrative audience research provides for broadcasters the "semblance of a general necessity elicited from the depths."

Arendt diagnoses the fundamental problem confronting the use of "scholarly" research in the service of mass-media corporations: It may well aid in the destruction of what it seeks to study—the life of subjects in society. But Arendt is, in America at least, fighting a losing battle. As nearly all the contributors of *Culture for the Millions?*—including Lazarsfeld—reveal, by the 1950s, the "official social sciences" have witnessed a shift in their chosen modus operandi and have adopted a generally conciliatory attitude toward the interpenetration of mass-communications studies as a discipline and market research as an economic tool. Thus, in *Culture for the Millions?* the ringing defense of the mass media and their benefits by Lazarsfeld, Stanton, and Edward Shils (who elsewhere calls Adorno a Marxist anti-American)[80] tends to predominate over and against those, like Arendt and Leo Lowenthal, who sound more cautionary notes.

Morrison, in his analysis of Lazarsfeld's contribution to the field of communications research, is clearly aware of how Lazarsfeld is implicated in the uneasy relationship between the market and the academy, and he writes that "a crucial question, however, is how far the external agency's 'concerns,' or interests, should be accepted by the academic community as worthy of attention, particularly if such concerns do not fit ethically with those of the staff to be engaged on the research, or fall outside their intellectual interests." Morrison then tries to absolve Lazarsfeld, suggesting that he maintained a degree of intellectual purity despite his business connections. But Morrison's defense betrays a certain naïveté about both the integrity of research and the links between economic interests and the academy and, in so doing, defaults to a somewhat romantic view of departmental funding. "If universities, however, wish their associated research institutes to engage in 'pure' research," he says, by way of excusing Lazarsfeld's willingness to follow the money, "then alternative sources of funds must be provided."[81] For Morrison, Lazarsfeld emerges as a heroic figure in the history of sociology for his resourcefulness in securing research funds while at the same time remaining pure. "In the case of Lazarsfeld," he insists, "his own manipulative skills allowed him to survive by satisfying the external agency's demands whilst at the same time not letting it interfere with what he considered the central task of his work." Lazarsfeld may have been acting like a "businessman," Morrison claims, when he was securing funds for his research, but business and the "pure" science Lazarsfeld conducted were two different things. "It is worth noting," Morrison concludes, "that the more applied the research of an institute, the less destructive such 'interference' is likely to be."[82]

This last statement highlights Adorno's incompatibility with Lazarsfeld and with administrative research in general. Morrison, a communications scholar, betrays an adherence to the commonly held notion that "applied" research somehow has privileged access to objective truth. As such, it is absolved of its relationship to business. However, Morrison refuses to consider this relationship dialectically, failing to acknowledge that a scientific methodology that develops within—and at the behest of—the system of commerce fundamentally transforms the object of its study. Market research divorces the idiosyncratic desires of human subjects from the statistical objects they become under the gaze of research. But it was precisely his insistence on thinking the interpenetration of subject and object, and therefore on thinking the system through the particulars, that characterized Adorno's approach to empirical research. This was not "cleverness," as Morrison insists ("cleverness dashed though with ignorance, and an arrogant ignorance at that"),[83] nor was it simply a difference between "quantitative" and "qualitative" approaches, as Morrison also claims. The "central task" of Lazarsfeld's work with PRRP was to measure the listening habits of radio audiences and in so doing to seek ways to bring the widest audience the best possible radio. But this task, no matter how progressive it was in the abstract, was nonetheless conditioned by the fact that the "best" radio was, in terms of marketing research, inevitably a function of quantity to the exclusion of quality. Whatever was deemed the best by the most was what the networks would produce.

For Adorno, however, the quantitative and qualitative were inseparable. A comprehensive understanding of an object had to incorporate the subjective encounter with the object, the social situation that determined the conditions of that encounter, and the methodologies used to measure and understand it. "No matter how instrumentally the moments of the mode of procedure are defined," Adorno writes, "their adequacy for the object is always still demanded, even if this is concealed." What was lacking in the methods espoused by Lazarsfeld—particularly in focus-group research that generalizes concepts about audience desires from particular data— was the adequacy of the method to its object. "Procedures are unproductive when they are lacking in such adequacy. In the method, the object must be treated in accord with its significance and importance, otherwise even the most polished method is bad." In short, the procedures of empirical research must ensure the dignity of the object of study by giving the object recourse to speak through the procedure itself. "This involves no less," Adorno claims, "than that, in the very form of the theory, the object must appear."[84]

These statements appear in "On the Logic of the Social Sciences," Adorno's response to Karl Popper in the 1961 symposium whose essays were published as *The Positivist Dispute in German Sociology.*[85] While the book *Culture for the Millions?* might have indicated the triumph of positivist administrative research in the United States (with an embattled Arendt as a lone holdout), *The Positivist Dispute* suggests both that theoretical approaches to the social sciences still have a necessary place and also that Adorno did indeed benefit from his introduction to the American social sciences. In a sense, what Adorno learned in his encounter with the American mass media and the empirical social sciences provided him the tools for a richer, more theoretically driven and nuanced version of social science research. For Adorno, theory isn't merely a tool to describe the objects collated by research, somehow distinct from those objects. Rather, theory is what makes the connection and disconnection between objects possible. Theory is what gives objects life, room to breathe, and, more importantly, the possibility of demonstrating how individual facts and opinions might be both part of a totalizing social system and yet also apart from that system. Thus, in *The Positivist Dispute,* Adorno strives to rescue theory from a presumption that the world could only be understood empirically from mere appearances while at the same time trying to preserve the sanctity of empirical objects. "Just as philosophy mistrusted the deceit of appearances and sought after interpretation," Adorno writes in *The Positivist Dispute*'s "Sociology and Empirical Research," "so the more smoothly the façade of society presents itself, the more profoundly does theory mistrust it."[86]

In saying this, Adorno takes a page from Friedrich Nietzsche, who was deeply suspicious of the natural sciences as a fetter on subjective will and insisted that interpretation was paramount. For Nietzsche, the natural sciences, at best, could only hope to do what philosophy did: interpret the world based on available evidence. "It is perhaps dawning on five or six minds," he writes in *Beyond Good and Evil,* "that physics, too, is only an interpretation and exegesis of the world (to suit us, if I may say so!) and *not* a world explanation."[87] Likewise for Adorno, while the object was of paramount importance, an assemblage of component facts could not speak to the whole. The capitulation of knowledge to the merely factual entailed the sacrifice by the social sciences of what was essential to philosophy. The pursuit of positivist objectivity entailed the loss of access to that which was vital and alive. "Theory seeks to give a name to what secretly holds the machinery together. The ardent desire for thought, to which the senselessness of what merely exists was once unbearable, has become secularized in the desire for the disenchantment. It seeks to raise the stone under which the monster lies brooding. In such knowledge alone meaning has been preserved for us."[88] For Adorno, the monster under the stone was, inevitably, the relations of economic production through which all the "facts" of the social situation are filtered. By not pausing to consider the nature of that monster, Adorno believes, the social sciences run the risk of presuming, on the basis of appearances, that one stone is pretty much the same as any other and of concentrating primarily on the evidence provided by those stones. However, it is precisely the unseen presence of the "monster" that gives the mundane stone its historical and material specificity, and only critical theory, according to Adorno—rather than administrative research—is adequate to lifting that stone and peering underneath.

Well before making this claim, in one of the most telling passages of *Minima Moralia*, Adorno insists that the continuous present disseminated by the culture industry and confirmed by empirical research told a story of history that prevented a genuine comprehension of history. What is essential is not the collection of stones, the seamless narrative or the self-contained data set, but rather the gaps in knowledge that escape the network of schematization burrowing beneath those phenomena. Here, Adorno inverts Stephen Daedalus's pretentious claim in *Ulysses* that "history . . . is a nightmare from which I am trying to awake."[89] Instead, he argues that the monstrous conditions of contemporary subjectivity are precisely those that are masked by the supposedly unassailable facts and their corollary—historicist, chronological progression. "Thought," Adorno writes, "waits to be woken one day by the memory of what has been missed, and to be transformed into teaching."[90] The challenge of modernity is to awaken not *from* the nightmare of history but *to* it, to rouse oneself from the seductive dream that the conditions of existence are noncontradictory. This awakening of thought is what Adorno calls "anamnesis," the memory of forgetting that forms such a crucial aspect of Adorno's writings on aesthetics, and this memory—of the gaps in knowledge—is the challenge posed in Adorno's reformulation of empirical research.

That Adorno is trying to implement this sophisticated approach to sociological research during his exile is evident in part in *Current of Music*, which offers, instead of audience data, the notion of a radio "physiognomy" in which audiences, producers, and technology form an ever-changing, contradictory body that mirrors the social system generally. And the full flowering of Adorno's sociology comes during his work with the AJC on *The Authoritarian Personality*. While a number of the conclusions drawn by the study, which suggested that many Americans in the 1940s harbored fascist tendencies, have been disproved, the methods of the project display an Adorno who worked diligently to bend Lazarsfeld's style of data gathering toward theoretical ends. In order to do this, however, Adorno and his colleagues had to confront the assumption that opinions could (and should) be measured directly. In the case of the Studies in Prejudice project, however, the direct empirical evidence of subjects' opinions was precisely what was least "true." How many people, after all, would answer "yes" to the question "Are you prejudiced?" Faced with this problem, Adorno and his colleagues devised what they came to call the F-scale, which asked questions designed to measure not people's prejudices but, rather, their adherence to irrational ideas. From those responses, Adorno and his colleagues were able to draw conclusions about the prevalence of prejudice and the tendency of citizens to follow authoritarian principles without ever having to ask the direct question.

The success of a text like *The Authoritarian Personality* is that it pulls a bait and switch on the reader. While it appears to satisfy the criteria of American sociological research methods, in reality it uses those protocols in its pursuit of the theoretical idea that people believe the opposite of what they profess. In "Scientific Experiences of a European Scholar in America," Adorno explains that "a work like *The Authoritarian Personality*, which, though much criticized, has never been charged with lacking familiarity with American materials and American procedures, was published in a fashion that did not attempt to conceal itself behind the customary facade of positivism in social science." Rather than privileging the empirical fetish that characterizes "American procedures," the success of *The Authoritarian Personality* derives from its "playfulness," which led the authors to devise the F-scale, whose empirical veneer permitted the authors the freedom to be "original, unconventional, imaginative, and directed toward fundamental issues."[91] This may be hyperbolic romanticism of the project on Adorno's part, but there is an unmistakable pride in his description of having used empiricism against itself, reversing

Lazarsfeld's poles so that administrative research is forced to do the bidding of a broader critique of the social whole. Further, the extensive revisions that the F-scale underwent and the diligence Adorno applied to its crafting should not go unremarked. In a memorandum to Horkheimer and the AJC, Adorno spells out just how vital an "indirect" questionnaire was to the success of the Berkeley Group's project. As he writes of the questionnaires:

> Anti-Semitism, ethnocentrism, and politico-economic reactionism or radicalism are topics about which many people are not prepared to speak with complete frankness. Thus, even at this surface ideological level it was necessary to employ a certain amount of indirectness. Subjects were never told what was the particular concern of the questionnaire, but only that they were taking part in a "survey of opinions about various issues of the day." . . . It was not possible, of course, to avoid statements prejudicial to minority groups, but care was taken in each case to allow the subject "a way out," that is to say, to make it possible for him to agree with such a statement while he was not "prejudiced" or "undemocratic."[92]

In short, what this indirect line of questioning was designed to do was both to gauge people's gullibility and to get subjects to "rationalize the irrational," to make the case for laws and violence directed against minority groups, to attribute otherworldly, mystical, or horrific attributes to entire populations. Throughout their exile work, particularly in *Dialectic of Enlightenment, Minima Moralia,* and *Eclipse of Reason,* Horkheimer and Adorno are keen to explain how rationality gives way to its opposite. Adorno's own skepticism concerning empirical research is conditioned by his awareness of how "science" or "the law" can be put in the service of extreme manifestations of insanity and give those manifestations the stamp of legitimacy. The indirect tactic of *The Authoritarian Personality* studies flows directly from these suspicions regarding the efficacy of "objective" science in a social situation that obscures actual social conditions. Since no subject would baldly admit to his or her anti-Semitic beliefs, the members of the Berkeley Group were charged with refining a testing procedure that would determine prejudice without asking about it. Their original anti-Semitism research was too direct:

> The issue of the "indirect approach" should be plainly faced. I see very well the difficulties it entails, but it is so basic an element of our whole study that it cannot possibly be dodged. Nor should it be diluted. The AS-scale, which does not include the question "Are you an Anti-Semite?"

but a number of overt questions pertaining to Jews cannot possibly be called indirect in the same sense as the more sophisticated questions of the F-scale.[93]

That the innovations of the F-scale questionnaires, which formed the centerpiece of *The Authoritarian Personality*, are Adorno's is confirmed in a letter Horkheimer sent in November 1944: "Your plan about integrating indirect indices into the general project is simply wonderful. I am very happy about it. The same thing goes for your hypothesis on the relationship of the underlying psychological tendencies and the rationalizations."[94]

This style of questionnaire operates contrary to traditional like/dislike methodologies exemplified by Lazarsfeld's and Stanton's program analyzer and its heirs; the development of the F-scale points to the fact that, for Adorno, the methods of research were themselves forms of mediation, means of transmitting data that altered the information between transmitter and receiver. A truly successful research methodology would therefore be one that acknowledged that the medium of research was the message—to borrow McLuhan's famous phrase—and recognized that the methodology most commensurate to the truth was often not the most direct one. With social science research, as in his writings on aesthetics, Adorno demolishes the concept of transparency and direct communication between subject and object. This strategy, we shall see, has crucial consequences for his writings about the mass media.

Accordingly, it is worth noting how Adorno attempted to circumvent the organizing principles of administrative research imposed by Lazarsfeld. In his memo to Lazarsfeld in response to the criticism of "Music in Radio" by Geoffrey Gorer, the Rockefeller Foundation's frequent consultant and watchdog on the project,[95] Adorno insists—as he does in "Procrustes"— that any account of an art form cannot simply consist of a description of its measurable phenomena. "It appears to me," he writes with regard to Gorer's reservations, "that in an artistic field such as music, any rigid distinction of 'scientific fact' with the esthetic judgment is naive."[96] Further, the concessions Adorno does make to positivism are dramatically impractical in their intricacy and draconian techniques. In one instance from the "Music in Radio" memorandum he suggests that broadcasters be convinced to air a piece of modern music twice, played the first time by an amateur, the second time by a professional trained to perform the piece. Reactions to perceived differences in performance would then be measured by questionnaires sent to listeners' homes. Or, in an even more bizarre and prohibitively expensive test, to gauge the destruction of aura wrought by music's reception in the home, Adorno suggests that researchers be dispatched to listeners' houses. There, they would note when during a specific piece of music the listener was distracted and when he or she paid attention. The notion that a study would take exactly as many researchers as there were participants can well be understood as a mocking jibe at the idea that anything short of full surveillance of the sort promised by Nielsen could possibly guarantee the faithful record of a listener's preferences.

Given Lazarsfeld's admission of the utility of research and the ends to which it is put in the fable, Adorno's criticism of administrative research, while often uncharitable, is not wrong. Age hardly mellowed this impression. In "Scientific Experiences of a European Scholar in America," although Adorno is perhaps kinder toward his colleagues on the various U.S. research projects (with the possible exception of the Mennonite jazz musician who was his assistant), he is nonetheless unrelenting in his critique of empirical research's deficient claim to be a privileged methodology. Further, he elaborates on his assertion in "Procrustes" that administrative research is, by virtue of its formal constraints, complicit with the logic of social domination. "It is hardly an accident that the representatives of a rigorous empiricism impose such restrictions upon the construction of theory that the reconstitution of the entire society and its laws of action is impeded," Adorno claims, introducing the notion of a conspiracy of bean counters. "The phenomena with which the sociology of the mass media must be concerned, particularly in America, cannot be separated from standardization, the transformation of artistic creations into consumer goods, and the calculated pseudo-individualization and similar manifestations of what is called *Verdinglichung*—'reification'—in German."[97] The integration of theory and research promised by Horkheimer, or theory's comfortable utility as proposed by Lazarsfeld, might betoken a fatal compromise on the part of the theorist. If one really cares about the sociology of mass media as well as the democratic principles sociologists claim to uphold, one must choose sides: "Whether one proceeds from a theory of society and interprets the allegedly reliably observed data as mere epiphenomena upon the theory, or, alternatively, regards the data as the essence of science and the theory as a mere abstraction derived from the ordering of data—these alternatives have far-reaching substantial consequences for the conception of society."[98]

If one were to level a final criticism at Lazarsfeld's "Remarks"—consistent with those already mentioned—it would be that in many respects the essay ignores the specificity of the particular mass medium to be studied.

Even in a notable exception like his *Radio and the Printed Page,* which has the express aim of determining variances in reception between two media, Lazarsfeld's emphasis is firmly placed on audience responses and reactions rather than on the constitutive elements that distinguish each form. Thus, the central question as to whether and how audiences receive a higher level of culture from the radio or from printed texts presumes that the raw material is fundamentally the same regardless of its method of delivery. Adorno refuses to make this presumption, and throughout his radio writings he tries to acknowledge the transformation the radio broadcast undergoes in its production, transmission, and reception. It is that specificity and its implications for a theory of time and space in modernity to which chapter 2 turns.

2 ADORNO IN SPONSOR-LAND
AUTHORITY ON THE RADIO

If, for pedagogical reasons, the whole truth cannot be told, at least
nothing but the truth should be told.

—Theodor W. Adorno

Among Max Horkheimer's papers, there is a draft of a curious letter composed
in the summer of 1940. Written to Elizabeth Rend Mitchell, the wife of
Charles E. Mitchell,[1] and asking for a donation of $1,500 to help Adorno
complete work on one of his projects, the correspondence contains the following, somewhat droll paragraph:

> My friend, Dr. T. W. Adorno, a member of our Institute, besides his work
> for us, directed the Music Study of the Princeton Radio Research Project,
> financed by the Rockefeller Foundation. He wrote great parts of his book
> "Current of Music," devoted to a theoretical analysis of the present social
> and aesthetic situation of music. As, at present, the music study of the
> Office of Radio Research (formerly Princeton Project) has stopped for
> lack of funds, the completion of Dr. Adorno's very important book is
> endangered. Moreover, the financial situation of the Institute would no
> longer permit Dr. Adorno to stay in New York. Like other members of the
> Institute he would have to retire to some small University town in the West.
> This would not only imply that he had to give up all of his chances and
> connections in New York, but also that the New York musical life would be
> deprived of his initiative which had just began to make itself felt here.[2]

Leaving aside the question of just how influential Adorno might have
been in the New York music scene, and also the fact that the "small

47

University town in the West" was, in fact, Los Angeles and its environs, the letter does draw an accurate thumbnail sketch of Adorno's experiences with Lazarsfeld, the PRRP, and the funds—or lack thereof—from the Rockefeller Foundation. As mentioned in chapter 1, the story of Adorno's relationship to PRRP and Lazarsfeld, as well as of his variable relationship with John Marshall, the man who controlled the Rockefeller Foundation's purse strings, is amply described in essays by both Adorno and Lazarsfeld, as well as in a number of postmortems by the Lazarsfeld scholar David Morrison.[3] But in the summer of 1940, the music section of PRRP was at something of a crossroads. In October 1939, Lazarsfeld and Marshall had arranged to have Adorno present his preliminary findings to a panel of music experts and radio industry heads, among them James Rowland Angell, a former president of Yale University, who had recently become the in-house "education counselor" at NBC.

Angell's presence at this meeting provides some insight into the obstacles that Adorno faced when expounding his brand of social critique to programmers and educators committed to a notion of radio's benevolence. Having only recently begun his post at NBC, Angell was appointed to give a certain weight to the network's claim that they were indeed providing a public service with their programming. The strategic nature of this hiring is best captured by a short publicity piece NBC issued in January 1939 touting Angell's decision to work for the network. The pamphlet, *The Place of Radio in Education*, includes a slew of newspaper editorials and testimonials "from leaders in business, education and public life," as well as the following statement from Lenox R. Lohr, president of NBC, that illustrates Angell's rhetorical importance:

> Broadcasting holds a mandate to operate "in the public interest, convenience and necessity." In other words, broadcasting is unique, for in many parts of the world radio is under rigid control and domination of governments. American broadcasting is untrammeled in its freedom to serve the public. It is in recognition of that responsibility that the National Broadcasting Company has concluded its arrangements to obtain the services and guidance of Dr. Angell in the important field of education through the air.[4]

Given this stated link between NBC's educational mission and American radio's "untrammeled . . . freedom," which purportedly stands in marked contrast to the "rigid control and domination" of radio in other parts of the world (read Germany, Italy, and the Soviet Union), one can only imagine the defensive posture assumed by Angell and his colleagues upon hearing Adorno, a German Jewish exile, claim in his presentation that, in America,

> radio music's ideological tendencies realize themselves objectively—that is, regardless of the intent of radio functionaries. There need be nothing subjectively malicious in the maintenance of vested interests. The major hypothesis for a study on the relation of vested interests to radio music is that music, under present radio auspices, serves to keep dormant critical analyses by listeners of their material social realities.[5]

Nor, given Lazarsfeld's attempt to collaborate with the networks in an effort to create the best radio programming possible, were the network executives prepared to entertain Adorno's nettlesome line of inquiry, which demanded of them that they "pose the question of the soporific effect of radio music upon social consciousness."[6] This was clearly a challenge that the radio experts were not expecting to consider, and Adorno's presentation, titled "On a Social Critique of Radio Music," was, to put it mildly, not received favorably.[7] The strident reaction against Adorno's work is best captured in the response of one of NBC's "music experts" quoted in a letter to Marshall from one of the network's programming chiefs:

> This paper is so full of factual errors and colored opinions, and its pretense at scientific procedure is so absurd in view of its numerous arbitrary assertions, that it is hardly worthy of serious consideration, except possibly as propaganda. In short, it seems to have an axiom to grind.[8]

In response to this charge, Marshall defended Adorno's work by claiming, "I know that it was intended to be a purely theoretical approach to the subject of music in broadcasting and that as such, axiom-grinding was its chief business. I recognize, of course, that a good bit of the theory involved was hardly original but felt that Adorno's formulation of it was in a good many ways illuminating."[9] Despite Marshall's seeming sympathy for Adorno, what followed was a protracted debate between Marshall and Lazarsfeld over the continued financial support of Adorno's work as well as over questions of how to smooth Adorno's prickly intellectual temperament and of the usefulness of his study as a program for change. By the early part of 1940, Marshall's support had curdled. In his diary entry from January 5, he writes that, while feeling "much engaged by the originality of Adorno's work . . . [t]he real issue is the utility of the study, and that utility must be measured by the effect which can be anticipated for it in remedying the present deficiencies of broadcast music." The problem, as Marshall saw it, was that given the connections of the study to high-level radio figures (and the support they were providing in terms of personnel and material), Adorno's critical tone "would be bound to put all those responsible for [radio] definitely on the defensive, with the probable result that they would be left more inclined to rationalize those deficiencies than to attempt any remedy for them."[10] Because of the antagonism Adorno's work displays toward the broadcasting industry, the only solution to the challenge Adorno presents is, Marshall claims, untenable:

> This leads J[ohn] M[arshall] to believe that Adorno at present could prepare a useful statement only if he had the collaboration of some one representative of the present system, but tolerant enough of Adorno's position to see what was useful in it and interpret that for people certain to be less tolerant. Finally, the tone of Adorno's paper leaves some doubt that Adorno would be able at present to collaborate in any such way. He seems psychologically engaged at the moment by his ability to recognize deficiencies in the broadcasting of music to an extent that makes questionable his own drive to find ways of remedying them.[11]

The result of this assessment was that "JM was not prepared to include any further provision for Adorno's going on with his work at present."[12] Although the negotiations and cajoling among Lazarsfeld, Marshall, and Adorno would drag on for nearly eighteen more months, the implications of Marshall's diary entry were clear: The plug was being pulled, and Adorno, who had dedicated most of his first years in America to the radio project, would not see the bulk of his work published. The plans for a book-length manuscript that would derive from the music department's work for PRRP were, at least as far as the Rockefeller Foundation was concerned, kaput.[13] As Marshall describes it, Adorno's situation and that of the radio studies were that

> he has some seven or eight studies which he began with Lazarsfeld which are now near completion. He can earn his living if he undertakes other research which is within the program of the International Institute for Social Research at Columbia, to which he is attached. But these studies which he began with Lazarsfeld and which he is at present most keenly interested in do not come within the Institute's program. Hence he cannot complete them unless he finds some further support.[14]

These then, were the circumstances that led to the letter asking for money from Mrs. Charles E. Mitchell. What makes this letter of interest, though, is less that it adequately describes the situation in which Adorno found himself under the threat of the denial of funds from the Rockefeller Foundation (albeit with some measure of hyperbole), and more that Adorno himself wrote this plea for a donation under Horkheimer's name and expected Horkheimer to sign and mail it. Attached to Mrs. Mitchell's letter in Horkheimer's archives is a note from Adorno that begins "Lieber Max, hier der Entwurf des Briefes an Mrs. Mitchell. Unter Umständen wäre es gut, noch den oder einen anderen über das Institut hinzuzufügen und ihr etwa auch das letzte Pamphlet beizulegen, wenn nicht die finanziellen Angaben des Pamphlets für den gegenwärtigen Zweck zu positiv klingen." (Dear Max, here is the draft of the letter to Mrs. Mitchell. Possibly it would be good to add a few sentences about the Institute and also to include for her the latest [Institute] pamphlet, if, for present purposes, the pamphlet's financial information doesn't sound too positive.)[15]

There is no reply to Adorno's note from Horkheimer, and it is unknown whether the request for aid was eventually sent to Mrs. Mitchell or to any other potential benefactor. But this letter illustrates precisely what Marshall's diary claims: Adorno had a huge manuscript about radio on his hands, and no means to complete and publish it. Notwithstanding the fact that this is essentially a fund-raising letter (and one written by Adorno himself), the claim that *Current of Music* is a "very important book" should not go unnoticed, for it indicates just how keenly Adorno himself felt about the significance of the radio work he was doing in America. The urgency to get *Current of Music* published is worth mentioning, because if one were to assess Adorno's writings on radio only on the basis of those essays published during his lifetime, one would necessarily conclude that radio was of relatively minor importance to the development of Adorno's aesthetic theories and of little consequence to his appreciation of America and the culture industry. Despite working as director of the music section of the PRRP from his arrival in the United States in 1938 until his move to Los Angeles in 1941, Adorno's published output on radio was comparatively meager. Of his writings specifically on the topic of radio, only three short pieces appear under his name between 1938 and 1953,[16] and Adorno contributed only one essay, "The Radio Symphony," to the *Radio Research* volumes, which record the results of PRRP's studies. But to base an assessment of Adorno's radio writings solely on the published output of the period would be to severely underestimate the centrality of radio in Adorno's thought. Indeed, within the last few years a number of publications have appeared that indicate just how extensive and how sophisticated Adorno's studies of the radio industry and broadcast programming were. In addition to two book-length essays—*The Psychological Technique of Martin Luther Thomas' Radio Addresses* and "Analytical Study of NBC's *Music Appreciation Hour*," both of which were written between 1938 and 1943 and which have been recently published—there also exists the mimeographed "Memorandum: Music in Radio" (161 single-spaced pages), which resides among Lazarsfeld's papers at Columbia University. And finally, there is *Current of Music* itself, which runs to nearly 700 printed pages and contains many of the components from the other radio writings. As Thomas Levin writes in "Elements of a Radio Theory: Adorno and the Princeton Radio Research Project," his introductory essay to Adorno's study of NBC's *Music Appreciation Hour*, "Adorno's serious interest in questions of popular culture and technology is . . . much more complex than has previously been acknowledged."[17] But while Levin's essay is an elegant introduction to Adorno's work with PRRP and its relationship to his pre-exile music writing, it nevertheless leaves out a discussion of the much larger texts Adorno produced while at work on the Princeton project. These exhaustive—sometimes exasperating—documents, unpublished during Adorno's lifetime, contain within their pages the kernels not only of the radio essays Adorno would actually publish during the exile period but also of those theories that would characterize Adorno's critique of the culture industry and his later philosophical writings.

This chapter seeks to place Adorno's analysis of the specificity of the radio mechanism in constellation with the radio networks' ideological and social agenda as evidenced both by their programming and by their publicity materials and their attempts to capture audiences and advertisers. By considering some of the means by which the radio networks of the 1930s and '40s produced, distributed, and marketed their sonic wares, I hope to suggest the urgency of Adorno's radio research, not only for his own period but also for our own.

In the memorandum "Music in Radio" Adorno writes, "One of the assumptions of this memorandum is that a unity between social and technical mechanisms actually exists."[18] And in *Current of Music* he claims that this social function

> is determined neither by the surface appearance of the particular contents
> which it transmits, nor by the conditioned reactions of the listeners, but
> by the actual technical structure of the radio phenomena which confront
> the listener. It is this structure, its social implications and relatedness to
> present social conditions, upon which a theoretical radio analysis ought to

be based. This structure displays irrational trends and it is apt to bewitch mischievously the laws of logic.[19]

As is made abundantly clear in "Music in Radio" and in *Current of Music,* Adorno considered the "logical," positivist methodological principles of Lazarsfeld's "administrative research" inadequate to the demands of a rigorous critique of radio as a social and technological medium. In opposition to the empiricist bent of his PRRP colleagues, in a memo entitled "Theses about the Idea and Form of Collaboration of the Princeton Radio Research Program," eventually published in *Current of Music,* Adorno makes the case for the primacy of a methodology that considers the phenomenon of radio as a whole rather than of a methodology that restricts itself to the interpretation of listener data. Accordingly, Adorno writes, "the work of the project is to be conducted subject to theoretical viewpoints," and the collection of survey data must, he claims, be subservient to that theoretical end. "That is," he continues "nowhere will the collection of facts be an aim in itself, except for special groups of problems upon which, for some reason or other, we must consciously concentrate our activity on fact-collecting. In general, however, facts are to be selected with reference to their applicability to a theory concerning the relationship between present-day radio and society. The preparation of statistical generalities, average numbers and so on, as well, is only a means to an end."[20]

Adorno's justification for this approach stems from his assumptions about the conditions of so-called individuals confronted by the culture industry. Surveys of "likes and dislikes," which Lazarsfeld espoused, assume that the individual has the capacity, in the face of mass manipulation of tastes and interests, to truly make individual choices. In contrast, Adorno believed that the culture industry standardizes musical experience and that in consequence the individual does not so much stand as a unique register of a particular response to cultural products as represent an index of the broader realities of that standardization. Extensive discussions with a handful of individuals can, Adorno believed, do the work of hundreds of surveys, but only if one conceives of the individual not as a unique and free-willed agent but as a symptom of the broader conditions of society. Hence, Adorno writes in his methodological protocol:

> To my mind, the justification for conducting individual analyses very thoroughly, instead of questioning or interviewing hundreds and hundreds of people in order to arrive at averages, lies in the conviction that the mechanism which works upon the individual, since it is the mechanism of

the one society, is identical in most cases. Consequently, if one succeeds in tracing back the "individual" psychology of a particular individual to this mechanism, the results will most likely hold good in general. The results, of course, must be checked. The usual positivist assertion, however, insisting that generalizations should not be made on the basis of individual experiences but that the investigator should rather try to get as many cases as possible and only then try to induce general rules, is based upon the fallacious assumption that the individual is absolutely "individual" and not the product of non-individual forces behind him.[21]

This is precisely the sort of logic that caused Adorno's detractors among the PRRP researchers and their supporters to react against him, his adherence to theory, and his supposed sloppiness, and it is no less the reason that critics of Adorno feel that he overstates and oversimplifies the actual effects of the standardization wrought by the culture industry. By adhering to the rigors of a theoretical critique, however, Adorno refused to accept that radio is merely a cultural good that could be made better or more educational for listeners. If one follows Adorno's arguments to their conclusion, one comes to understand radio as a symptom of an entire network of social processes. This network threatens to transform not only the relationships among society, technology, and subjects but also the very nature of subjectivity itself. Moreover, an adequate analysis of radio phenomena can never derive from the same techniques that radio itself uses to sell its wares. As Adorno writes in the introduction to the version of "On a Social Critique of Radio Music" presented to PRRP and its collection of experts, "The logical form of [audience research] is moulded according to the ideal of a skilled manipulation of the masses."[22] By that criterion, Lazarsfeld's brand of research is ineluctably tied to the principles of commodity exchange that demand that all cultural goods be transformed into exchange values. "Whatever its content may be," Adorno writes, excoriating Lazarsfeld's methods while defending his own,

> it is a type of investigation that follows essentially the pattern of market analysis even if it appears to be completely remote from any selling purpose. For I am fully aware that this type of research applies to intentions so highly divergent that it seems arbitrary to speak about administrative research in general. It might be research of an *exploitive* [sic] character, i.e. guided by the desire to induce as large a layer of the population as possible to buy a certain commodity. Or it may be what Dr. Lazarsfeld calls *benevolent* administrative research, putting questions, such as, "How can we bring good music to as large a number of listeners

as possible?" Still it appears to me that by their very structure both these
types of research are more closely akin than they present themselves
materially.[23]

Adorno begins the later, published version of this work, "A Social Critique of Radio Music," with Lazarsfeld's question: "How can good music
be conveyed to the largest possible audience?" But via a series of corollary questions, Adorno seeks to illustrate the paradoxes of the listening
situation: "Does a symphony on the air remain a symphony? . . . And as
to the number of people who listen to 'good music': *how* do they listen to
it? Do they listen to a Beethoven Symphony in a concentrated mood? Can
they do so even if they want to?" Adorno thus transforms Lazarsfeld's original question and asks whether the very act of *broadcasting* "good" music
"make[s] the ideal of bringing good music to large numbers of people altogether illusory."[24] This shift in Adorno's focus is crucial, if only to understanding how antithetical Adorno's and Lazarsfeld's agendas were, as well
as the genuine incompatibility of their methods. Given the skepticism embedded in Adorno's question about the illusory possibilities of broadcasting good music, there is very little chance that Adorno would—or even
could—have accommodated himself to the demands of administrative
research placed on him by PRRP and the radio networks. For whatever
shortsightedness Marshall may have displayed when denying Adorno his
requested funds, he proved remarkably astute in realizing that any hope
of mediating or interpreting Adorno through the intervention of some industry representative would be a failure. If, after all, a central concern of
Adorno's radio work is the way the radio industry and the bureaus that
research it, by virtue of their technical and social constraints, reduce the
complexity of artworks and consign subjects to atomized, reified patterns
of consumption, then to subject Adorno to the same simplification by some
"representative of the system" would have fundamentally undermined his
theoretical project.

The increasingly transparent collusion between government agencies,
entertainment conglomerates, and economic interests that Adorno identified in his radio writings is blatantly revealed both in the history of the
radio research project and in the pages of the radio network documents
that helped form his critique. But Adorno's vain attempts to see *Current of
Music* published and Marshall's recognition of the inability of such a work
to reach any but deaf ears sadly resonate with our own era. For those who
live in the United States today, the interpenetrations between government

and corporate interests are the norm—business as usual. But at a moment like ours, when criticism of the links among business, government, and the academy is explicitly deemed antipatriotic and government officials tell us that we have to "watch what we say"[25] lest we come under suspicion for challenging the conventional mandate for silence, it is all the more necessary to examine Adorno's intellectual defense against these trends in the 1930s and '40s. By examining the complex issues raised by Adorno's radio theories and the industry-produced pamphlets and publicity manuals, one can approach a fuller understanding of Adorno's critique of the culture industry. And what gives Adorno's writings continuing vitality is that he was writing at a time when, not unlike today, many people firmly believed that the mass media, particularly the radio, were in fact the voices of freedom and democracy.

Consider one of the many documents that illustrate the stakes of Adorno's radio writings: In a 1938 promotional book called *Musical Leadership Maintained by NBC,* there is an intriguing page of photographs containing nothing but pictures of serious musicians playing and holding their instruments (Figure 4). The fact that these are "serious" musicians is conveyed both by their expressions, dour and intense, and by the photos' captions, which inform the reader that they are looking at not just any musicians with their instruments but musicians with famous, historically significant instruments. In the top photo, heavy-browed men stand in front of an NBC microphone in a room full of cherub-covered frescoes. In this room, we read, "Paganini's violin was played for the first time over the air in a broadcast from Genoa, Italy." Beneath this image is another photograph of a musician and his instrument; once again the NBC microphone is prominent. In this luxurious chamber stands, we are told, "the immortal Wagner's own piano upon which he composed many of his famous operatic scores." Like Niccolò Paganini's violin, Richard Wagner's piano, courtesy of NBC, was "heard in an overseas broadcast from Bayreuth, Germany." Still a third photo, again with microphone and ornate tapestry (this one with a bare-chested African), shows "Chopin's piano played during an overseas broadcast from Warsaw, Poland."

In contrast to the sumptuous settings of the first three photos, the fourth image on the page is relatively austere. The wall covering is subdued and the instrument being played, a piano, is mundane—just a piano, not a famous composer's piano. Still, we learn that this broadcast has historical significance of its own; we are looking, the caption explains, at "Max Jordan, NBC's European representative announc[ing] a concert from the

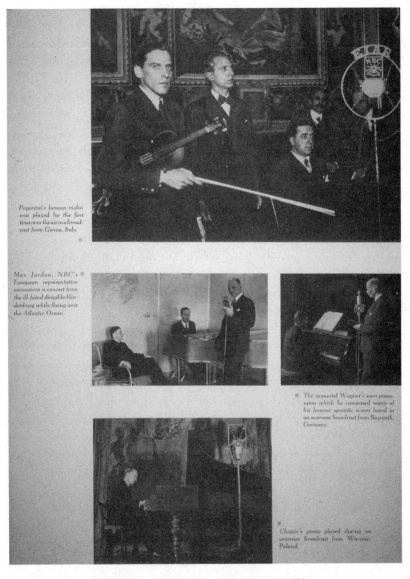

Paganini's famous violin
was played for the first
time over the air in a broadcast from Genoa, Italy.

Max Jordan, NBC's
European representative
announces a concert from
the ill-fated dirigible Hindenburg while flying over
the Atlantic Ocean.

The immortal Wagner's own piano,
upon which he composed many of
his famous operatic scores heard in
an overseas broadcast from Bayreuth,
Germany.

Chopin's piano played during an
overseas broadcast from Warsaw,
Poland.

Figure 4. From National Broadcasting Company, *Musical Leadership Maintained by NBC*
(New York: National Broadcasting Company, 1938), 24. Courtesy of NBC.

ill-fated dirigible Hindenburg while flying over the Atlantic Ocean."[26]
Considering this page as a whole, it is worth noticing that each of the
photos makes reference to an Axis country or, in the case of Poland, a
country that Germany will soon overrun. Although this collage of serious
musicians is meant to convey NBC's musical leadership, the historical and
geographic settings of the photographs make a compelling case that NBC's
musical broadcasts aspire to something much grander. Originating from
the center of world-historical events, NBC equates being "serious" about
one's music (by fetishizing master instruments) with being serious about
the European crisis. That the link between the broadcast of "serious"
music over the radio and the seriousness of events in the days prior to
World War II is being used by NBC to attract audiences and sell them
to advertisers is the apparent, if unspoken, strategy of the collage. Further,
NBC's assertion of musical *leadership* in Germany, Italy, and Poland likewise helps rhetorically assure listeners that the network, wielding Paganini's
violin, will get its audience and sponsors through troubled times. Looking
at these images today, *Musical Leadership* implies that in response to the
rise of fascism, Americans could rely on the "benevolent" leadership of
the networks just as they could rely on the benevolent leadership of their
government.[27]

The implicit link that *Musical Leadership Maintained by NBC* draws
between the supposed "value" of "serious" music on the radio, the rise of
European authoritarianism, and the leadership of networks was not lost on
Adorno. It goes almost without saying that the connection between fascism
and the mass dissemination of cultural goods is of central importance in
Adorno's writings while he was in exile,[28] and much of Adorno's criticism
of radio music and its conditions of performance can be seen condensed
in this one page of *Musical Leadership Maintained by NBC*. It should come
as no surprise, then, when reading Adorno's writings on radio, to realize
that Adorno himself looked at these same photos of serious musicians and
serious instruments with a degree of bitter irony as his worst suspicions
regarding "musical fetishism" were confirmed. It is in fact from *Musical
Leadership* that one of Adorno's favorite jabs at the networks comes. In
"A Social Critique of Radio Music," he writes:

> Whereas only the expert is able to distinguish a "Strad" from a good mod-
> ern fiddle, and whereas he is often least preoccupied with the tone quality
> of the fiddles, the layman, induced to treat these instruments as commodi-
> ties, gives them a disproportionate attention and adoration. One radio com-
> pany went so far as to arrange a cycle of broadcasts looking, not primarily

to the music played nor even to the performance, but to what might be called an acoustic exhibition of famous instruments such as Paganini's violin and Chopin's piano. This shows how far the commodity attitude in radio music goes, though under a cloak of culture and erudition.[29]

An examination of Adorno's writings that derived from his work as musical director for the PRRP, including the "Memorandum: Music in Radio" and *Current of Music*, makes clear that Adorno had fairly extensive access to the networks' promotional materials for his work and to *Musical Leadership* specifically.[30] When Adorno levels criticism at a specific aspect of the broadcast networks' treatment of music, he often does so making reference to "that NBC publicity publication" to bolster his argument. *Current of Music* contains an entire section titled "Some Remarks on a Propaganda Publication of NBC," and while the "Propaganda Publication" is never named, a comparison between Adorno's descriptions and the various sections of *Musical Leadership* reveals them to be one and the same document. Thus, when attempting to draw a connection between the broadcast of folk music and the National Socialist fetishization of the *Volk*, Adorno quotes a passage from *Musical Leadership Maintained by NBC* verbatim: "Folk music . . . simple melodies handed down orally from one generation to another and played or sung by people for their own enjoyment have provided some of the most interesting series of programs sponsored by the NBC."[31] To Adorno's mind, this nostalgia for traditional music has unsavory implications and confirms the link between NBC's musical programming and the situation in Europe from which he fled. "A direct connection with nationalist tendencies cannot," Adorno insists, "be overlooked here."[32]

Adorno's statements can be elaborated with a closer examination of *Musical Leadership* itself. Perhaps not surprisingly, the picture Adorno evokes in the section of the memorandum titled "The Role of Folk Music" appears on the page directly opposite the serious-musicians-with-serious-instruments collage and constitutes part of NBC's promotion of its folk-music programming (Figure 5). In contrast to the photos on the serious-music page, in these photos, jug-eared men grin over their fiddles, an open-shirted banjo player poses astride his instrument, and women in everyday wear form a "Folk" trio. While the serious musicians appear in rich surroundings, thereby asserting their "cultured" status, the photos on the folk-music page are shot outdoors, conveying the music's more "primitive" connections to nature. In effect, the folk collage operates as a down-home counterpoint to the collage highlighting the Paganini violin and the Chopin piano, suggesting that from fiddle tunes to violin concertos and

Figure 5. From *Musical Leadership Maintained by NBC*, 25. Courtesy of NBC.

from raw nature in the United States to the cultured interiors of Europe, NBC led the way.[33]

The folk-music page's appeal to authoritarianism is more direct than the relatively subtle overtones of the serious-music collage. The caption under the fiddlers explains that it portrays the "First broadcast of American Folk Music from White Top." The compendium of "firsts" here and throughout *Musical Leadership Maintained by NBC* predictably conforms to the marketing logic of the new-and-improved. However, the caption continues, "Many players traveled long distances by horseback and on foot to play native airs handed down by first white settlers." Through this statement, one can read the erasure of African music traditions from American folk-music history as well as the belief that "settler" music usurps the primacy of truly "native" art. While different in affect, the folk-music and serious-music pages perform similar ideological work, work that depends on a belief in the inherent superiority of Western cultures. Although the photographs of folk musicians make a direct appeal to racial authoritarianism, it is nonetheless perfectly complemented by the inherent belief in the great men and moments of Western "culture" made by the serious-music page.

Adorno's use of *Musical Leadership Maintained by NBC* invites an analysis of other network-produced publicity materials to gain a more nuanced understanding of the inextricable links between Adorno's radio texts on the one hand and his analysis of authoritarianism on the other. Although Adorno's critique of the culture industry is often dismissed as elitist, there is ample evidence, particularly in those documents produced by radio networks for potential sponsors, that his insistence that there were links between the mass media and the psychological techniques of fascism is extremely well-founded. Indeed, as he writes in *Current of Music,* the foreclosure of any productive use of radio by the masses can be gleaned directly from the pages of publicity manuals like *Musical Leadership Maintained by NBC.* "A perusal of a publicity release of any major network," he claims, "will show that the greatest positive emphasis is placed upon those very features which we regarded as the strongest enemies to radio functioning suitably for its material and its bringing the listener into a living relation with the material."[34]

Thus, any discussion of Adorno's radio writings should first of all remember that what Adorno has to say about radio bears a strong affinity to what he has to say about the degeneration of musical experience in general, particularly as he describes this situation in "On the Fetish-Character in

Music and the Regression of Listening" (1938) and "The Culture Industry" (1947).[35] In fact, the section "Types of Musical Conduct" that appears
in *Introduction to the Sociology of Music* (1952) and that describes characters ranging from the "expert" to the "jitterbug" and the "anti-musical
type," was written more than a decade earlier as part of Adorno's analysis
of radio listening.[36]

There is probably little need to revisit in detail the various arguments
Adorno makes regarding the regression of serious music in modernity.
These are amply described in Adorno's own work as well as in the work of
musicologists and Adorno scholars almost too numerous to mention.[37]
However, it should be said in passing that many of the key themes Adorno
sounds in his musical works—"atomization," "quotation listening," "fetishization," and so on—are equally vital Adorno's to radio essays. However,
while Adorno claims that the type of music suited to the radio—jazz and
popular hits—is symptomatic of a general decline in musical understanding, the radio itself is not to blame for that decline. Radio broadcasting
may exacerbate and accelerate the demise of certain forms of musical experience, but it is not, as Adorno is keen to note, the cause of those trends.

When looking at the radio essays, therefore, it is important to designate
those aspects of Adorno's critique that derive directly from radio transmissions themselves, and it must be emphasized that in his writings Adorno
is nothing if not insistent on the specificity of the radio mechanism. In
this regard, he is far more rigorous than his colleagues on the PRRP, who
tended to consider radio broadcasts—particularly as they were received
by the audiences under study—as isolated from their status as technologically mediated goods. But, as Jacques Attali writes in a work owing a profound debt to Adorno, one can never separate the performance from its
mediation. "The form of the music," Attali insists, "is always influenced
by the transmitter and the medium."[38] If one were therefore to summarize
what is perhaps the central, unifying element of Adorno's radio writings, it
would be this: Radio, by virtue of its psychological, technical, and social
conditions of production, transmission, and reception, represents a unique
cultural medium that cannot, in analysis, simply be made analogous to live
music or other live performances. One can no more understand the psychological effects of a broadcast apart from the realities of its technological
preconditions than one can divorce a broadcast from its function within
an increasingly monopolized system of distribution. Attempts to separate
out any of these components and examine them in isolation cause one to
fundamentally err and miss how each level—psychological, technological,

and sociological—conditions the others. A performance, its reception, and the technical and economic circumstances of its mass mediation must be, Adorno claims, considered as a unity, albeit a unity fraught with possible contradictions and tensions. This unity Adorno terms radio's "face" or "physiognomics" (with full awareness that he is indulging a paradoxical visual metaphor), and this "face" of radio is what gives the medium its unique "voice."

Regarding the unity presented by radio physiognomics and the radio voice, Adorno writes:

> It is this intention to connect scientific processes of different levels with the phenomenon from which they are abstracted which finally guides our physiognomic endeavors. We may confess here that the axiom which governs all these attempts is our conviction that the unity of the radio phenomenon, in itself, as far as it really has the structure of a unity, is simply the unity of society which determines all the individual and apparently accidental features. In our approach we try to combine sociological, psychological and technological aspects because we believe that they are only "aspects" of our society and, in the last analysis, that they may be reduced to fundamental categories of our society.[39]

Since the radio mirrors and transmits aspects of society generally, the implications of this physiognomic approach extend far beyond "the radio" per se. By virtue of radio's ability to fuse these various levels of cultural production and consumption, as well as by virtue of the mechanism's capacity to blur the divisions between public and private space—and indeed between all private spaces, because radio invades multiple homes at once—Adorno's theory of radio is, in many respects, a theory of the conditions of modern subjectivity.

Adorno's radio writings reveal a sensitivity to how the medium presents a unique problem for theorists of aesthetic consumption. Not only can people receive a standardized, reproducible work without having to leave their own homes (something that was at least theoretically made possible by magazines and newspapers), but also, because the sites of production and consumption are linked via the technologies of wireless transmission, multiple and geographically far-flung consumers can experience those performances simultaneously. In this regard, and because radio and television share similar business models, radio is a much more direct predecessor of television than is cinema. Furthermore, radio presents a challenge to a theorist of the political economy for the way it transforms the home into the site of the production of exchange value on a large scale. Although even today most listeners assume that radio is "free," radio networks actually transform listeners into workers by selling their ears to advertisers. What is in fact free about radio is the "attention labor," as Jonathan Beller calls it (although in the context of cinema studies), which listeners provide to the networks at no charge.[40] Adorno is, of course, acutely aware of the "productivity" of culture and the means by which leisure is converted into labor, but as we shall shortly see, so too are the network programmers and publicity agents of the 1930s and '40s.

The means by which the radio eradicates the distinction between public and private spheres is its "illusion of closeness," which, Adorno claims, "is as intimately associated with the 'radio voice' as the subject matter of radio physiognomics."[41] This illusion that the radio voice is physically with the listener is what gives the medium its unique authority over listeners. The radio voice enters the home by way of the transmitter and, by filling up a listener's small surroundings, purports to speak directly to that listener while in fact speaking to the multitudes. This inescapable yet invisible closeness is, Adorno claims, precisely what gives the radio its authoritarian character. "The very fact that they are confronted by 'voices,'" he writes in *Current of Music*, "without being able to argue with the person who is speaking, or even may feel somewhat in the dark about who is speaking—the machine or the man—may help to establish the authority of the tool." Because there is no one to argue with, Adorno argues, the voice becomes the voice of truth, indeed, even of God. "The absence of visible persons makes the 'radio voice' appear more objective and infallible than a live voice; and the mystery of a machine which can speak may be felt in atavistic layers of our psychical life."[42]

Of course, statements such as these paint a distinctly pessimistic portrait of the authoritarian nature of the radio voice, and they are precisely the reason Adorno draws the ire of his peers and of contemporary scholars. But the rhetorical link Adorno describes between the radio voice and the voice of the Almighty is hardly hyperbolic given the ways the networks framed their own programming. To take the most obvious example, in a 1941 publicity pamphlet—called *The Word of God*, no less—NBC touts the influence and success of its religious programming by claiming that "no written word can adequately portray the comfort and joy which these programs have brought to the lives of the churched and unchurched alike nor tell the thrilling story of the new, fresh promise wrought by The Word of God."[43] This statement reveals a number of strategies implicit in the network's call to faith. First, by claiming that the "written word" is inadequate to conveying the joys of religious faith, *The Word of God* implies that radio renders the Bible, the Torah, and the Koran superannuated and in fact supersedes them. Antiquated holy scriptures are geared to a community of faithful, while "churched and unchurched alike" will benefit from NBC's religious programming. Additionally, by uniting the title of this publication—*The Word of God*—with the "fresh promise wrought" on the network's listeners, NBC implicitly links itself with the voice of divinity. In the testimonials from the clergy and religious figures that follow in the pamphlet, this equation between the network's broadcasts and holy decree is made more explicit, but with the added twist that the spiritual authority of the network is wedded to its economic mission. As the Right Reverend Monsignor Fulton J. Sheen,[44] host of *The Catholic Hour,* writes:

> There is no corporation in the entire United States which has made such
> a contribution to religion as the National Broadcasting Company. The
> broadcasting of religious programs is just as much a part of its policy as
> advertising is the policy of commercial companies. Thanks to its generosity
> it has built the largest pulpit in the history of the world, and in the space of
> thirty minutes makes it possible for the speaker to address more souls than
> St. Paul did in all his missionary journeys.[45]

That there is a telling if unintentional elision here between advertising and the promulgation of faith reflects both the religious overtones of the radio business as well as the business of religion, and this conflation implicitly confirms Adorno's suspicions about the authoritarian character of the radio voice—as well as the networks' designs on the general conversion of its listeners into faithful consumers of its wares. If, for Lazarsfeld, voting and buying were one and the same, for Sheen, preaching and marketing were coequal, and the advertisers are analogous to the clergy. Resistance to their proclamations is nothing short of heresy. Adorno completed the long study of the Christian radio demagogue Martin Luther Thomas, part of the Studies in Prejudice project for the Institute of Social Research and the AJC, around 1943. Thus, by the time he wrote of the near-divine radio voice, in *Current of Music,* he was, no doubt, well aware of the insidious potential of this most personal of proselytizing media. This potential was made abundantly clear in publications like *The Word of God,* a text that came, after all, not from some fringe figure like Thomas or a noted demagogue like Father Charles E. Coughlin, but from what was then the largest radio broadcasting network in the country.

Before rejoining the issue of how radio networks, through their publicity and programming, assault their listeners and condition them to adapt to authoritarian demands, it is worth noting two further claims Adorno makes regarding the closeness and ubiquity of the radio voice. These elements, particularly at the time Adorno is writing, are unique to the medium and distinguish radio from other forms of communication. First, radio outdoes print media like newspapers and magazines in its ability to communicate to the extent that the radio broadcast seems to appeal to the listener directly, that is, without apparent mediation. As Adorno notes, the radio voice exceeds in its capacities the "intermediary, objectivating stage of printing which helps to clarify the difference between fiction and reality."[46] *The Word of God*, which equates the radio voice with divine truth, confirms radio's privileged relation to the real. Indeed, if the radio outdoes the Bible, as *The Word of God* implies, radio then represents the most significant communications advance since Johannes Gutenberg's press, from which the first publication was, after all, the "Good Book." Friedrich Kittler, in his book *Gramophone, Film, Typewriter,* confirms the capacity of electronically transmitted sound to re-form and produce any number of manipulable realities, thereby exceeding the possibilities of written expression. "The 'sound of music in my ear' can exist only once mouthpieces and microphones are capable of recording any whisper. As if there were no distance between the recorded voice and listening ears, as if voices traveled along the transmitting bones of acoustic self-perception directly from the mouth into the ear's labyrinth, hallucinations become real."[47]

When thinking of radio's capacity to remake reality, any number of hysterical responses to radio broadcasts could be invoked, the most obvious being Orson Welles's *War of the Worlds* program, the effects of which were studied by PRRP. In the book that resulted from the Welles study, Hadley Cantril's attempts to draw conclusions about the mass hysteria the broadcast provoked inevitably lead him to a comparison with the radio techniques of the National Socialists and to the suggestion that the economic circumstances then prevalent in the United States made Americans as susceptible to manipulation as Germans:

> That "the course of world history" has affected us is a truism. But this course of history contains more than war crises. Just what has happened is too familiar to be recited here. Probably more important than anything else, the highly disturbed economic conditions many Americans have experienced for the past decade, the consequent unemployment, the prolonged discrepancies between family incomes, the inability of both

young and old to plan for the future have engendered a widespread feeling of insecurity. . . . Individuals are sooner or later likely to rebel at a situation which is far from satisfactory and which they cannot understand. . . . The whole tactics of Hitler show the importance he places on providing directed relief to bewildered souls. If they are not already sufficiently bewildered, bewilderment can be manufactured by sufficient propaganda.[48]

While Adorno was certainly sensitive to the implications of Welles's broadcast, perhaps a more pertinent example of radio's capacity to transform hallucinations into concrete political consequences was the Nazi-sponsored raid on a German radio station that served as the flimsy pretense for Germany to attack Poland in World War II. As often proved the case, Joseph Goebbels and his cronies realized the primacy of the "simulated" gesture over the authentic event. The organizer of the raid, Alfred Helmut Naujocks, in his own affidavit about his role in the radio station raid, reveals the (sham) force of the radio voice:

On or about August 10, 1939, the chief of the S.D. [the Sicherheitsdienst, or Security Police], Heydrich, personally ordered me to simulate an attack on the radio station near Gleiwitz near the Polish border and to make it appear that the attacking force consisted of Poles. Heydrich said: "Practical proof is needed for these attacks of the Poles for the foreign press as well as for German propaganda." My instructions were to seize the radio station and to hold it long enough to permit a Polish speaking German who would be put at my disposal to broadcast a speech in Polish. Heydrich told me that this speech should state that the time had come for conflict between Germans and Poles. . . . Heydrich also told me that he expected an attack on Poland by Germany in a few days.[49]

Although few people were actually deceived by this ruse, the motives for arranging this pretense should be clear: Radio constructs and affirms reality.[50]

The second consequence of radio's direct entry into the home is that this "illusion of closeness" is not a unitary phenomenon but instead happens simultaneously in multiple locations. In both *Current of Music* and the memorandum "Music in Radio," Adorno cites a proto-Orwellian example from Guenter Stern that describes the ubiquity of the radio voice:

When one leaves his house, the music of the loudspeaker still resounds in his ear. He is still in it—it is nowhere. One takes ten steps and the same music sounds from a neighbor's house. Now, when there is music here as well, one finds music here and there, localized, rammed into place like two stakes. But, at the same time, "here" it is the same music which was heard "there." "Here" Mr. X continues singing what he has started to sing "there." One continues walking. At the third house X3 continues again, accompanied by X2, and very vaguely echoed by the cautious X of the first house.[51]

This capacity of radio to homogenize space by virtue of its simultaneous broadcast provokes Adorno to recuperate the argument that Walter Benjamin, in "The Work of Art in the Age of Mechanical Reproduction," makes concerning the destruction of aura. Namely, Benjamin argues that media like cinema and radio, by virtue of both their reproducibility and their dissemination of a series of "shocks," deny audiences the capacity to experience them with the near-reverent contemplation accorded earlier aesthetic forms. Rather than lamenting this historical transformation, however, Benjamin instead tries to claim the potentially progressive and liberatory aspects of the "distraction" with which audiences confront modernity's art forms. The shock Stern experiences on hearing the same music pouring from separate households is, Adorno claims, anecdotal evidence of Benjamin's broader theoretical premise. In conditions of general reproducibility, the uniqueness of the live performance is diluted and its effects fundamentally altered. "Benjamin treats the difference between the uniqueness and reproducibility of the work of art from the point of view of a fundamental historical change—terms which can enlighten Stern's . . . points and which can help to understand the shock he mentions no longer in 'existential' concepts, but in social and historical ones."[52]

While provisionally reconciling himself to Benjamin's arguments, Adorno also offers an important caveat that derives from his conception of music as a priori reproducible. "Now," he says, by way of cautioning against fully embracing Benjamin's "Artwork" essay as corresponding to musical concepts, "it is obvious that this theory cannot be directly applied to music because there is no conceivable music, except perhaps improvisations and they do not count, which is not based upon the idea of reproducibility."[53] Nevertheless, while acknowledging that Benjamin's argument more properly applies in the visual register and works better as a theory of cinema, he does admit that something in the electronic rebroadcast of music corresponds to Benjamin's analysis:

> However, we must acknowledge that in music something very closely akin to Benjamin's observation can be found. *The authenticity which Benjamin*

attributes in the visual arts to the original must be attributed to live
reproduction in music. This live reproduction has its "here"—either the
concert room or the opera—and its "now"—the very moment it is executed.
And what Benjamin calls the "aura" of the original certainly constitutes an
essential part of the live reproduction. It is exactly this aura which leads
people to be eager to attend a live performance even if they cannot follow
the music as well from their cheap seat as they could have followed it in
front of their radio set.[54]

In his response to Benjamin's essay "On Some Motifs in Baudelaire"—
a work that bears strong affinities to the "Artwork" piece—Adorno
famously chides Benjamin that his "dialectics lacked mediation" and goes
on to reprimand him for ignoring the way the shock experiences of modernity can only be read through the relations of production. "Materialist
determination of cultural traits is only possible," he insists, "if it is mediated through the *total social process.*"[55] Adorno's statements resonate with
his general critique of the Benjaminian destruction of aura, as it is spelled
out not only in the "Artwork" essay but also in Benjamin's treatment of the
"profane illuminations" of the surrealists. To Adorno's mind, the ready-
mades and collages of the surrealists or the editing techniques of Charlie
Chaplin's films fail as rejoinders to the dehumanization of the individual
for the way that each ultimately valorizes the notion of individual genius
and creativity. A new aura—that of the autonomous artist—stands in for
the aura that the artwork putatively destroys. But if Benjamin's analysis of
the destruction of aura is elsewhere unsatisfactory because of the absence
of mediation, in *Current of Music,* Adorno is able to redeem the concept
of aura—and its destruction—precisely because of the social and technological mediation wrought by radio. Adorno can make this argument only
because the industrial process of radio's production, transmission, and consumption so closely mirrors that of the "total social process." The unity of
radio's "physiognomy" is, Adorno claims, "simply the unity of society which
determines all the individual and apparently accidental features" of human
subjects. As Giorgio Agamben writes, in an essay generally critical of
Adorno, what makes Adorno compelling is that, by virtue of his insistence
on mediation, he is able to close the gap between traditional concepts of
"base" and "superstructure" and reveal them as mutually determining (and
mutually enslaving) for the modern subject:

Was it not Engels himself who . . . stated that only *in the final instance* is
production the determining historical factor? The yawning gap between

structure and superstructure opened by this "in the final instance" is
bridged by Adorno through the appeal to "mediation" and the "total social
process," thanks to which "good" speculative theory is forearmed against
any "direct interference." This "universal mediation, which in both Hegel
and Marx establishes totality," is the unassailable guarantee of Marxist
orthodoxy in Adorno's critique, whereby his own doctrinal solidity is
confirmed.[56]

Because of its unified physiognomy, radio destroys the aura of the original, site-specific performance. And yet, in so doing, the radio broadcast
reinscribes an authoritarian aura both through its contents and through its
technological form. First, its contents are standardized. As the Stern anec-
dote describes, the listening experience and spatial differences are homog-
enized. "The standardization which we mean," Adorno writes, explaining
this phenomenon, "is the more or less authoritarian offer of identical material to a great number of people." Ubiquity functions authoritatively regardless of the relative merits of the broadcast: "It would hold good even
if there were no standardization of programs. This standardization, in a
way, is the essence of radio itself."[57]

It is worth noting, however, that Adorno is unwilling to divorce the
ubiquity of radio broadcasts from the "standardization of programs" themselves; throughout Adorno's radio critique, particularly in "A Social Critique of Radio Music," his barbs are explicitly pointed at the reification of
the artworks as a function of the political economy. In a commodity society,
the profit motive is paramount; hence "human needs are satisfied only incidentally, as it were. The basic condition of production affects the form of
the product as well as human interrelationships."[58] The supposedly subjective aspects of an autonomous artwork—the "ethereal and the sublime"—
congeal into objects, "trade marks." As such, music on the radio becomes
culinary, an object of lip-smacking consumption. Radio broadcasts achieve
"the ideal of Aunt Jemima ready-mix for pancakes extended to the field of
music," Adorno sadly insists. "The listener suspends all intellectual activity when dealing with music and is content with consuming and evaluating
its gustatory qualities—just as if the music that tasted best were also the
best possible music."[59] This reduction of the musical work to a commodity
fetish is "very much like sports spectatoritis which promotes a retrogressive and sometimes even infantile person."[60]

The business practices of the networks, particularly in the era when all
programs were explicitly linked to specific advertisers, demanded a certain
leveling of the programming to entice the greatest number of listeners.

Since the individual attributes of a given broadcast are less important than its ratings, the qualities of the program are made into a function of the quantity of listeners (that is, the number of advertising dollars generated). In classic Marxian terms, use value is transformed into exchange value, and in more Adornian language, what was formally an end in itself (the aesthetic truth content of a program) is transformed into a means to earn revenue.

But one doesn't have to take Adorno's word for it—or Marx's. The networks themselves confirm the notion that their programs operate within a system of equivalences and extol the transformation of quality into quantity. In the 1926 advertisement that announced the formation of NBC, the agenda is clear:

> The market for receiving sets in the future will be determined by the quantity and quality of the programs broadcast.
>
> We say quantity because they must be diversified enough so that some of them will appeal to all possible listeners.
>
> We say quality because each program must be the best kind. If that ideal were to be reached, no home in the United States could afford to be without a radio receiving set.[61]

Although both "quantity" and "quality" are the stated goals of this manifesto, it is apparent—and not just from the order of paragraphs—that the quality of the program is secondary to the quantity of listeners and radio owners. Even when quality is privileged ("each program must be the best kind") that excellence is transformed into a function of the general colonization of the domestic sphere, such that "no home in the United States could afford to be without a radio receiving set." Thus, even though programs may actually differ from one another in fundamental, substantive ways, they are ultimately reduced to being identical in a system of equivalences, plugged into the radio machine like interchangeable parts.

This consumerist element of electronic transmission has implications for any sort of socially responsible aesthetics. "A Social Critique of Radio Music" intervenes at the point where the ideological effects of the radio transmission and the complementary mystification of social antagonisms are intertwined. "Music under present radio auspices serves to keep listeners from criticizing social realities; in short it has a soporific effect upon social consciousness."[62] This is the ideological effect of atomized listening. And it is precisely atomization, repetition, and exchangeability that breed the familiarity by which we come to "know" our sonic possessions. As such, even while diversity proliferates on the airwaves, individuality is foreclosed by the fact that all the programs do exactly the same things. Despite the existence of 1930s and '40s programs such as *Art for Your Sake* and *Music and You*, which purport to offer something of value for the development and edification of audiences, genuine individual needs remain unfulfilled. Listeners are forced to accommodate their tastes to equivalent programming choices and in so doing find their subjectivities fundamentally impoverished. This aspect of the standardization among radio broadcasts is captured nowhere more eloquently or succinctly than in Kenneth Fearing's poem "Radio Blues," written—not uncoincidentally—at the same time that Adorno was employed by PRRP. In the poem, no matter how many radio channels are available, something is still missing:

> 9000, 10,000;
> Would you like to tune in on your own life, gone somewhere far away?[63]

As the choices on the radio dial geometrically expand, Fearing's listener is increasingly unable to hear himself and his experiences on the radio, until at last his individual existence becomes the ghost of a memory.

While the standardization of radio, characterized by the ubiquity of radio broadcasts and the transformation of quality into quantity, is a fundamental part of the radio's sociological makeup, Adorno is also acutely aware of the technological transformations wrought on the artwork by the radio mechanism. These transformations—themselves a function of standardization—cut right to the heart of Adorno's concerns about the degeneration of musical experience. The radio broadcast (particularly of the symphony, but also of other musical forms), by virtue of its technological limitations, irrevocably transforms and mutilates the original work, and the radio networks are invested in making this transformation invisible for the purpose of their commercial interests.

As Kittler suggests, the industrial reproduction of sound all but necessitates some "noise" in transmission. "Technological media operate against a background of noise because their data travel along physical channels; as in blurring in the case of film or the sound of the needle in the case of the gramophone, that noise determines their signal-to-noise ratio. . . . Noise is emitted by the channels media have to cross."[64] As early as 1929, Adorno was contemplating the effects of the sound of the mechanism on the artwork. In "The Form of the Phonographic Record" he indicates that even the negative aspects of technologization and reification can reverse themselves when the mechanical destruction of the artwork stands as the

mute yet living witness to what has been destroyed. In a relatively conciliatory mode, Adorno suggests that truth content can be, in part, a function
of technologization: "There is no doubt that, as music is removed by the
phonograph record from the realm of live production, it absorbs into itself,
in this process of petrifaction, the very life that would otherwise vanish. The
dead art rescues the ephemeral and perishing art as the only one alive.
Therein may lie the phonograph record's most profound justification, which
cannot be impugned by an aesthetic objection to reification."[65] In the case
of the record, what rescues the musical work is that what made it unique—
the ephemeral, transitory nature of live performance—is transformed into
a concrete object. Ossification stands as the testament to mobility.

However, it would be unwise to conflate Adorno's dialectical approach
to the phonograph with his critique of electronic reproduction generally.
While the commodity form of the record represents the life-in-death of the
artwork, the radio performance, particularly before the era of home recording, presents as transitory a phenomenon as did the live performance (for
the listener at least). What remains, and what draws Adorno's critique, is
not the solidity of the record but the realities of sound engineering. And
so, in "The Radio Symphony," Adorno examines the effect of electronic
mediation on Beethoven's Fifth Symphony and laments the capitulation of
the symphonic performance to the technical constraints of transmission.[66]
Turning a critical ear toward everything from the disappearing second vio-
lins to the radio "hear-stripe" (the sound of the mechanism), Adorno concludes that the music bearing the name "The Fifth Symphony" is, when
played over the radio, really no symphony at all. From this analysis, he
proposes a theory of the broadcast symphony in which its mode of reproduction is integral to the social appreciation of its form.

Among the many technical problems Adorno identifies in the radio symphony is its reduction of the absolute intensities (magnitudes) of sound.
Absolute magnitudes give the "life symphony" the power to "absorb" its
parts into the organized whole as well as the power to engulf the listener.
When these magnitudes are reduced to a narrow range by electronic transmission, this diminution poses a threat to the very structure of the symphony. Using the first movement of the Fifth as an example, Adorno claims
that the "creation *ex nihilo,* as it were, which is so highly significant in
Beethoven" is undermined by the flattening performed by the radio. "As
soon as it is reduced to the medium range between piano and forte, the
Beethoven symphony is deprived of the secret of origin as well as the
might of unveiling." The dialectical relation that powers the Fifth, "which

makes out of the Nothing of the first bars virtually the Everything of the total movement . . . is missed before it has been actually started."[67] That which gives the Fifth its power is made impotent and unpalatable when every sound is blended into sonic mayonnaise.

Lest one think of this strictly as the cultural elitism of an "expert" listener, one should note that Adorno is consistent in his argument across the range of technological media and aesthetic forms, elsewhere extending his critique to television and film.[68] But on the radio, the sonic leveling of the "unity of the manifold" and the "manifoldness of that unity" has a number of consequences that ultimately suggest an insidious function for radio within the political economy. If the ubiquity of the radio broadcast at the level of programming reflected the transformation of quality into quantity, the leveling of the absolute magnitudes of the Fifth Symphony reduces the music itself to a system of equivalences. Instead of a music experience that would permit the listener to hear the rebellion of subjectivity within and against the hyperrationalized demands of form—a fundamental element of an artwork's truth content—by mixing the symphony down so that it fits the comfortable confines of the living room, the experience of subjectivity offered by the symphony is evacuated.

By reducing the absolute intensities of the Fifth, radio renders the symphony the musical analogue of the relations of production—a hyperrationalized system of equivalences. But this effect on the Fifth consigns Beethoven to a more retrograde position within the history of composition. Rather than standing as the voice of free, enlightened subjectivity (as Adorno will argue in his Beethoven essays), Beethoven becomes instead a musical calculator characteristic of the worst type of rationalized baroque music—precisely the type of music Beethoven historically transcends. As Susan McClary writes of the historical implications of composition based on a system of equivalences and hierarchical relations, this form of music corresponds to a worldview in which capitalism, the market, and industrial production represent the natural order of things: "This music shapes itself in terms of bourgeois ideology (its goal orientation, obsessive control of greater and greater spans of time, its willful striving, delayed gratification and defiance of norms). . . . The tonal procedures developed by the emerging bourgeoisie to articulate their sense of the world here become presented as what we, in fact, want to believe they are: eternal, universal truths."[69]

In *Noise*, Attali makes this link between the political economy and the economy of rationalized musical composition even more explicit, suggesting that the effort to exhaust all harmonic combinations both precedes and reflects Taylorist principles of industrial production:

> Thus by listening to music, we can interpret the growth of the European economy and the political economy of the eighteenth and nineteenth centuries, not as an incomprehensible and miraculous accumulation of value, but in the context of the idea of combinatorics: eighteenth-century science made possible a broader range of combinations of raw materials; it allowed the exploration of larger aggregates and their representation in simple terms. . . . Efficiency required, for a time, gigantism and the scientific division of labor."[70]

While Attali may overstate this link between the rise of the bourgeoisie and the development of compositional styles, Adorno's critique of the effect of electronic reproduction on music essentially argues for the validity of Attali's thesis, if only within the historically specific confines of radio broadcasting. With regard to Beethoven, therefore, Adorno implies that the Fifth Symphony is transformed from the expression of subjective freedom into the resignation of the subject to the demands of atomization and the complete capitulation to an alienating formal logic.

But a further aspect of electronic manipulation makes the relationship between radio music and capital accumulation even clearer. One of the fundamental mutilations visited on the symphony by the sound engineer is that the engineer's manipulations reinsert the listener into homogeneous, linear time. A crucial characteristic of the first movement of the Fifth Symphony, Adorno claims, is that by virtue of its careful construction, "one has the feeling that the movement doesn't take seven or fifteen moments or more, but virtually one moment." Contrary to the failure of romantic symphonies or the numbing repetition of Guy Lombardo's music, the "life symphony" will instead produce a "suspension of time consciousness."[71]

One should note that this suspension of time consciousness invites a consideration of the connections between Adorno and Kant's aesthetic theories. In the *Critique of Judgment*, Kant explains that measurements of apprehension, because of their numerical nature (counting cannot, by its nature, take place instantaneously), must take place in measurable time. Comprehension, on the other hand—the way one approaches the absolute magnitudes of the sublime—is an instantaneous intuition. Note the resonance between what Adorno calls the "authentic experience" of the "ethereal and sublime" Beethoven movement and the judgment of the sublime in Kant. As Kant explains, "Comprehending a *multiplicity in a unity* (of intuition rather than of thought), and hence comprehending in one instant what is apprehended successively, is a regression that in turn *cancels the condition of time in the imagination's progression* and makes *simultaneity* intuitable."[72] By thinking of the sublime as a simultaneity, the imagination bumps up against the limits of its own rational and measured inner sense. To the extent that this limit threatens to overwhelm the subject, the sublime would be contrapurposive. However, Kant claims, because this capacity to think simultaneity is necessary to estimate the magnitude of the sublime, it becomes the source of the spark upon which subjectivity can be kindled. Therefore, Kant continues, "this same violence that the imagination inflicts on the subject is still judged purposive for the whole vocation of the mind."[73] The result of this encounter is a dialectic of pleasure in unpleasure, for the imagination's struggle toward the unbounded whole reveals the purposiveness of our more rational, measured apprehension. Thus, for Kant, the capacity to judge the sublime—the play of the faculties on which subjectivity is founded—is irrevocably bound to aesthetic judgment:

> The quality of the feeling of the sublime consists in its being a feeling, accompanying an object, of displeasure about our aesthetic power of judging, yet of a displeasure that we present at the same time as purposive. What makes this possible is that the subject's own inability uncovers in him the consciousness of an unlimited ability which is also his, and that the mind can judge this ability aesthetically only by that inability.[74]

With regard to Adorno's radio theory, it is crucial to recognize that what Kant claims as the terrain for the aesthetic object is the fundamental challenge that lets the subject know it is a subject. And, importantly, the very foundation of individuality is that suspension of time consciousness that is denied the listener by the radio symphony. Following Adorno's line of reasoning, I would further argue that, instead of removing its listeners from time, when electronically manipulated and broadcast, the radio symphony thrusts them back into regulated, chronological, homogeneous time—the time of the workplace. The idea that under current conditions of reproduction all time is homogeneous—and therefore quantifiable and exchangeable as capital—is a notion of central importance in Marxian economic theory, and one that has relevance to the transmission of the symphony by a radio network. If what makes a symphony unique is that it offers the listener an opportunity to experience heterogeneous time, nontime, when it is reinserted into the rigors of regular time the work once again becomes just that—work. The symphony is time on the clock, either time when the listener gets paid or time when he pays for the network through his attention to a sponsored broadcast for a certain measurable period.

Adorno's concerns here are primarily technological. The radio, in the 1940s at least, was not adequate to the sonic demands of the symphony. But Adorno also reserves some criticism for the rearrangement of symphonic works so that they are suitable for a radio broadcast. This practice also has implications for the transformation of music time into labor time. Consider the remarks of a Muzak executive about the type of programming marketed to factories and offices: "When the employee arrives in the morning, he is generally in a good mood, and the music will be calm. Toward ten thirty, he begins to feel a little tired, tense, so we give him a lift with the appropriate music. Toward the middle of the afternoon, he is probably feeling tired again: we wake him up again with a rhythmic tune, often faster than the morning's."[75] Here the music—and one should remember how blandly arranged Muzak tunes were—has the function of regulating time in such a fashion that all time has the same affect. That is, every period of the day is exactly like every other; music makes each moment equally productive.

To the degree that radio music standardizes time in modernity, it also renders each historical epoch equivalent and exchangeable. Indeed, during the spring of 1939, when Adorno was writing his radio essays and cautioning against the medium's authoritarian logic, a Columbia workshop production broadcast by CBS baldly claimed that radio transcends history and thereby controls it. In verses that evoke the fundamentalist fire of the early American Congregational minister Jonathan Edwards's "Sinners in the Hands of an Angry God," the program *"Seems Radio Is Here to Stay"* admonishes its listeners:

> Think hard upon these words which tumble toward you through the night:
> > The race of man is shrewd and silly, brutal and benign
> > And full of sudden starts and tardy reckonings.

All those that doubt radio's primacy are reminded that not only will radio outlive them, but it has also, theoretically, preceded human history:

> Do you grant Radio is here to stay?
> > Then grant this further:
> > That the mystic ethers were established well before the first word
> passed between two men.[76]

As in NBC's *The Word of God*, in *"Seems Radio Is Here to Stay"* there is a rhetorical connection drawn between the radio voice and divine wisdom. In the case of the CBS program, God becomes both the radio engineer and the head of the Federal Communication Commission (FCC); the radio is his holy instrument:

> Meanwhile some homage to the High Commissioner
> > Who first assigned these frequencies to earth,
> > Who marked these airlanes out.
> > He is the same who fixed the stars in place,
> > Who set afire the sun and froze the moon and dug the furrows wherein
> oceans flow,
> > Who put some molecules together in a way
> > To make a man.

The power of creation is then transformed into the power to broadcast material electronically:

> He holds the formula for genesis and death.
> His hand rests on a dial bigger than infinity.[77]

"Seems Radio Is Here to Stay" was broadcast on April 24, 1939, and makes a strong case not for the extremism of Adorno's critique of radio but for its restraint. His PRRP colleagues and the radio executives gathered at the presentation of "On a Social Critique of Radio Music" took issue with the notion that the "'broke' farmer is consoled by the radio-instilled belief that Toscanini is playing for him and him alone, and that an order of things that allows him to hear Toscanini compensates for farm products, or that even though he is ploughing under cotton, radio is giving him culture." Still, a look at the script and accompanying illustrations of *"Seems Radio Is Here to Stay"* would appear to more than confirm Adorno's provocative claim.

Thus, in one of the illustrations from the script (Figure 6),[78] Shakespeare is plucked from his England of circa 1600 and rests on a tree stump chatting with a cowboy, two Depression-era workers, and a young woman, presumably an office worker. The image, which links the Bard to recognizable nineteenth- and twentieth-century American figures, speaks both to radio's capacity to bring culture to the working class and to its ability to homogenize history. Widely divergent periods and locales are seamlessly wedded to one another in apparently natural settings. But while the image of Shakespeare—a clichéd icon of "culture"—seems to suggest the benevolence of radio's mission to bring listeners into contact with the greats, elsewhere *"Seems Radio Is Here to Stay"* reveals that this reduction of history to interchangeable components has a specific economic purpose. Almost inevitably, Beethoven becomes the image for the marketing potential of the dissolution of historical specificity (Figure 7).[79] Hovering like the head of Oz[80] and radiating energy waves between a symphony and its myriad listeners, poor Beethoven gets disinterred to serve the interests of the network:

O BEETHOVEN!

O LUDWIG!

HAVE YOU GOT YOUR HEARING BACK?

WE CALL YOUR HALLOWED BONES!

WE SHOUT

Do we disturb your dust?

How restful is your rest there in Vienna, anyway?

Death is too long a leisure, we suspect,

For one of such invention.

You must be out assembling harmonies somewhere.

But listen, Master: hear:

MUSIC: SNEAK IN WITH SECOND MOVEMENT OF BEETHOVEN'S FIFTH SYMPHONY

There are more ears attending you tonight

Than ever you imagined could perceive a note:

All at once; this instant.

More by millions, than you ever saw

In continents of concert halls.

Your music gets around these days.

On plains, on mountains and on shores you never heard of,

You are heard tonight.[81]

Many of the themes Adorno addresses in his radio writings appear directly in this verse: the ubiquity of the broadcast, the idea that music—particularly Beethoven's—can be assembled like an industrial product, and the notion that music is a portable good that "gets around." The network, whose voice can raise the dead, holds the exclusive power to affect history and the history of the artwork. Just as Adorno writes in "The Radio Symphony," under the conditions of radio broadcasting, Beethoven's Fifth becomes the instrument not for the liberation of subjectivity but, "in continents of concert halls," for the wide-scale colonization of listeners and their conversion into consumers. In light of the explicit strategies of a text like *"Seems Radio Is Here to Stay,"* Adorno's thoughts on radio, often dismissed as "too theoretical" by his more empirically minded colleagues, take on the qualities of reportage.

One of Adorno's favorite quotations, taken from Francis H. Bradley, was "When everything is bad, it must be good to know the worst."[82] Although *"Seems Radio Is Here to Stay"* is genuinely awful in what it suggests about the controlling power of radio, the dissolution of history, and the manipulation of listeners, the worst is still to come. Despite the fact that in return for the use of the airways radio networks (and ultimately television networks) were ostensibly supposed to act in "the public interest," both network documents and Adorno's criticism of radio reveal that that benevolence transformed itself into a particularly troubling paternalism, one that depended equally on the authority of the radio networks and the infantilization of the listener. In the war-era document *Broadcasting in the Public Interest,* NBC acknowledges the unique power that radio has over its listeners, especially children: "The effect of radio broadcasting on the thinking of men and women is ever widening. The thoughts and reasoning of their children are forming under the influence of the voices and music that pour from the loudspeaker into their homes."[83] Nevertheless, while NBC claims that the effect radio has on children is one of the reasons why radio broadcasting

Figure 6. Columbia Broadcasting System, *"Seems Radio Is Here to Stay": A Columbia Workshop Production by Norman Corwin,* illustrations by Rudolph Charles von Ripper (New York: Columbia Broadcasting System, 1939), 16.

must proceed responsibly, as Adorno will argue—and the networks' other publicity materials will confirm—there is a coordinated effort on the part of the networks to infantilize their listeners, their advertisers, and even their employees for the purpose of what can only be considered social control and domination.

As Lorenz Jäger notes in his biography of Adorno, something about him was acutely sensitive and empathetic to the experiences of childhood. "Adorno was particularly productive," Jäger claims, "when he was able to call on his memories of childhood and use them in a theoretical context. His ability to play with the dialectics of childhood and maturity gave him the means by which to react and intervene."[84] For Adorno, childhood represented both the dangers of intellectual regression and a nostalgic arena of pure possibility, when the mind was free and uncolonized by the preprogrammed thoughts of an alienating society: "The giant egg from which the monster of the Last Judgment can creep forth at any moment is so big because we were so small the first time that we looked at an egg and shuddered."[85] Although Jäger at times tends to paint Adorno as an arrested adolescent, there is something in his assessment of Adorno's affinity for childhood that rings true, particularly with regard to Adorno's radio work.

Figure 7. *"Seems Radio Is Here to Stay,* 12. Illustration by Rudolph Charles von Ripper.

On the one hand, the radio networks were actively engaged in reducing their listeners and advertisers to the status of children; on the other, they were molding children into certain types of consumers, thereby limiting their experiences. Adorno's intervention into the social realities of radio during his exile years often took into account this paradoxical status of children in the networks' eyes.

In the memorandum "Music in Radio," for instance, Adorno writes that he hopes to develop "a theory of the 'infantile' ear within the framework of this project."[86] While in the memorandum itself this proposed theory sees no further development, it is clear that the question of how the culture industry forces regression on its audiences is never far from Adorno's mind. One of the fundamental elements of cultural industrial domination is its success in provoking childish enthusiasm for its products while at the same time requiring a simplistic response to its increasingly facile intellectual demands. Indeed, one of Adorno's central musical concepts, "the regression of listening," implies the general infantilization of the listening public whereby "the very function of hearing recedes to stages in the development of our entire social order which otherwise would have been overcome much earlier."[87]

Adorno's concern with this regressive tendency is particularly acute in his "Analytical Study of NBC's *Music Appreciation Hour*," no less so because the show was designed to educate children. In fact, one of Adorno's main arguments in this essay is that conductor Walter Damrosch's *Music Appreciation Hour* fails so utterly in its attempt to educate children that it perpetuates an infantile response that denies them a vigorous relationship to music. "It will be shown," he writes, "that not only is the purely musical part of this program insufficient musically and pedagogically, but that it also leads to a fictitious musical world ruled by names and personalities, stylistic labels, and pre-digested values which cannot possibly be 'experienced' by the audience of the *Music Appreciation Hour*."[88] There is something almost touching about the sensitivity Adorno displays to children and child psychology in this essay. If the *Music Appreciation Hour* strives to entrap its students in a "fictitious" fantasy world, in so doing, it makes them mini adults bound to the consumerist realities of reification and fetishized listening. In contrast, Adorno offers a kind of child psychology *Aufhebung*, whereby breaking the news about the real world to children enables them to retain a kernel of childhood innocence in their subsequent "enlightened" response to music. Thus, in a poetic passage of the essay, Adorno attempts to rescue musical experience by refusing the development of music listening advocated by Damrosch and instead privileging an "irrational" response to the material:

> It may suffice to mention that a person who is in a real life relation with music does not like music because as a child he liked to see a flute, then later because music imitated a thunderstorm, and finally because he learned to listen to music as music, but that the deciding childhood experiences are much more like a shock. More prototypical as stimulus is the experience of the child who lies awake in his bed while a string quartet plays in an adjoining room, and who is suddenly so overwhelmed by the excitement of the music that he forgets to sleep and listens breathlessly.[89]

The Proustian overtone of this passage is not coincidental. The recuperation of what is lost in the subject's atomization, the taste of freedom continually dissolving into the tisane of mechanized listening, is precisely the memory that Adorno hopes to restore and that is categorically denied children by the *Music Appreciation Hour*. Furthermore, the overwhelming sensuous shock of musical experience is what modern subjects are forced to manage in the more regulated reduction of all music to the *Erfahrung* of music "appreciation." However, at the same time that they are taught to accommodate the sensuality of music, Adorno insists that students are denied access to the so-called adult world under the belief that "there are certain things one should not tell children." The development of a true appreciation of the work is hindered when, for example, *Tristan und Isolde* is purged of any reference to adultery. "If one is afraid to speak of adultery," Adorno chides, "one had better not speak about *Tristan*. One had better not even play it."[90]

Instead of a life relationship with music, or even an overwhelming memory of musical experience, Adorno argues that children are subjected to a particularly pernicious brand of commodified logic that seeks to make music into a consumer good, and they are encouraged to hoard their "musical treasures" like card collectors. By cultivating a fetish for great composers and a "hankering for instruments," as well as by oversimplifying musical theory and historiography, the *Music Appreciation Hour* equates a love of music with, to use one of Adorno's pet terms, "sports spectatoritis." Adorno insists, "The *Music Appreciation Hour* destroys respect for the work, its meaning, and its achievement by transposing it into the effect it has upon the listener and inculcating in him composer-fetishism which becomes virtually identical with the 'fun' he derives from viewing a World Series baseball game."[91] In that it concerns itself with the effect of music on individuals rather than on its historical and social roots, the *Music Appreciation Hour* is not so different from Lazarsfeld's administrative research. This focus on the listener reveals itself as focus on the consumer, and the insistence that music is "fun" belies an effort to associate music with a commodity. "Something must be pleasing and worth its money to be admitted to the market," Adorno explains, suggesting that the focus of the *Hour* should be directed elsewhere than on audience effects. "On the contrary, the work of art really raises postulates of its own, and it is more essential for the listener to please the Beethoven symphony than for the Beethoven symphony to please him."[92]

A basic element of the "keeping the score" mentality that is the pedagogical principle of the *Music Appreciation Hour* is the insistent emphasis on the melody at the expense of "musically complete unity within the manifoldness." In this regard, Adorno offers a number of examples directly from the *Music Appreciation Hour*. However, no example more perfectly summarizes the emphasis on the melody as a function of musical ownership than a statement found in the *"Music Appreciation Hour" Instructor's Manual* from the 1931–32 season: "Music that is known and remembered until it can be whistled or sung, or can be reviewed silently in the mind, becomes loved, and is heard with appreciation."[93] The reduction of music to its stripped-down components (comparable to a car enthusiast's admiration of detailing) results, Adorno says, in a type of musical Babbittry. The student is required to hoard knowledge while at the same time being made the slave of a cult of personality perpetuated through the aura conferred by the mechanism on the composer and the orchestra conductor.

"What can we do to get the most from what the radio fairy brings?" the *Music Appreciation Hour* asks. This question speaks to concerns regarding both the infantilization of the listener and the transparency of the mechanism's authoritarian elements. According to the *Music Appreciation Hour*, the home of the radio fairy isn't part of a complex network of social, technological, and economic processes; it is a magic box. Those who control the box are therefore themselves invested with magic powers. As a result of this mystification of the mechanism, the student is rendered not merely infantile but also, at the same time, subject to its authority, helpless to break free of the alienating logic that lies behind the radio's mystification. "The *Music Appreciation Hour*," Adorno argues, "first cheapens music, and then teaches its pupils to adore musicians as spiritual leaders. This contradiction, basic to the whole approach, makes any destruction of fetishes impossible."[94]

In his essay analyzing the *Music Appreciation Hour,* Adorno paints Damrosch as the cultural dictator whose authority over the listeners is at once naturalized and rationalized. But his is the authority of the bureaucrat, whose power derives not from his own merits but from the nature of authority itself. It is worth noting the parallels between the image of Damrosch and Adorno's descriptions of the radio demagogue Martin Luther Thomas. Both deploy the technique of the "great little man" who defers to higher authority while at the same time cementing control over the listener. A crucial theme in Adorno's exile writings is that the belief in authority qua authority is what conditions subjects to embrace their own exploitation in the workplace. The musical education offered by the *Music Appreciation Hour* offers a special case of this ideological training. From the attention to the division of labor within the orchestra to the authority accorded as if by magic to the conductors (and composers), the program naturalizes hierarchical relations not unlike those the students will encounter when they grow up.

Remarking on the analogy between the symphony and the factory, Attali describes the conditions of musical production in terms of the authoritarian systems Adorno identifies in the *Music Appreciation Hour.* The orchestra's

> constitution and its organization are also figures of power in the industrial economy. The musicians—who are anonymous and hierarchically ranked, and in general salaried, productive workers—execute an external algorithm, a "score," which does what its name implies: it allocates their parts. . . . They are the image of productive labor in society. Each of them produces only a part of the whole having no value in itself. . . . The orchestra leader appears as the image of the legitimate and rational organizer of a production whose size necessitates a coordinator, but dictates that he not make noise. He is thus the representation of economic power, presumed capable of setting in motion, without conflict, harmoniously, the program of history traced by the composer.[95]

An objection might be raised that the *Music Appreciation Hour* was, after all, a children's program, and that therefore a certain measure of oversimplification and even socialization was—if regrettable—to be expected. However, a survey of publicity materials produced by NBC and CBS in the 1930s and '40s confirms that the phrase "Musical Leadership Maintained by NBC" had ominous, Pied-Piper overtones for adults as well as for children. It is striking how often the tone and style of children's books are employed by the networks for their publicity materials. In these documents, the twinned strategy of infantilization and authoritarian command characterizes the networks' responses to their listeners, their sponsors, and their workers in a manner that is even more disturbing given European events and the "defense of freedom" in which the networks were purportedly engaged. In light of these publicity materials, the network of social control and domination was more baldly apparent than even Adorno diagnosed and feared.

The keystone of this control is the maintenance of the illusion of transparency. The notions that one could go "behind the radio dial" and that radio is a magical production are cultivated in a number of publications, often with a more or less explicit insistence that what one would find is not the real activities of a media conglomerate but a fantasyland. "If you could manage by some dexterous sleight-of-hand to go behind your radio dial," begins the 1943 publication *What Goes On behind Your Radio Dial?* "you would find yourself in a wonderland far surpassing anything dreamed up by the most imaginative storyteller."[96]

Of course, since the listener presumably does not have magical powers—or access to a radio station—they then must stipulate to what follows. In the pamphlet, the evocation of the fantastic—with its accompanying overtones of pulp science fiction—creates a picture of radio production as a site where anything could happen instantaneously. As though the physical and technological principles of radio broadcasting weren't fantastic enough, by evacuating the radio of its concrete technological innovations *What Goes On behind Your Radio Dial?* insists on circumventing the laws of physics altogether. The dissolution of temporal and spatial constraints effected by the transparency of technological mediation prefaces an even more radical conquest of geography and time. The document claims that this utopian "Wonderland" "is the nerve center of world news, where renowned contributors, analysts and news men are on the alert 24 hours a day listening for the faintest murmur of news that may swell in seconds to the thunder of history making sentences."[97] Here, the implied claim made by *Musical Leadership Maintained by NBC* that the network was at the vanguard of world-historical events is made plain, with the added wrinkle that, as the "nerve center of world news," NBC, like the human brain, has the capacity to decide which stimuli it chooses to act upon, thereby deciding what constitutes history. Moreover, since that determination is made in the form of "history making sentences" uttered by its "contributors, analysts, and news men," these radio employees are, by extension, themselves world-historical figures. The authority conferred within this wonderland implies control not simply of contingent historical events but of absolute truth and absolute power, irrevocable and inescapable. The radio wonderland, the publication claims, once again revisiting the idea that the radio and God speak with one voice, "is a modern cathedral of the air, where the ancient wisdoms of all faiths are given the power to penetrate steel and stone, and carry their truths to the most remote corners of the earth." And of course, who has command of this pulpit's awe-inspiring power? Naturally, it is "The National Broadcasting Company, a name to conjure with the Wonderland of Radio."[98]

To accuse publicity materials of hyperbole is hardly sporting, but what is noteworthy about this tactic is the way it blithely expects NBC listeners to capitulate to the fantasy of the wonderland in the same way that the children listening to the *Music Appreciation Hour* are asked to believe in the radio fairy. In both instances, this infantilism is rhetorically masked and maintained by a knowing tone that, despite the fatuous fantasy they are asked to swallow, assures the audience that they are really the ones "in the know" and thus have freedom. Thus, adult sophistication is invoked in *What Goes On behind Your Radio Dial?* by the claim that in addition to a "nerve center" and a cathedral, the wonderland is "a gay night spot where the torrid wailing of a trumpet sinks to a whisper, as an idolized voice croons the words of the latest hit song."[99] Cannily, the suggestion of sexual abandon in the torrid wails and whispers is forced to comply with the demands of the idol. Divinity, even if it's a secular singing idol, holds sway—pleasure must have its purpose. There is, in this technique, a certain resonance between *What Goes On behind Your Radio Dial?* and the demagoguery of the radio personality Martin Luther Thomas. Among Thomas's techniques, Adorno claims, is the "if you only knew" device, which deploys innuendo to convince listeners that, should they follow along, they will be granted access to a mysterious, inconceivable world about which "outsiders" will remain ignorant. The teasing come-on in the title of *What Goes On behind Your Radio Dial?* taps into the audience's desire to be among the in-group, but the mystery, Adorno writes, "allows for an unchecked play of the imagination and invites all sorts of speculation, enhanced by the fact that the masses today, because they feel themselves to be objects of social processes, are anxious to learn what is going on behind the scenes."[100] The tantalizing hints at radio's sensuality, as well as the promise of the divine, softens up the listeners, who, in their desire to be admitted to both the harem and the holy of holies, will capitulate to almost anything. Thus, what Adorno says of a demagogue like Thomas can well be applied to the mainstream major network:

> The "if you only knew" device is of paramount importance with regard to this desire. Innuendo is a psychological means of making people feel that they already are members of that closed group which strives to catch them. The assumption that one understands something which is not plainly said, a winking of the eye, as it were, presupposes a kind of esoteric "intelligence" which tends to make accomplices of speaker and listener. The overtone of this "intelligence" is invariably a threatening one. . . . The "if you only knew" device promises to reveal the secret to those who join the racket and pay their tithe. But it also implies the promise that they will some day participate in the night of long knives, the Utopia of the racket.[101]

Further, I would argue that *What Goes On behind Your Radio Dial?* takes the notion of freedom and transforms it into the freedom to listen to NBC and in turn NBC's freedom to monopolize the listening public. The document includes a patently historicist exercise in which the story of radio is told with reference to Abraham Lincoln, Franklin D. Roosevelt, Pearl Harbor, and Jack's beanstalk and during which NBC, through careful omissions, writes itself back into Frank Conrad's garage for KDKA's first radio broadcast of the Harding–Cox election results in 1920. Although NBC didn't begin broadcasting until 1926, the implication of this narrative is not unlike what CBS tries to suggest in *"Seems Radio Is Here to Stay":* Since radio transcends history, the corporation that controls the airwaves has the authority to rewrite history as it sees fit. By inextricably fusing its own history with that of America, NBC implies that it is a shadow state demanding privileges and rights equal to those of the United States. Thus, after co-opting the history of the U.S. nation-state as the history of NBC, *What Goes On behind Your Radio Dial?* co-opts FDR's "Four Freedoms" of democracy, transforms them into "American Radio's . . . Four Freedoms," and declares NBC a government. "The Wonderland of American Radio, lying behind your radio dial," as the text describes this secret state, "has its law and order just as any well governed country must have. It is a government based on American Radio's own Four Freedoms—expressing the very essence of the American system of free radio."[102]

What are these four freedoms? Essentially they are the freedom for NBC to go about its business: "Freedom to Listen," "Freedom Not to Listen," "Freedom to Broadcast," and "Freedom From Fees and Licenses." It is worth noting a couple of features of these so-called freedoms that gesticulate about the audience's choices while secretly picking their pockets. The "Freedom Not to Listen," for example, is meant to celebrate the listener's program choices and the variety of options Americans have, unlike "listeners in foreign lands." What merits attention here is that NBC highlights the listeners' freedom not to listen to a specific program but not their freedom to turn off their radios. "American broadcasters provide a wealth of program variety. If the American listener doesn't like the program he is hearing, he simply tunes in other stations until he finds a program that suits his mood."[103] What is unsettling, if characteristically "American," about this "freedom" is not that a listener would calibrate his or her moods to the radio but that he or she would never be in the mood to stop listening altogether. Nowhere in *What Goes On behind Your Radio Dial?* is it suggested that the radio is not on. Here, NBC confirms the eerie Big Brother aspects of Adorno's discussion of radio's ubiquity in the "Music in Radio" memorandum and *Current of Music*. Since everyone is assumed to have the radio on at all times, NBC can mobilize large segments of the population simply through a single tone. In fact, in response to the attack on Pearl Harbor, it did just that, as *What Goes On behind Your Radio Dial?* admits with the matter-of-factness of a fait accompli. As the attack became known, the text boasts, "at NBC, the famous Fourth Chime was added instantly to the customary three chime signature which follows the close of every program. You probably heard it as you listened in your own home on that day of infamy. It was the prearranged emergency signal to all NBC engineers and key personnel to report immediately to their posts for special duty."[104] In a sense, *What Goes On behind Your Radio Dial?* one-ups Adorno. A network doesn't need a whole symphony or even a single movement to manipulate the masses. It can mobilize the populace with a single, well-placed note.

The metaphor of the radio wonderland is an important trope in NBC publicity materials and is extended to the sales pitch for potential sponsors in a mock children's book called *Alice in Sponsor-Land* (1941). The tactics employed by this bit of marketing are comparable to those used by *What Goes On behind Your Radio Dial?* In this case, Alice, a potential radio sponsor "who didn't know beans about radio," is led through the Wonderland of the NBC Red[105] weekly schedule (again, as the pictures illustrate, just behind the radio dial) by the advertising firm of "Hatter, Hare, Dormouse and Chaos." At each stop along the journey, fantastical creatures introduce Alice to a different day of the week and the wonders of the network's offerings. What distinguishes the advertising pitch from the materials designed for public consumption is that, under the guise of a children's book, the reader is hit with an onslaught of statistical information that confirms NBC's primacy in the broadcasting industry. The claim made by the repeated reference to NBC Red's motto, that it is "the Network Most People Listen to Most," is corroborated by the extensive statistical commentary delivered by the Dormouse and by an automated book "which could turn its own pages and answer questions put to it."[106]

In effect, Alice, the potential sponsor, is subjected to an *avant la lettre* PowerPoint presentation. Here, the Dormouse is "Sponsor-Land's" equivalent of the market researcher, but his "damn data" is continually belittled by the other characters: "'Every time I tried to get across some salient fact,' [the] Dormouse said, 'the Hatter treated me shabbily and I don't like it.'"[107] However, ridiculing statistics paradoxically acts to assure their authority. Since they are "the" facts, accessible to any bean counter, best to let the good people at NBC, Gallup, Nielsen, and Crossley compile them and provide the gist; the important businessman has better things to think about. The effect is ultimately to suggest that NBC has done the thinking for the advertiser, and the advertiser has only to capitulate to NBC Red's control to earn his pecuniary reward. The connection between submission and profit heaven is made explicit when, in yet another example of the denigration of research that confirms its authority, Alice asks about the concrete benefits of advertising on NBC Red:

> "Notes or no notes" said Alice, "I think the queen brought up an interesting point, not only about Saturday daytime, but about all time on the Red—namely, how does it pay out?"
>
> "Beautifully," said the Dormouse. "Statistics show—"
>
> "Never mind, George," interrupted the Hatter. "There's a much better answer waiting for us over on the next page."[108]

The next page, it turns out, is the image of businessman heaven (Figure 8). Still wearing their jackets, vests, and ties, portly tycoons carouse with naked cherubs, smoking cigars, drinking, and singing a song that confirms that the NBC wonderland is in fact a utopia: "ANY TIME IS GOOD TIME ON NBC RED."

> "What's this?" asked Alice. "—Heaven?"
>
> "You might call it that," replied the Hare. "Actually it's the next best thing—the Contented Advertisers' Club Membership is automatic for Red Network clients."
>
> "The one thing that keeps clients happy," explained the Hatter, "is sales. And the Red produces them—in abundance. The reason for *that* of

course, is because the Red's the Network Most People Listen to Most. It's sort of an un-vicious circle, you see."[109]

One of the repeated refrains of the network marketing publications from the 1930s and '40s—and one explicitly reiterated by *Alice in Sponsor-Land* as the characters march through the Red network's weekly schedule—is that radio networks capture the "psychological moments" of audience's daily lives and use that psychological information to deliver listeners to their sponsors. This notion that the networks somehow have privileged access to the audience's psyche is still in evidence nearly a decade later in the illustrated CBS publication *We Don't Know Why They Listen (so much!)*, whose cover image features a suspiciously Freud-like analyst counseling a patient who happily caresses his fetishized radio. Although in *Alice in Sponsor-Land* the statistical measurements of radio listening were denigrated, they were nonetheless present. In *We Don't Know Why They Listen*, the "damn data" disappears almost entirely. Instead, in images of cartoonish nude figures walking around in the minds of the book's radio listeners, the advertiser is treated to the suggestion that the successful radio program

Figure 8. National Broadcasting Company, *Alice in Sponsor-Land: A Chronicle of the Adventures of Alice, the Hatter, the March Hare, and the Dormouse in That Twentieth Century Wonderland on the Other Side of Your Radio Loudspeaker,* illustrated by Bernard Tobey (New York: National Broadcasting Company, 1941), 40. Courtesy of NBC.

is a combination of alchemy and psychosexual intuition. Moreover, CBS insists, sponsors would be better off leaving the magic and the match-making to the radio "analysts":

> Nobody knows precisely why more people are listening to radio more. But the fact that they do is very clear. And pretty important. Today the network advertiser is reaching bigger audiences than any advertiser has ever reached before—and at less cost! This fact has unusual significance for him as the need for the most economical medium daily becomes more demanding. Maybe they're in love with radio. Arithmetic alone cannot explain it. Any more than statistics can explain the structure of a love affair."[110]

Once again advertisers are encouraged to leave it to the network to bring them listeners. The simplicity of the sentences corresponds to the patriarchal tone of the message. And in this case, the imagery is more crudely violent. Hence, later in *We Don't Know Why They Listen*, on one page the developing techniques of radio marketing are equated with the tools of capture and murder, as images of fishing lures and nets are abandoned for an image of a gun. On the following page, the fruits of this arms escalation are revealed, as a big fish, filled with the smiling, yet nonetheless severed, heads of listeners, is proudly displayed to the advertisers. The fact that the faces are smiling does little to obviate the fact that they are the catch of the day, ready to be devoured.

In a sense, the images of Freud and naked men and women in *We Don't Know Why They Listen* confirm one of Adorno's most deeply held and problematic principles: the centrality of the unconscious in audiences' responses to the culture industry. Although in *Minima Moralia* Adorno famously claims that "in psycho-analysis, nothing is true except the exaggerations,"[111] the importance of Freud in Adorno's work cannot, itself, be overexaggerated. "We may take it for granted, as an indubitable result of modern psychology," he writes in "Memorandum: Music in Radio," "that unconscious facts influence the behavior of the individual much more than the conscious facts."[112] Throughout Adorno's work on the mass media, there is an insistence that a full understanding of the effects their products have on modern subjects can only be achieved by considering the relationship between consciously held beliefs and unconscious, often irrational drives. And it is because the unconscious plays such a large role in the way people's desires are molded and gratified by the culture industry that purely empirical sociological studies will often fall short.

As Martin Jay relates, "the more radical, even utopian implications" of the Freudian tradition were not embraced by Adorno to the same extent as they were by Herbert Marcuse. "He was, certainly, always a highly selective disciple," Jay insists.[113] Nevertheless, when it came to understanding the roots of authoritarianism, Adorno strove to mobilize Freud for the cause. Freud is perhaps most helpful, Adorno claims in "Freudian Theory and the Pattern of Fascist Propaganda," in understanding the "massification" of the public accomplished by the culture industry. "He tries," Adorno writes of Freud, "to find out which psychological forces result in the transformation of individuals into a mass." And then, as though putting into words the unspoken implications of the naked figures and neurotic patient in CBS's *We Don't Know Why They Listen,* Adorno continues, "In accordance with general psychoanalytic theory, Freud believes that the bond which integrates individuals into a mass is of a libidinal nature."[114] And yet, in authoritarian mass psychology, the energies of the libido are no longer aimed at the preservation of the individual (which would be rational) but instead are marshaled in the service of the subject's self-destruction (his loss of subjectivity). Thus, Adorno claims, authoritarianism relies on the "internalization" of irrational impulses, which, because they are shared by so many, become systemic and appear rational. "Under prevailing conditions," Adorno claims, "the irrationality of fascist propaganda becomes rational in the sense of instinctual economy. For if the status quo is taken for granted and petrified, a much greater effort is needed to see through it than to adjust to it and to obtain at least some gratification with the existent—the focal point of fascist propaganda."[115]

For Adorno then, contra CBS's publicity claim, we *do* know why audiences listen so much, and the reasons have everything to do with the images of Freud, sex, and murdered bodies in CBS's publicity manual. The radio provides gratification for the audience's libidinal energies, but it does so in a way that unifies listeners with other subjects and transforms their rational interests into willing self-exploitation. But it is important to note two things about how Adorno understands psychology: First, although he is often accused of doing so, Adorno is careful not to convict the audience of pure passivity; at the same time, however, he doesn't blame audiences for their self-destruction. Audiences actively seek their gratification, but the social and economic realities of their listening situation channel those impulses into destructive ends. Although Kathy Newman, in her book *Radio Active,* argues that audiences were rational agents and often actively resisted the consumerist logic of radio networks and their advertisers, surveying radio networks' publicity materials from the period gives one a sense of how the networks were equally engaged in cultivating audiences' irrational activity for their own ends. This ability of the culture industry to capitalize on the dialectic between irrational impulses was one of the centerpieces of Adorno's (and Horkheimer's) critique of the culture industry. As the characters in *Alice in Sponsor-Land* reveal, the networks were increasingly savvy about the psychology of their audience in this regard:

> "Oh," said Alice, "—that means Saturday morning's a good time to tell them to put your product on their shopping lists!"
>
> "A *good time!*" exclaimed the Queen. "Heavens to Betsy—it's one of the *best!*" In fact, it's a *psychological moment.* You not only nail your housewives in time to put a bug in their ear, but you also reach the other members of the family—men, women, and children.[116]

This relationship between rational and irrational impulses is at play in many of the networks' children's-book-style documents. If in *Alice in Sponsor-Land* and *We Don't Know Why They Listen* the advertising executive is encouraged to eschew data and give way to irrational impulses, the flip side of this impulse is displayed in yet another of the networks' "children's" books from 1940, where the prospective sponsor is asked to accord rationality the power of magic. In NBC's *It's Not Done with Mirrors*, the irrationalism of the wonderland is replaced by the hyperrationalism of the modern industrial city. On the cover (Figure 9), a magician stands in front of a mirror that transposes the title letters. Here, however, the looking glass as a transparent passageway to the radio wonderland has been rendered powerless. Whereas in other publicity documents the reader is instilled with a desire to believe in the "magic" of the radio, in this text the magician is portrayed as an antiquated opposition to industrial organization and, consequently, decidedly premodern and foreign. "Don't mind the Swami," the book begins, leaving little doubt as to its cultural sensitivity toward the turbaned caricature painting a sign with the words "UNFAIR TO ORGANIZED MAGICIANS":

> He's our "little man upon the stair"—one Abdullah Q. Dazzalian, frustrated Mullah of Magic Mirrors, who came to find out just how it *is* done, and who wouldn't stay out of this book.[117]

It's Not Done with Mirrors is able to capitalize simultaneously on ridicule of the traditions of the Middle East and on an attack on organized labor. In illustrations by the frequent *New Yorker* contributor Peter Arno,[118] the

Figure 9. From National Broadcasting Company, *It's Not Done with Mirrors* (New York: National Broadcasting Company, 1940), cover illustration. Courtesy of NBC and the Peter Arno Estate.

turbaned "Mullah" is pictured picketing in front of the giant RCA building while the crowds—all in Western clothes—teem into the building,
which, with its jutting, phallic, modernist structure, is meant to convey the
rational world of Western commerce and communications confronted by
the irrationality of its lone, extremist protester (Figure 10).

Here again we are reminded that NBC Red is the network "Most People
Listen to Most," but in the place of *Alice in Sponsor-Land*'s denigration of
"damn data," in *It's Not Done with Mirrors*, statistics and scientific research are valorized. Nevertheless, for all their importance, the facts are no
less mystified in this text. Here, when an advertiser talks to "an expert on
coverage and audience measurement," what he hears will be just another
sort of magic words: "He'll speak the language of field strength, mail analysis, coincidental and recall ratings, audimeters and the like."[119] Still, the
advertiser should not be dismayed, for once again he's in good hands, and
NBC can translate the techno-speak into the universal language; "there's
a common ground on which we all can meet, to our own good profit." NBC
Red boils down sophisticated audience research into a very simple equation—that of capital exchange. "In a word," the text claims, "it's 'getting-
the-most-out-of-your-advertising-budget.' And the way to do that, in radio,
is to find out *which network most people listen to most*."[120] Here we see the
inherent flaw in the formal principle of Lazarsfeld's version of administrative research: Marketing research's inherent "usefulness" is inextricably
bound to the maximization of profits. As such—and this is exactly Adorno's
challenge in his presentation of "On a Social Critique of Radio Music"—
administrative research can never be "benevolent" if its very nature is the
mechanism by which the alienation of labor is furthered.

However, despite the usefulness of market research for the network,
It's Not Done with Mirrors manages to mystify the relationship between
empiricism and profits by suggesting that the process of data gathering is
so organizationally complex that comprehending it is beyond the grasp of
mere mortals. Thus, while magic is denigrated, statistics themselves are
transformed into a new and more potent form of magic. The litany of magic
words used by the expert on coverage ("field strength, mail analysis, coincidental and recall ratings, audimeters and the like") are the "open sesames"
to this magic kingdom. But instead of the cave of the forty thieves, *It's
Not Done with Mirrors* presents the transparent synthesis of humans and
machines within the high-rises of media moguls.

Confronted with the sterile efficiency of the networks' technical profi-
ciency, the "Mullah" has a moment of crisis: "Our little man who wasn't

Figure 10. From *It's Not Done with Mirrors*, 2. Courtesy of NBC and the Peter Arno Estate.

there sees the engineers' magic with sighs of despair."[121] But even if it is magic, at least the engineering room is a recognizable—if stylized—work site, replete with electronic consoles and turbines. The big juju happens under the auspices of the research staff (Figure 11). In a massive room, countless letters and listener surveys, shunted in from some postal ether, are collated and tabulated with—even in a static cartoon—unbelievable speed and precision. The secretarial staff logs each survey and passes it off to a male figure who files the responses in a box corresponding to their time zone or city size. The results are then tabulated on giant blackboards with the legends "Day Most" or "Night Regular." The parade of people in the airy corridor in the background, as well as the increasing pile of letters, conveys the endless repetition of the scene. While the image implies an organizational hyperreality, the caption suggests that this is magic on a much grander scale than our "Mullah" can muster: "Take a card—any card—what's the use, I'm a sap! These people take cards from all over the map."[122] The parlor trick pales in comparison to the power of an organization that can determine anyone's preference anywhere.

As in *Alice in Sponsor-Land*, faced with the magic of radio, be it the irrational wonderland or the hyperrational organization of the industrial workplace, the sponsor has no choice but to capitulate to what the network commands. The illusion of free choice is proffered. A ream of statistics is followed by the statements "These clinch the evidence offered by programs and facilities. But you can judge the results yourself."[123] However, given the overwhelming "evidence" provided by the research statistics as to the popularity and profitability of NBC Red, the claim that one can judge for oneself rings hollow. Judging for oneself takes on the aspect of willful ignorance and recalcitrance embodied by a figure like our turbaned fanatic.

Better to fall in line, the text rhetorically argues, than to assert an independence from statistics and reveal oneself as bucking the system; best to give in to the reified logic of positivism. That this is the predominant concern of *It's Not Done with Mirrors* is driven home by the image of sponsors in their overcoats trundling past an expressionless secretary into a nameless room (Figure 12). Were it not for the single, maniacally grinning gentleman doffing his cap on the way out, clearly satisfied with his service, one might suspect that the thronging businessman were marching to their dooms.

Despite the horrific resonance of this image, it could perhaps go without saying that the radio Adorno encountered seems not only more quaint and benign than our own but also, in many regards, more progressive.

Figure 11. From *It's Not Done with Mirrors*, 13. Courtesy of NBC and the Peter Arno
Estate.

Figure 12. From *It's Not Done with Mirrors*, 16. Courtesy of NBC and the Peter Arno Estate.

Notwithstanding the faults Adorno found with the radio, faults that ultimately contain within them the seeds of an authoritarian approach to audiences, there is something almost touching about the notion that for-profit national radio and television networks would dedicate as much time as NBC and CBS did to educational programming, the arts, and "classical" music. In her book *Radio Active,* Kathy Newman argues that audiences were hardly the docile, passive consumers we might imagine them being in the 1930s and '40s, and she details numerous program and product boycotts as well as a range of political actions staged by angry listeners. One of the things that strikes me about Newman's research, as well as about the material I have uncovered in writing this chapter, is how much material the networks actually did offer audiences that gave them space for rejoinder. Despite Adorno's impressions, much of the publicity and marketing material I have found indicates that a great number of radio personnel did in fact believe that they served the "public interest," even if they turned a handy profit doing so. Adorno's insight—and one could say his genius— was that he saw through the positive attributes of radio broadcasting to the infantilization and the nascent authoritarianism that lay just below the surface of its smiling sonic countenance.

It should also be apparent that Adorno's most dire pronouncements about radio in the 1930s and '40s seem much more applicable when examining contemporary radio culture. Partly this has to do with the relaxing of FCC laws concerning station ownership in a given locale. Clear Channel and Infinity Broadcasting far surpass the ambitions of CBS and NBC in the 1930s, airing multiple formats on multiple stations in every market, something that the older networks were legally precluded from doing. Today's radio listener has increasingly fewer choices that do not conform to the standardized programming of these media giants. That hegemony has also brought with it new breeds of demagogues whose techniques, perhaps reflecting their audience, are more blatant and coarse and whose reach is substantially broader than anything Martin Luther Thomas could have imagined.[124] And finally, lest we think that the rhetorical strategy to link a mass-media technology to the "word of God" was merely an old-fashioned yet convenient metaphor, consider what former FCC chair Michael Powell said of digital recording technology during a speech at the 2003 International Consumer Electronics Show: "My favorite product that I got for Christmas is TiVo. TiVo is God in my household. I can't wait to walk in the house each day to see what it has recorded for me."[125] Whereas once it was the box that transmitted God's word, today the box is God Itself. A fertile and fascinating study could be performed linking the entirety of Adorno's radio writings to contemporary broadcasting practices, but until such a study is available I will simply offer that Adorno wasn't retrograde; he was ahead of his time. And the businessman is still smiling maniacally, but the line of bodies behind him has only grown longer.

If this discussion of radio has strayed into a discussion of images and even into developments in video technology, it perhaps does so in line with Adorno's own intellectual trajectory. After the music section of PRRP folded, Adorno turned his attentions more explicitly to the questions of authoritarianism and anti-Semitism in his work for the AJC and the Studies in Prejudice project, work that would result in *The Authoritarian Personality*. In those studies, Adorno was forced to move beyond radio and music to confront and at times deploy the power of mass-reproduced images. While pictures like those in *It's Not Done with Mirrors* tend to confirm Adorno's worst suspicions about the authoritarian nature of radio broadcasting, when Adorno shifts his attention to mass-produced artworks consumed visually, the awesome breadth and incisiveness of his radio critique is faced with challenges that don't quite translate into the visual register.

Despite John Marshall's claim that Adorno was "psychologically engaged . . . by his ability to recognize deficiencies in the broadcasting of music to an extent that makes questionable his own drive to find ways of remedying them,"[126] there is ample evidence, both in his PRRP writings and in his studies of radio demagogues, that—*pace* his subsequent admonitions, in the essay "Commitment," that art should counter coercion through form alone—Adorno was in fact able to conceive of his project in practical terms. Although many of the suggestions for productive empirical research in "Music in Radio" and *Current of Music* were patently absurd,[127] he does nevertheless offer a number of suggestions for alternative radio practices in accordance with his understanding of the medium as a physiognomic unity. On the one hand, Adorno's suggestions seek to highlight the technological mediation essential to radio transmission by altering the design of the radio set. "It is obvious . . . that the preservation of what appeared to be individualistic features of radio technique are completely inconsistent," he writes. "If our radio sets, for instance, look like hallowed and sacred shrines, each like a miniature tabernacle, this certainly is not in keeping with the idea of radio as a mechanical tool." In order to circumvent the tendency to confuse the voice of the radio with the word of God, Adorno claims that "a modern architect, Mr. Kramer, has developed the idea of a new type of radio set which does not look like a shrine or a piece of furniture, but which looks instead like the machine which it actually is. Thus, they look 'better' than the older sets." Adorno then holds out the tantalizing but probably unfulfilled promise that he and "Mr. Kramer" would prepare a memo on the subject for future publication.[128]

If a redesigned radio was to highlight the functionality of the mechanism—calling a tool a tool, as it were—then Adorno's sonic suggestions proceed in a similar track. For Adorno, the dream radio would also be a musical instrument. Given the inadequacies of radio transmission and the degeneration inflicted on music by its broadcast, Adorno asks, in "Music in Radio," "How can an uninterrupted scale of every color of sound possibly be produced arbitrarily by an instrument which would be independent of the contingencies of all musical instruments now used or those which have ever been used in the past?" In response he answers that should the radio transmitter be mobilized as a musical instrument as well as a form of mediation, it would obviate the gap between the radio and its raw material, sound. "If this actually could be achieved," Adorno conjectures, "the whole difference between musical production and reproduction would disappear. That is, the composer would fix the work directly upon the apparatus which would have at its disposal every physically possibly musical possibility." As evidence of this utopian union of composition and its broadcast, Adorno cites the development of certain electronic musical instruments, among them the Meissner electronic "violin," the Hammond organ, and the theremin, for which "the idea is that we no longer 'broadcast over the radio,' but 'play on the radio' in the sense that one plays on a violin."[129]

Today, thanks to the Beach Boys' "Good Vibrations," as well to countless horror films, Leon Theremin's invention has become familiar, if only for its clichéd otherworldliness.[130] In 1938, however, the theremin was a relatively young instrument whose potential for use in composition was only just being explored,[131] and there was some hope that the theremin and its electronic siblings would revolutionize musical broadcasting and composition as music truly (as in *"Seems Radio Is Here to Stay"*) pulled "from the ether."[132] The effect of the theremin, Adorno claims, is "especially noteworthy when considered within the context of our theories." [133] If, for Adorno, the radio fails to adequately transmit natural sound, the theremin succeeds by "dispensing with the necessity of imitating a natural sound altogether."[134] Or perhaps, to expand the notion of natural sound, the theremin locates nature within the radio mechanism itself, making broadcast equipment and performance one and the same. The result is a music that, though removed from the "natural" world, collapses the gap between performer, broadcaster, and receiver and attains a vitality otherwise deprived of instruments by the radio. Thus, the mechanization of the theremin and its integral relation to radio engineering are the key to its liberation: "As the interpreter's command of the sound producing medium increases, the sound itself becomes more capable of conveying genuine elements of subjective musical expression and at the same time it becomes less mechanical."[135]

But for Adorno the possibilities of the theremin and its electronic peers remained strictly theoretical, as did his suggestions for a redesigned, utilitarian radio receiver. As far-fetched as some of these suggestions may seem, they nevertheless reveal an Adorno far more open to certain possibilities for praxis than is generally acknowledged, and what gives those suggestions weight is Adorno's encyclopedic knowledge of musical theory and history. However, one of the fundamental problems Adorno encountered in his radio research was that few listeners were as "expert" as he was, and thus they could not hear how the radio manipulated its objects and hence its audiences. Although the fact that Adorno was sensitive to this quandary is demonstrated throughout the radio writings, it is perhaps this gap between Adorno and the average listener that more than any other factor precludes translating his theories into practical experiments on radio listening.

But the question of translating aesthetic and social theory into performance was not to end with the abortive suggestions in the radio projects. In 1941, Adorno did move to the West, although not to "some small University town" as the letter to Mrs. Mitchell warned. Instead, following the ailing Horkheimer, Theodor and Gretl Adorno made their way to Southern California. While there, not only would Adorno find himself in an exile community that mingled freely with the stars of the Hollywood firmament, but he would also witness, firsthand, the day-to-day life of the culture industry that he had only just begun to glimpse while working among radio personnel in New York. Adorno's time in Hollywood, which resulted in some of his most important theoretical work, would also produce his most sustained and yet ultimately frustrating attempt to put his theoretical principles into aesthetic practice. Although with the question of music's transformation via the radio Adorno was on fairly sure footing, when it came to the transmission of visual information via film, he was on somewhat less easy ground. Nevertheless, as I detail in chapter 3, it is in Adorno's and Horkheimer's surprising efforts to make a film in Hollywood that one sees not only a somewhat charming naïveté on Adorno's part but also the subtlety of his theoretical insights and the depth of his dedication to a truly democratic culture.

3 *BELOW THE SURFACE*
FRANKFURT GOES TO HOLLYWOOD

The starry-eyed one seems to have failed—anyone who counts on the
movies is throwing himself on Satan's mercies.
—Thomas Mann

In *City of Nets*, Otto Friedrich's exceptional snapshot of Hollywood in the
1940s, the author makes room for a brief mention of the Institute of Social
Research. Suggesting that the "whole group" from the "Frankfurt Institute"
came to Los Angeles at the invitation of Ernst Simmel, one of the founders
of the Berlin Psychoanalytic Institute and Judy Garland's sometime analyst, Friedrich goes on to claim:

> These Frankfurt exiles cherished the idea of synthesizing Marx and Freud
> in their critique of modern society, and although they never accomplished
> anything very substantial, they did their best to serve as an irritant even
> in southern California. Blessed with foundation grants from the East,
> they staged little seminars, attended by fellow exiles like Brecht and
> Feuchtwanger, on various cultural topics, the significance of jazz or the
> movies.[1]

Except for the part about the foundation grants, there is very little about
Friedrich's thumbnail sketch that is wholly accurate. Here is not the place
to argue whether or not the Institute's goal was to synthesize Marx and
Freud or indeed whether Adorno could ever be claimed as a champion of
synthesis of any sort, but Friedrich's account provides other more concrete
errors with which to contend. For instance, while Horkheimer and Adorno

(and ultimately Marcuse) did travel to California beginning in the early 1940s, by no means did the "whole group" transfer to the West Coast. In fact, the Institute maintained its office, headed by Pollock, at Columbia University throughout most of the decade, and such key members of the Institute as Lowenthal, Franz Neumann, and Marcuse, due to various research projects for Voice of America and the OSS, remained on the East Coast throughout the war. Further, as is well documented by Adorno's biographers and historians of the Institute as well as in Horkheimer's own correspondence, the move to California was predicated not on an invitation from Simmel but on Horkheimer's poor health and the need for a more hospitable climate.

Friedrich's factual slips are troubling, especially given how assiduously researched *City of Nets* is otherwise.[2] But I am much more interested in his claim that the Institute "never accomplished anything very substantial" while in their Hollywood environs. Leaving aside the question of the influence or importance of *Dialectic of Enlightenment, Minima Moralia,* or *The Authoritarian Personality,* each of which was written during the years Adorno and Horkheimer spent in California,[3] Adorno also collaborated on *Composing for the Films* with Hanns Eisler and advised Thomas Mann on the musical sections of *Doctor Faustus.* The first of these was one of the earliest and most trenchant analyses of cinematic music; the second, arguably the most important novel to emerge from the German intellectuals in exile.

However, it could well be argued that each of these texts, while historically and intellectually important, is marginal to the broader business of Hollywood filmmaking, and even when Adorno is writing about cinema, as he does in *Composing for the Films,* he is ultimately concerned not so much with movies per se as he is with the degeneration of music listening. In addition, one could say that Friedrich's argument refers not so much to the Institute's overall influence but to its effect on the movie-making community specifically.

Here too, however, the claim needs some revising. I do not wish to suggest that Horkheimer and Adorno were by any means central Hollywood players, but it does seem that Friedrich's dismissal of Adorno's and Horkheimer's California work is symptomatic of a general critical concession that the two—especially Adorno—had very little productive to say about the popular cinema and to the representatives of the motion picture industry.

The record among Adorno's critics is spotty. While Martin Jay writes that among the scholars who followed in Adorno's footsteps, "one of the keenest areas of interest has been Adorno's scattered remarks on film,"[4] subsequent writings about Adorno on cinema tend to portray him as the same "mandarin cultural conservative" that Jay does.[5] Writings about Adorno's sensitivity to cinema range from Claudia Gorbman's insinuation that Adorno was not in fact Eisler's collaborator on *Composing for the Films*[6] to Harvey Gross's memoir of the Los Angeles exile, which claims that Adorno "consciously resisted every compulsion to 'adjust' to the American scene."[7] That the American scene is, to Gross's mind, synonymous with the film industry is evident in the absence of any reference to the many film personalities Adorno encountered in Hollywood, émigré or not. Even Adorno's friend, the filmmaker and scholar Alexander Kluge, claimed that "Adorno had no knowledge of the production sphere. He did not deal with it. He was interested in what Marcel Proust did, with what music did."[8]

Among the critical engagements with Adorno's writings on cinema that do acknowledge his contribution to the medium, perhaps the most sustained and sophisticated consideration comes from Miriam Hansen. Both by using Adorno's writings and by deploying certain of Adorno's interlocutors (Benjamin, Kracauer), Hansen has perhaps done more than any other scholar to suggest that Adorno does not dismiss cinema out of hand.[9] Rather, she claims that Adorno recognized, albeit late in life, the inherent aesthetic potentials of cinema and argued that by abandoning the pretense of aping the novel and resisting the mimetic impulse to present "realistic" events, the motion picture could become its own unique form of "writing." This notion of film as writing, she claims, "is reframed in the context of an alternative practice."[10] By virtue of seeking out its own combinatory techniques—that is, through montage, sonic disjunctions, and so on—the cinema can thereby strive toward the aesthetic truth content of more distancing and opaque aesthetic forms such as writing and music. The difficulty the spectator encountered in interpreting a cinematic text would provide the irritant against which subjectivity could react and so resist its own domination:

> If an aesthetics of film is advised to reconstruct an associational mode of experience in constellations akin to writing, this means nothing less than that it should aspire to the level of self-conscious construction by which— in Adorno's view—all truly modern art assumes the function of dialectical theory. Only then would film cease to be a script, which imposes a literal reading on the spectator, and become *écriture*—which requires critical deciphering.[11]

But if Hansen is genuinely supportive of Adorno as a film theorist and insists that *Composing for the Films* might be a good place to start when reconsidering Adorno's relationship to Hollywood filmmaking practices, she nonetheless focuses her critique on the late Adorno, who was writing in response to filmmakers like Michelangelo Antonioni and Kluge, rather than on the Adorno living in the shadows of the major studios in the 1940s. Despite Adorno's proximity to the dream factory from 1941 to 1953, this relationship tends to be overlooked. As Hansen herself admits, "the invocation of Adorno's writings on film and mass culture amounts to little more than a ritualistic gesture, reiterating the familiar charges of elitism, pessimism, and high modernist myopia."[12]

Hence, the most succinct summary of the canonical account of Adorno's incapacity to find something fruitful in Hollywood texts appears in Andreas Huyssen's essay "Adorno in Reverse: From Hollywood to Richard Wagner":

> While Adorno recognized that there were limitations to the reification of human subjects through the culture industry which made resistance thinkable at the level of the subject, he never asked himself whether perhaps such limitations could be located in the mass cultural commodities themselves. Such limits do indeed become evident when one begins to analyze in detail the signifying strategies of specific cultural commodities and the mesh of gratification, displacement and production of desires which are invariable [*sic*] put into play in their production and consumption.[13]

Huyssen's argument about Adorno's inability to concede to cultural-industrial objects the potential for subjective liberation is exemplary, but it is also typical of a utopian longing expressed by many of Adorno's critics that generally proceeds on two levels. First, there is the belief that the "signifying strategies" of mass-media texts could be used to wrestle those texts and their consumers away from the context of their industrial production. Second, there is the corollary wish that Adorno would articulate strategies for how these signifying practices could be put into socially and politically progressive action. Those familiar with Adorno's later works on the social function of art will recognize that he is constitutionally unable to make those sorts of concessions, not only to mass-media texts but also to "authentic" works of art. Adorno's reluctance to attribute a defined praxis to the artwork is consistent with his skepticism regarding the subject's diminished agency in industrial society. In "Commitment," for example, Adorno inveighs against the arrogance of modern subjects who, convinced of their agency in a time of objective powerlessness, force art to do what they themselves cannot, namely, to resist the coercions of a world that "continues to hold a pistol to the heads of human beings."[14] Further, Adorno's insistence that the autonomous artwork need neither be productive nor participate in an overt political challenge to the status quo is a vital element of *Aesthetic Theory:* "By crystallizing in itself as something unique to itself, rather than complying with existing social norms and qualifying as something 'socially useful,' [the artwork] criticizes society by merely existing, for which puritans of all stripes condemn it." The notion that a text should be useful *for* something is anathema to Adorno because it transforms the artwork into a means rather than an end in itself. "What is social in art is its immanent movement against society," Adorno argues, "not its manifest opinions."[15]

With regard to popular culture specifically, Adorno generally does confirm the common perception that he finds little in popular cinema and television as aesthetic practices. Statements such as the one from *Minima Moralia* that "every visit to the cinema leaves me, against all my vigilance, stupider and worse"[16] leave very little room for anyone to argue that Adorno intellectually embraced Hollywood filmmaking. But against this sentiment, against Friedrich's assertions, and against the dearth of Adorno scholarship regarding his actual relationship to the motion picture industry, I would like to offer a number of pieces of evidence that suggest a somewhat closer relationship among Horkheimer and Adorno, the Hollywood community, and the "signifying strategies" of narrative film and television than to date has been acknowledged. In so doing, I am not attempting to resituate Adorno and Horkheimer as integral parts of the Hollywood establishment. Nor am I interested in rescuing popular culture for Adorno—or from him, for that matter. Rather, I hope to provide a corrective for a general lack of consideration of the historical, geographic, and social milieu into which Adorno found himself thrust in the 1940s. In so doing, I suggest that we might reconsider Adorno's criticisms of cinema and television as deriving not (as conventional wisdom would have it) from Adorno's aloofness and elitism but rather from his intimate knowledge of the practices and personnel of the U.S. film industry.

It is true that, unlike in his work on the physiognomics of radio, Adorno fails to articulate a theory of the unified, contradictory bodies of movies and television on the order of *Current of Music.* And although his work on mass-mediated images never culminates in as sustained a critique as do his writings on broadcast sound, his apparent lack of critical engagement masks a more concerted attempt on Adorno's part to participate in film-making practices themselves.

Part of the problem Adorno confronted in the cinema was an overwhelming incapacity of the spectator to intellectually account for what he or she was asked to see and understand. To Adorno's mind, this blindness in the way audiences confront movies and television was a symptom of their subjective destruction and the winnowing of their intellectual capacities. If anything, Adorno's attempts to make sense of—and even use—mass-produced images illustrates the fundamental failure of vision at the heart of motion pictures and motion-picture spectatorship. His comments about the types of misreadings cultivated by movies and television and—in a different register—about the phantasmagoric works of Wagner both anticipate and refine many of the themes that will dominate subsequent film theory. These insights, combined with a richer understanding of Adorno's Hollywood years, argue for a continuing reassessment of Adorno's importance to the discipline of cinema studies.

Before addressing Adorno's direct relationship with Hollywood, I should perhaps say something about Adorno's coauthorship of *Composing for the Films*, because it is after all the only text Adorno wrote during his stay in the United States that is explicitly and predominately about cinema. Any claim one might make that Adorno is giving sustained thought to the importance of filmmaking on contemporary consciousness begins with this text. Although most scholars generally accept that Adorno and Eisler wrote the manuscript together, in her work on Eisler, Gorbman is implicitly doubtful. While refusing to come down directly on one side or the other of the authorship question, throughout her essay Gorbman insists on referring to *Composing for the Films* as Eisler's without acknowledging Adorno. Further, in a footnote describing the genesis of the book, she quotes Gunter Mayer, the editor of Eisler's *Musik und Politik*, as saying that "Adorno's . . . claim of authorship is highly questionable."[17]

A letter found in the Rockefeller Foundation Archives may perhaps settle the matter and bear out Adorno's claim. At the outset of the film-music project, Eisler went to the Rockefeller Foundation requesting a research grant in much the same way as Adorno had done for *Current of Music*. Unlike Adorno, however, Eisler was successful in his request, and in January of 1940, he was granted $20,160 for a two-year study of film music, during which he was to rescore a number of Hollywood films to "gauge audience reaction to the different versions presented" and, more generally, to interrogate the "problem of music in relation to the content of film—

rudimentary esthetics of film and music."[18] In 1942, the grant was renewed for one year, and for a while Eisler submitted regular, if somewhat thin, up-dates on his progress to John Marshall at the Rockefeller Foundation.

However, after a long period of silence, in July 1946, a letter arrived in Marshall's office stating the following:

> We gladly take the opportunity to inform you about the state of affairs concerning the book on film music.
>
>   As early as late in 1942 we decided to pool our theoretical ideas and practical experiences and to write the book together. The German manuscript was finished in summer 1944. Publication was held up by difficulties of translation. Now, however, the English manuscript is ready to go into print as soon as a few minor changes have been agreed upon between the Oxford University Press and ourselves. The book should be out not later than sometime in fall or winter. We should gladly let you have a copy of the English manuscript but unfortunately we have none. . . .
>
>   Sincerely yours,
>   Hanns Eisler
>   T. W. Adorno[19]

There is a certain element of deadpan payback in the letter, since Adorno had been denied Rockefeller funds to complete his radio music project. Despite his earlier battles with Marshall and Lazarsfeld, Adorno, in a back-handed way, had received his support from the foundation after all, even if it had to come in the form of a collaboration with Eisler. And instead of *Current of Music*, which had to wait sixty years to see publication, the world got *Composing for the Films*.

According to this letter, by the time Adorno got involved in the film music project, he was already living in Los Angeles, and through Eisler, Schoenberg, and other émigrés, Adorno was able to make contact with a number of filmmakers, actors, writers, and composers.[20] But there is ample evidence that even before moving to Los Angeles, Adorno and Horkheimer were thinking about the problems presented by cinema and movie people. In a letter Adorno wrote before joining Horkheimer in Los Angeles, Adorno worried about leaving too much of his furniture behind in New York, both because he feared losing the last vestiges of "empirisches Europa"—his authentic Europe—but also because he had heard that Hollywood was an "open house" society where literally anyone could stop by unannounced and unexpected.[21]

A survey of the correspondence between Adorno and Horkheimer con-firms how interconnected that society was, particularly among the exiles, and reveals Adorno's and Horkheimer's familiarity and intimacy with the glitterati of Hollywood. References to dinners with Greta Garbo, Lotte Lenya, Kurt Weill, and Schoenberg are followed by notes about parties attended by Chaplin, where Adorno gets imitated and good-naturedly ridiculed.[22] Moreover, skimming the pages of *Variety* and the *Hollywood Reporter*, one learns that Adorno and Horkheimer were not simply retiring docents holding "little seminars," as Friedrich suggests, but instead were out on the social circuit, attending premiers, and appearing—as "world-famous authors"—in the daily notices. For example, in 1943, the *Hollywood Reporter* printed the following description of what must have been a nearly unimaginable evening:

> Exiled Notables at Showing of "Rhine"
>
> World-famous authors, consuls-general, and educators forced to flee from Germany or from their now-occupied native lands joined motion picture stars last night in a unique "Premiere in Exile" at Warner Bros. Hollywood Theatre. They saw the Motion Picture version of "Watch on the Rhine" starring Bette Davis and Paul Lukas.
>
> Present as the guests of Harry M. Warner and Jack L. Warner were Thomas Mann, Heinrich Mann, Bruno Frank, Emil Ludwig, Lion Feuchtwanger, Bert Brecht, Dr. T. N. Adorno [*sic*], and Prof. Max Horkheimer.

Now, obviously, Horkheimer and Adorno could credit some of their "world fame" to the reflected glow from the Manns, Feuchtwanger, and Brecht (and the misspelling of Adorno's name testifies to his minor celebrity), but it is clear not only that the two traveled in fairly select company among the émigrés but also that they were known to the broader Hollywood community.

But perhaps more telling evidence that Institute members were on the Hollywood radar for the content and quality of their work (rather than simply for their exile status) appears in documents found in Horkheimer's FBI files. In September and early October 1948, there was a flurry of activity in the ongoing investigation of the Institute and its members when the Hollywood gossip columnist Walter Winchell[23] forwarded the following anonymous telegram to J. Edgar Hoover:

> SEPT. 29TH. 1948.
> WALTER WINCHELL, c/o DAILY MIRROR
> SCOOP FOR YOUR PAPER AND RADIO BROADCAST
> DIVORCE CASE BEFORE JUDGE BAIRD, LOS ANGELES, CALIF., WILL EXPOSE THE

COMMUNIST CREW AT COLUMBIA COLLEGE [*sic*]. IT INVOLVES DR. FELIX WEIL, DR. MAX HORKHEIMER, AND DR. FREDERICK POLLACK [*sic*], OF THE INSTITUTE OF SOCIAL RESEARCH, 429 WEST 117TH ST., NEW YORK CITY.

THIS INSTITUTE BESIDES HARBORING COMMUNISTS, IS A COVER-ALL FOR TAX EVASION. INCOME TAX MEN SHOULD TAKE NOTE[24]

As I discuss in the introduction, this telegram was merely a sheet in the reams of material gathered during the ongoing investigation into the activities of the Institute of Social Research and its members. But as Winchell's tip and the *Hollywood Reporter* notice reveal, Adorno and Horkheimer were, during the 1940s, fixtures in the Hollywood landscape, bit players perhaps, but nevertheless not without a certain staying power. And not without influence either: Horkheimer maintained a lifelong friendship with the émigré film director William Dieterle, which survived through the exile period into both men's old age. Among Horkheimer's papers can be found early drafts of the screenplays that Dieterle was set to direct, to which Horkheimer and, at times, Adorno appended extensive suggestions for improvement. Indeed, it seems that Horkheimer made a habit of forwarding Dieterle's scripts to Adorno to get the younger man's opinions on the projects.[25]

Adorno's comments on one of these, *Syncopation* (1942), are especially interesting given the subject matter, a fairly typical romance set against the backdrop of a jazz nightclub.[26] While Adorno at first claims that compared to previous film scripts from Dieterle he has seen, "der Film ist dies Mal absolut harmlos . . . ein B-film" (This time the film is absolutely harmless . . . a B-Film),[27] in a long follow-up telegram, Adorno reveals a sensitivity to the subtleties of jazz not usually associated with his other writings on the topic: "My private opinion that it will be a flop again because of lack of clarity of musical issue. Praise basic idea of advocating jazz in its boldest form."[28] Accordingly, Adorno suggests an alternative to the film's original script, an alternative that runs completely against the grain of both the film's romantic narrative logic and the racial imperatives of Hollywood. Adorno opines that in the climactic jazz contest of the original script, which pits the white romantic lead Johnny (eventually played by Jackie Cooper) against the black bandleader Reggie, "Reggie should win." This assertion has more to do with the relative merits of different jazz styles than with the overarching narrative logic of the film, which has Johnny trying to win the affections of Kit, the female lead (Bonita Granville).

Perhaps recognizing the contradictions his solution entails, as well as the impossibility of having the black bandleader victorious in a multiracial

Hollywood film, Adorno continues, "Johnny defeated with his big band should make good in jam session with small ensemble. Reggie's band ought to be early hot style. Johnny's sophisticated swing Browning's sweet Lombardo style."[29] The implication here is that, upon abandoning the "sweet Lombardo style," the white bandleader, Johnny, would attain something more musically legitimate—that is, the type of music Reggie plays. Indeed, as if to illustrate the impossibility of such a conclusion in 1940s Hollywood, in the final version of the film, the character of Reggie has been transformed into a tertiary character, the son of Kit's maid and a New Orleans trumpeter whose "Rag Time" music reminds Kit of her bayou home. Nevertheless, Adorno's assertions concerning the contest are intriguing given his previous statements in "On Jazz" and his review of the book *Jazz, Hot and Hybrid,* both of which were published in the *Zeitschrift* and which suggested that the privileged place of African Americans in jazz history is actually a cynical ploy by the white music establishment to create a synthetically "native" art form, one that celebrates figures like "King" Louis Armstrong in order to ultimately parody (and thus dialectically solidify) the actual oppression of blacks in America.[30]

If Adorno's advice for Dieterle is perhaps inconsistent with Adorno's other writings on jazz,[31] his suggestion for the climax of the film offers a vision of jazz as a redemptive force. "Scene in record shop ought to be high spot," he continues. "Suggest Kit playing six different records for different customers. Customers furiously open boxes. Six records should make satanic concert which by and by is integrated into one mighty jazz piece."[32] The image of the cinematic DJ spinning separate records until they mesh into a unity is a provocative one given the way it anticipates the performance techniques of hip-hop and techno DJs as they try to seamlessly mesh the samples and drum breaks of preexisting compositions. However, as with many of Adorno's more outlandish suggestions for research protocols during the PRRP, the execution of this scene, which would involve both intensely complicated visual editing as well as an extremely sophisticated musical score, is far beyond the financial and technical parameters of "ein B-film."

But however unworkable this scene is in practical terms,[33] it does reveal a certain utopian vision that Adorno holds out for jazz and cinema alike. One of Adorno's primary criticisms of jazz is that the musician, in "getting into and out of trouble," eventually reveals that his free-willed, improvisational spirit is in reality tied to musical and economic rules over which he has no control. The breaks in the jazz performance that offer the illusion of individuality are forced to conform to a greater, more powerful musical logic and resolve themselves into the dominant theme, thereby consigning the individual to the logic of standardization. In Adorno's imagined climax for *Syncopation,* however, while the disparate musical pieces are integrated into a whole, this integration comes at the expense of the individual pieces and therefore at the expense of a record industry that prizes atomized, trademark personalities and easily recognizable hooks. No single record could contain the "satanic" might of the resulting six-record climax, which by resolving itself in a "unity of the manifold" would become, for Adorno, a kind of utopian jazz symphony.

At the level of cinematic practice, what the record-shop scene indicates is the inversion of the relative importance of music and image that is in line with what Adorno and Eisler promote in *Composing for the Films.* Whereas the tendency in narrative films is to use music as a supplement for the diegetic action, Adorno and Eisler propose a cinema in which the screenwriter and the composer would work as equal partners, with music playing an integral part in the film's narrative drive. Eisler offers a somewhat uninspiring account of how his score for *Hangmen Also Die* helps portray the solidarity of the anti-Nazi resistance, but Adorno's account of a cinematic jazz apocalypse offers a far more compelling description of a synthesis of music and image where a complex musical activity would go beyond supplementing the inadequacies of the film's visual narrative and instead become the story itself.

It could well be argued that these offhanded remarks about a mediocre film from 1941 anticipate Adorno's sophisticated, yet much later, account of the way the cinema's salvation is contained not in its manifest content but in the spaces between its images. "Whatever is 'uncinematic' in . . . film," Adorno writes in "Transparencies on Film," "gives it the power to express, as with hollow eyes, the emptiness of time."[34] What is potentially expressive about cinema is not the *flow* of images, one into the next, which is ultimately an illusion of unfettered movement, a transparency of a reality divorced from its conditions of production. Instead, Adorno finds the utopian potential for film in the gaps between determinate images: "It is in the discontinuity of that movement that the images of the interior monologue resemble the phenomenon of writing: the latter similarly moving before our eyes while fixed in discrete signs."[35] In the sound film, these gaps are generally elided and obscured by music. In his description of the climactic performance in *Syncopation,* however, the images are inadequate to convey the complicated interplay of dissonance and harmony that is—

at least in Adorno's fantasy film—the central concern of the plot. Neverthe-less, the pictures of the impoverished individual record players are still cru-cial to convey their incommensurability to the musical resolution to which the film aspires. In essence, Adorno's version of the film self-consciously announces that the important narrative and formal issues will be resolved somewhere other than in the visible content, beyond the manifest spec-tacle.[36] In this interpretation, cinema would be adequate to questions of subjectivity and alienation only by acknowledging that it wasn't giving its spectators the whole picture. As Adorno will ultimately say in "Trans-parencies on Film," contrary to the spectator-based theories that argue that the driving force of cinema is its ability to provoke the threat of absence, cinema instead offers illusory plenitude and wholeness.

In a sense, Adorno's critique of cinema is an extension of his general critique of the mimetic impulse in art. For Adorno, the mimetic impulse—realist art's pretense of showing nature as it is—proposes a utopian rec-onciliation through art between human beings and the natural world that humans have subjugated. The effort to mirror nature is doomed to failure by virtue of the irrevocable dialectical transformation that humans and nature enact on one another. Nevertheless, Hansen writes, "throughout modern art history, the mimetic impulse has also objectified itself in the bent toward imitation, in the futile attempt to close the gap with the object by doubling it."[37] The more the artwork strives for realism, the more it distances itself from reality, and the more art tries to approximate life, the more it accom-modates itself to the death of nature. However, the death of nature in the artwork is precisely what enables art to enter into the system of exchange as a commodity. Just as dead labor is the secret history of exchange value, dead nature is the necessary foundation for the artwork. This is especially true of cinema, which purports to have a privileged relationship with the natural world. But the realist film only more forcefully objectifies nature, rendering it a thing. In re-creating the world, narrative film only distances itself from that world and enters into an ever-tightening spiral of exchange. Since it can only embody the world by re-presenting it, the cinema epito-mizes a promise perpetually broken. Hence, Adorno claims that most films "are advertisements for themselves," offering the veneer of coherent reality while denying the spectator access to the real. As such, "every commer-cial film is actually only the preview of that which it promises and will never deliver."[38]

But this insight into the unity and consistency of the moving image is most fully fleshed out not in Adorno's cinematic writings but rather in his discussions of that composer whose work shares the strongest affinity with cinema, Richard Wagner. While many of the musical themes Adorno addresses in *In Search of Wagner*—leitmotiv, gesture, color—can be mapped directly onto his critique of the totalizing qualities of cinematic music in *Composing for the Films,* Adorno's description of Wagner's ability to produce a "phantasmagoric" reality through his music dramas closely corresponds to the capacity of cinema and television to create equally illusory realities for the delectation of their audiences. For Adorno, the notion of the artwork as phantasmagoria, "the concept of illusion as the absolute reality of the unreal,"[39] is closely bound up with Marx's well-known analysis of commodity fetishism in *Capital:* The transformation of the commodity into an object of exchange value obscures the actual labor that produces it. This mystification of labor power is a necessary aspect of the subject's reification. Marx writes:

> The commodity-form, and the value relation of the products of labor within which it appears, have absolutely no connection with the physical nature of the commodity and the material relations arising out of this. It is nothing but a definite social relation between men themselves which assumes here, for them, *the phantasmagoric form of a relation between things.*[40]

For his part, Adorno shifts the question of the phantasmagoria to the realm of the aesthetic object, claiming that the formal principles of Wagnerian music drama likewise display the "occultation of production by means of the outward appearance of the product." By virtue of its structural totality, the artwork appears to be natural: "The product presents itself as self-producing," that is to say, not the result of relations of production. Adorno continues:

> In the absence of any glimpse of the underlying forces or conditions of its production, this outer appearance can lay claim to the status of being. Its perfection is at the same time the perfection of the illusion that the work of art is a reality *sui generis* that constitutes itself in the absolute without having to renounce its claim to the image of the world.[41]

In Adorno's account, the artwork gets to have it both ways, portraying the relations between human beings while appearing not to derive from them, masquerading as wholly natural while carrying about its business among historical subjects. From this description of the illusory coherence of the artwork, Adorno draws the link to "phantasmagoria as the point at which aesthetic appearance becomes a function of the character of the commodity," and implicitly invokes the way, in Marx's commodity form, the relations among subjects takes on the character of the relations among things:

> As a commodity it purveys illusions. The absolute reality of the unreal is nothing but the reality of a phenomenon that not only strives unceasingly to spirit away its own origins in human labor, but also, inseparably from this process and in thrall to exchange value, assiduously emphasizes its use value, stressing that this is authentic reality, that it is "no imitation"— and all this in order to further the cause of exchange value.[42]

What is striking about these statements is that although they are specifically aimed at Wagner's music dramas, they also resonate strongly with Adorno's critique of the commodity character of texts of the culture industry, particularly cinema. Although parts of the Wagner book were written between 1937 and 1938, that is, well before his Hollywood years, Adorno's dialectical argument concerning the coherence of the Wagnerian world could, appropriately, be applied to the industrial practices of Hollywood filmmaking. The more faithful the text's mimetic adherence to the real world, the more synthetic is its construction and the more fully the work is a creature of the political economy. "Where the dream is most exalted," Adorno laments, "the commodity is closest to hand. The phantasmagoria tends toward dream not merely as the deluded wish-fulfillment of would-be buyers, but chiefly to conceal the labor that has gone into making it."[43]

That Adorno's analysis of the phantasmagoric vision of Wagner's *Gesamt-kunstwerk*, the total and totalizing work of art, is in reality a critique of cinema in utero[44] is made abundantly clear in *Dialectic of Enlightenment* in statements like "Those who are so absorbed by the world of the movie— by its images, gestures, and words—that they are unable to supply what really makes it a world, do not have to dwell on particular points of its mechanics during a screening."[45] The unified consistency of the drama— cinematic or musical—brooks no interrogation of the contradictory forces that go into its construction. Indeed, cinema marks an advance on the stage and on Wagner's musical theater. As Adorno famously writes in the essay "The Culture Industry":

> The more intensely and flawlessly [the filmmaker's] techniques duplicate empirical objects, the easier it is today for the illusion to prevail that the outside world is the straightforward continuation of that presented on screen. . . . Real life is becoming indistinguishable from the movies. The sound film, far surpassing the theater of illusion, leaves no room for

imagination or reflection on the part of the audience, who is unable to respond within the structure of the film, yet deviate from its precise detail without losing the thread of the story; hence the film forces its victims to equate it directly with reality.[46]

But while cinema ultimately outdoes Wagner with its unprecedented success at producing the phantasmagoric commodity, in its consideration of the spectating subject, *In Search of Wagner* bears an uncanny resemblance to some of the seminal texts of film theory. Consider, for example, how Adorno anticipates Laura Mulvey's appropriation of the Lacanian mirror stage when he discusses the encounter between the monolithic drama and the defenseless spectator: "[The phantasmagoria] mirrors subjectivity by confronting the subject with the product of its own labor, but in such a way that the labor that has gone into it is no longer identifiable. The dreamer encounters his own image impotently, as if it were a miracle, and is held fast in the inexorable circle of his own labor, as if it would last forever."[47] Here, as in Mulvey's "Visual Pleasure and the Narrative Cinema," the spectator faces a more powerful, more perfect vision of the world, one that reinforces the inadequacy of the spectator and the potency of the screened image. But whereas Mulvey's argument about the power of the cinematic image relies on notions of castration anxiety and the cinematic text's capacity to provoke the threat of absence, Adorno's critique of phantasmagoria focuses on its seamlessness and its privileged relationship to the commodity form. As such, Adorno's critique more closely resembles that of such theorists as Christian Metz and—perhaps more directly—Jean Louis Baudry. As Gregor Stemmrich describes it, for Baudry, the cinematic "apparatus" is involved in the ideological work of grafting the unique and anomalous subject into the larger network of society in such a way that the subject no longer recognizes the distinction between its desires and those of the outside world. For Stemmrich, the union of cinema and spectator is explicitly "phantasmic":

As Baudry explains: "Just as the mirror assembles the fragmented body in a sort of imaginary integration of the self, the transcendental self unites the discontinuous fragments of phenomena, of lived experience into unifying meaning. Through it each fragment assumes meaning by being integrated into an 'organic' unity. " Lacan's starting point was the premise that the subject was structured by the experience of lack, and thus constitutively characterized by the wish for transcendental unity, fullness and omnipotence. For Baudry, this cinema fulfils this wish in a unique way by producing a phantasmification of the subject. The cinematic apparatus is intended to be internalized in order to maintain a fiction without which the state apparatus could not function ideologically: the fiction of an autonomous and transcendental subject, which as the self-conception of an individual that believes itself to be free and unique is accompanied by a denial of real social coercion. For Baudry, the only way to break through this phantasmification was to make its production obvious.[48]

The success of phantasmagoric texts lies not so much in their capacity to terrify as in their capacity to reassure the spectator that his subjectivity, alienated though it may be in reality, resonates harmonically with the illusion up on the screen. "The might of industrial society is lodged in men's minds," Adorno explains, by way of describing the bonds between the culture industry and the subject. As a result, the spectator does not consume the cinematic commodity passively or in distraction, as Benjamin would claim, but instead labors on the broadcast or projection to continually produce the coherent object he has come to expect. Contrary to Mulvey's analysis, the viewer will watch in spite of terror, not because of it:

> The entertainments manufacturers know that their products will be consumed with alertness even when the customer is distraught, for each of them is a model of the huge economic machinery which has always sustained the masses, whether at work or at leisure—which is akin to work. From every sound film and every broadcast program the social effect can be inferred which is exclusive to none but is shared by all alike. The culture industry as a whole has molded men as a type unfailingly reproduced in every product.[49]

Whereas Mulvey's spectator looks at the screen and sees the ever-present threat of deprivation, castration, and absence against which he must be always vigilant, Adorno's spectator beholds the phantasmagoria and perceives a crystalline perfection in whose service he must constantly labor—without, of course, considering his activity labor. What is interesting about Adorno's analysis of the phantasmagoria, as well as of motion picture texts, is that he describes a situation in which not only do subjects see too little of the latent network of social and historical conditions that go into making up the world but also individuals see too much, assuming that there are cogent and coherent links between a given text's surface elements that tell the "whole story."

As Jonathan Crary explains in *Techniques of the Observer,* the question of how subjects put together various visual stimuli as a coherent message and, conversely, how that message has been interrogated and ruptured is very much intertwined with the history of the last two centuries.[50] According to Crary, Adorno's critique of the phantasmagoria and cinema situates him firmly within a tradition of European theorists whose suspicions of the capacity of subjects to adequately envision the empirical world coincide with the development of optical inventions that rely on the viewer's capacity to trick themselves. Items like the stereoscope, which uses two images seen from slightly different angles to produce the image of three-dimensional space, or like such cinematic ancestors as the phenakisto-scope, whose rotating series of pictures creates the illusion of movement through the persistence of vision, depend on human beings' capacity to literally see something that isn't there. This capacity for self-delusion is accentuated—or perhaps capitalized upon—by a socialization of our vision: We tend to see what we've seen before. As Crary notes, Nietzsche was particularly sensitive to the way preexisting knowledge tempers our vision: "Our eye finds it more comfortable to respond to a given stimulus by reproducing once more an image that it has produced many times before, instead of registering what is different and new in an impression."[51]

Nietzsche's statements and Crary's analysis of visual technologies can help us situate historically Adorno's analysis of phantasmagoria and its relationship to cinema spectatorship and ultimately to Adorno's critique of prejudice. But it is also worth noting the ways Adorno's concern for the illusory coherence presented by the artwork echoes the early writings of Maurice Merleau-Ponty, particularly his analysis of perception, which, written in 1945, is roughly contemporaneous with *Dialectic of Enlightenment*. In the opening pages of *Phenomenology of Perception*, Merleau-Ponty outlines the problem and the fundamental error confronting modern subjects, conditioned to the primacy of empirical methods:

> We think we know perfectly well what "seeing," "hearing," "sensing" are, because perception has long presented us with objects which are coloured or which emit sounds. When we try to analyze it, we transpose these objects into consciousness. We commit what psychologists call "the experience error," which means that what we know to be in things themselves we immediately take as being in our consciousness of them. We make perception out of things perceived. And since perceived things themselves are obviously accessible only through perception, we end by understanding neither. We are caught up in a world and we do not succeed in extricating ourselves from it in order to achieve consciousness of the world.[52]

The problem, it would seem, is that despite trying to disappear or to naturalize itself, the *social* (being "caught up in a world") is the inescapable truth of vision. The social is the bad conscience of the empirical, and ultimately social relations transform subjective perception into a vision of the world consistent with those relations. "So the question," Merleau-Ponty claims, "is whether attentive perceptions, the subject's concentration on one point of the visual field, do not instead of revealing the 'normal sensation' substitute a special set-up for the original phenomenon."[53] In a manner akin to Adorno's analysis of mimesis and the reified subject, Merleau-Ponty suggests that this type of perception forces the subject to confront the object *as* an object, thus obscuring the object's social, "subjective" existence. "The determinate quality by which empiricism tried to define sensation is an object, not an element, of consciousness, indeed it is the very lately developed object of scientific consciousness. For these two reasons, it conceals rather than reveals subjectivity."[54] Instead of a focused attention on a unified world, which, as Merleau-Ponty argues, "is supported by no evidence provided by consciousness," the solution for the problem posed by perception is to recognize the productive potential of gaps, caesurae, disunity. "We must," he insists, "recognize the indeterminate as a positive phenomenon."[55] Despite the many differences between Adornian "negative" dialectics and phenomenological critique, Merleau-Ponty's assertion bears a strong affinity to much of Adorno's overall philosophical project. As Adorno famously writes—in the same year that *The Phenomenology of Perception* was published—"the whole is the untrue," and throughout Adorno's career, he will play up the importance of "the cavities between what things claim to be and what they are."[56]

Indeed, much of Adorno's writings on cinema and television deals with the tendency of the culture industry to purvey a glossy, coherent surface as the image of the world and of spectators to willingly participate in that process by adapting themselves to one-dimensional (or two-dimensional, as the case may be) information. As such, Adorno's critique of cinema often echoes his critique of positivism.[57] By virtue of the fact that television and cinematic texts privilege a uniform and univocal interpretation, they likewise deny any substantive access to interior subjective life. For Adorno, this evacuation of the subject mirrors the lived relations of human beings in contemporary society. As Adorno frequently laments, "Life has become appearance." What the interaction between spectators and cinematic images generally illustrates is that "people who are no more than component parts of machinery act as if they still had the capacity to act as

subjects, and as if something depended on their actions."[58] While Adorno
is often chided for not being sensitive to visual mass media, I tend to
believe that such criticism is itself shortsighted for refusing to recognize
that Adorno—in very nuanced ways—conceives of cinema as part of a
continuum of aesthetic productions.

On this score it is worth considering how thoroughly Adorno's statements regarding the phantasmagoria and cinema anticipate Guy Debord's
Society of the Spectacle, in which he writes that "the spectacle is not a
collection of images; rather, it is a social relationship between people that
is mediated by images."[59] Debord argues that the explosion of the world
of images is inseparable from the increasing sedimentation of the political
economy into all aspects of existence: "For what the spectacle expresses
is the total practice of one particular economic and social formation; it
is, so to speak, that formation's agenda. It is also the historical moment by
which we happen to be governed."[60] But Debord's statements must be considered as an echo of the opening words of *Minima Moralia,* a book written
twenty years before *The Society of the Spectacle:*

> What the philosophers once knew as life has become the sphere of private
> existence and now of mere consumption, dragged along as an appendage
> of the process of material production, without autonomy, or substance of its
> own. . . . Should the appearance of life, which the sphere of consumption
> itself defends for such bad reasons, be once entirely effaced, then the
> monstrosity of absolute production will triumph.[61]

While this is Adorno at his most pessimistic, the resonance between
Minima Moralia and Debord's work is telling for the way it illustrates
Adorno's sensitivity to a world dominated by images and appearances.
Adorno is nothing if not acutely aware of the pressures put on the subject
to function as though there were only smooth surfaces, aiding the integration of the individual into the exchange logic of production and consumption and forcing the subject to live its social life on the basis of those
surface attributes. One of Adorno's fundamental concerns is the way that
the arts contribute to this process, and this hollowing out of the subject is
one of the central issues in "How to Look at Television," an essay written
at the end of Adorno's American exile. Whereas the serialized novel of the
nineteenth century offered the reader a glimmer of a free interior for the
individual, on the television, which offers only surface characterization,
the situation has substantially changed: "The accent on inwardness, inner
conflicts, and psychological ambivalence (which plays so large a role in

earlier popular novels and on which their originality rests) have given way to unproblematic, cliché-like characterization."[62] The prevalence of this "hollow character" of television subjects results in the spectator's reading faculties degenerating while the latent content escapes his or her diminished critical vision, opening the door for manipulation:

> As a matter of fact, the hidden message may be more important than the overt, since this hidden message will escape the controls of consciousness, will not be "looked through," will not be warded off by sales resistance, but is likely to sink into the spectator's mind. . . . This falls in line with the suspicion widely shared, though hard to corroborate by exact data, that the majority of television shows today aim at producing, or at least reproducing the very smugness, intellectual passivity and gullibility that seem to fit with totalitarian creeds even if the explicit surface message of the shows may be anti-totalitarian.[63]

It is not, therefore, completely accurate to say that the problem Adorno encounters is subjects' inability to read past the surface elements of cinematic and televisual texts. Rather, Adorno implies that the spectator/reader, accustomed to interfacing with texts only superficially, tends to reproduce the latent content as the manifest content. Hence, the problem presented by cinema and television is neither that viewers miss things, blind to elements in the visual field, nor that audiences passively consume the visual narrative. Instead, Adorno stresses that audiences are *too* active, but at the surface level; they see too much of what is not there while seeing too little of the social relations behind images. As with Merleau-Ponty's insistence on indeterminacy, Adorno confronts this problem by privileging the gaps in motion-picture texts against the illusory, palliative wholeness and coherence that movies and TV shows construct.

The notion that the formal properties of mass-produced images limit the subject's ability to see the underpinning social and historical origins of their entertainment commodities is strongly rooted in Adorno's work on the Studies in Prejudice project. Despite his claim to the contrary in "How to Look at Television," Adorno did in fact have access to data that corroborated his arguments concerning the totalitarian elements of cinema and television spectatorship, even if that evidence was primarily anecdotal. Further, that evidence points very strongly to the subject's willingness to participate with the culture industry not only in creating a coherent picture of the "natural" world, as Adorno suggests in *Dialectic of Enlightenment* and *In Search of Wagner*, but also in assigning the Jew and other minorities a very specific—and ultimately derisory—place in that world.

As one reads in the *Authoritarian Personality*, Adorno and his colleagues made use of a number of visual studies that they hoped would help indirectly gauge the latent prejudice of their focus-interview subjects. The pictures published in the volume only represent part of the story, however. Indeed, as part of the ongoing research conducted by the Institute of Social Research and the AJC, a variety of image-reading experiments were attempted, often with limited success.[64] The problem, the researchers continually discovered, was not only that interview subjects were routinely unable to interpret any but the surface elements of an image, but also that often, as Nietzsche's earlier statement suggests, subjects were likely to read images as a function of preexisting suppositions instead of reading the specific image at hand.

Two examples of this phenomenon are particularly illustrative of Adorno's assertions in "How to Look at Television" and reveal that spectators are more likely to read a parody of totalitarianism as pro prejudice than they are to ferret out the antitotalitarian message of supposedly progressive texts. What is all the more disturbing about these experiments is that each of them makes use of a cartoon, and the inability of the large majority of adults to understand their simple satirical elements casts into question the critical faculties of all levels of the population.

In 1946, a research unit of the AJC in New York[65] showed a number of cartoons featuring "Mr. Biggott" to a group of 150 white, non-Jewish, working-class men. The cartoons, featuring the pointy-headed Mr. Biggott, deathly afraid of contact with anyone but "Native-born, white, seventh-generation Americans," was intended to be distributed among churches and schools to parody and denigrate xenophobia, anti-Semitism, and racial prejudice. In one typical cartoon, Mr. Biggott upbraids a clergyman outside a church, saying, "Was it necessary, Reverend, to emphasize the Lord's— er—Jewish background in your sermon?"[66]

As the report on the program indicates, rather than succeeding at humorously displaying the backwardness of prejudice, the cartoons were misunderstood by two-thirds of the respondents:

> It was found that only one third of the respondents understood the message correctly. About one third understood the message to be the opposite of what it was really intended to be: they thought the cartoons were intended to promote prejudice. The rest either saw no message at all, or grasped only a very blurred version of it.[67]

A subsequent report later that year, dealing specifically with "Biggott and the Minister," confirmed the boomerang effect of the cartoon. "This guy's like all ministers," one respondent complains, siding with Mr. Biggott, "they stick up for [the Jews]. They don't believe half of what they're preaching about."[68] The conclusion of both reports is that, especially among working-class readers, the Mr. Biggott cartoons would effectively be counterproductive, encouraging people to read them as supportive of prejudice.

While the Mr. Biggott studies targeted the working class, a year earlier, another cartoon study had inadvertently drawn attention to the literal-mindedness of law enforcement officials and news reporters. In a memo sent to John Slawson, executive director of AJC, Lazarsfeld describes an incident that occurred while his colleagues were doing research for AJC, this time about a cartoon called "The Ghosts Go West":

> On Saturday Morning, August 25th, an interviewer from our office was
> pre-testing the revised version of the questionnaire in Central Park, which
> is adjacent to our office, when she was approached by a policeman who
> inquired into her activities. It seemed that she was violating a park
> regulation by interviewing people within the park. (We have frequently
> done such pre-test interviews in Central Park before.) The policeman was
> inclined to dismiss her simply with a notice of the park regulation but he
> was so attracted by the "subversive" nature of the cartoon that he took her
> to the precinct station. The officers there were also inclined to let her go
> with a warning except for the nature of the cartoon, which all of them
> misunderstood. Finally, the sergeant in charge called Dr. Berelson who
> identified the interviewer, and she was released with a summons.[69]

To compound matters, after the incident in the park, a reporter from the International News service called Lazarsfeld to investigate the story. As Lazarsfeld explains, "The reporter had seen a copy of the cartoon and perhaps had one at the time. He inquired into the nature of our office, its connection with Columbia, its activity in the park—all of this because, as it turned out, he, too, had seen the cartoon as a measure for promoting anti-Semitism rather than countering it."[70]

Slawson forwarded Lazarsfeld's memo to Horkheimer, and it could well be imagined that episodes such as the reaction to the Mr. Biggott cartoon and the arrest in Central Park are precisely what Adorno has in mind in the television essay when he evokes the "suspicion widely shared" that certain images provoke "the very smugness, intellectual passivity and gullibility that seem to fit with totalitarian creeds." Subjects conditioned to accepting at face value what they are presented and accustomed to receiving only glossy surfaces that invite no deeper consideration may have lost the capacity to look beyond those surfaces. That this symptom was most consistently expressed in the working class paints a pessimistic picture of any potential for class consciousness and a progressive response to the images of popular culture.

But what is equally fascinating about these responses is their tendency to produce elements in the manifest content that are not necessarily present but that nonetheless correspond with a coherent (by prejudiced standards) worldview. In the mind of the average spectator, even the antiprejudice cartoons were transformed into anti-Semitic tracts to fit with the predominant logic of mass culture. Further, although perhaps not surprisingly, the representatives of the press and the police endorsed this transformed worldview by virtue of their inability (or unwillingness) to interpret these images as anything other than anti-Semitic. The Central Park episode in particular illustrates the difficulty of combating ideology and of tearing off the veils of false consciousness adorning the products of the culture industry. Since the law and the press ultimately proved complicit in promoting these one-dimensional reading practices and were subject to the same perversion of vision, a genuine disincentive to critical engagement with the objects of culture was manifested. In a way, the cartoon experiments suggest a 1940s updating of the situation prevalent in the France of 1848 that Marx diagnoses in *The Eighteenth Brumaire of Louis Bonaparte.* Unable to recognize and understand their historical situation, deluded by a collaborationist press, and threatened by an authoritarian *gendarmerie,* the proletariat was doomed to act against their interests, allow despotism to reign, and reproduce the conditions of their own oppression.

Now, this is undoubtedly a dour way of looking at the results of these experiments, and one that is consistent with the most pessimistic—yet generally accepted—version of Adorno: sour, skeptical, and ever on guard against the affronts of the culture industry against the embattled subject, a kind of Marxian Mr. Biggott. What is perhaps not so generally accepted, but what Adorno's all-too-brief remarks on *Syncopation* reveal, is Adorno's abiding interest in exploiting those elements of motion pictures that encourage the subject to see what isn't there and miss what is. In this light, Adorno's exile writings on film merit reassessment. Instead of the monolithic film text, against which no subject could hope to do anything other than grow "stupider and worse," Adorno offers a vision of the motion picture in which subjectivity survives at the margins, just offscreen and out of view. In his remarks on the Dieterle film, Adorno betrays a belief that even in a supposedly one-dimensional and rigorously commercial medium, there are opportunities to tap into expansive interior worlds. How is it, one could well ask, that in supposedly bankrupt aesthetic forms, one could mine lost veins of subjectivity?

This question is too seldom asked about Adorno's work on cinema, particularly when considering the years Adorno spent in Los Angeles. But it is a question that remains to be addressed. Not only do Adorno's relationships with filmmakers raise the issue of his influence and interest in Hollywood matters, but so too does the fact that, for an extended if ultimately unfruitful period, Adorno and Horkheimer helped craft a film of their own.

In Max Horkheimer's papers, there is a brief, one-page résumé of Adorno's work, no doubt prepared for some bureaucratic purpose, grant proposal, job application, or visa update. Attached to the document is a single-spaced typed list cataloging many of the projects with which Adorno was involved at the time (probably 1949). The list runs to forty-seven items, and includes both well known texts (*Minima Moralia, The Authoritarian Personality*) and pieces that subsequently came to light in the years after Adorno's exile (the monographs on NBC's *Music Appreciation Hour* and on Martin Luther Thomas). More to the point, there are also two separate listings for a *Filmbuch*.[71] There is some confusion over what projects exactly these entries refer to. The *Filmbuch* could easily refer to *Composing for the Films*, but that text had a title well before the list was compiled. Perhaps, if Adorno was concerned about the associations with the then politically toxic Eisler,[72] as many have claimed was the reason why his name was left off the original publication, he would have referred to the project simply as *Filmbuch*. But that interpretation is complicated somewhat both by the second reference and by translation of the term itself. While *Filmbuch* can mean "book about film" it can also mean "film script."

The notion that Adorno would collaborate on a film script is not so far-fetched.[73] In the protocol for the "Research Project on Anti-Semitism," which appeared first in volume 9 of *Studies in Philosophy and Social Science* and subsequently in the collection *"The Stars Down to Earth" and Other Essays on the Irrational in Culture*, Adorno and his colleagues in the Institute[74] argue that "anti-Semitism is one of the dangers inherent in all most recent culture." To prove that point, they outline a multipart study that will "combine historical, psychological, and economic research with experimental studies."[75] The "Research Project" essay would become the template for much of the published Studies in Prejudice work done in collaboration with the AJC, but what I am most interested in here is the last component of the project, the "experimental section." Here Adorno suggests an investigation, carried out in a manner not unlike Lazarsfeld's program analysis, that would "provide a series of experimental situations which approximate as closely as possible the concrete conditions of present day life" in order to develop a typology of anti-Semitic traits.[76]

But how is the reaction to "the concrete conditions of present day life" to be gauged? Adorno continues, "The most satisfactory method of experimentation appears to be the use of certain films designed to be presented to subjects of different regional and social groups." Adorno presents the reader with the paradox of modernity: real life—that is to say, the actual social relations of subjects—is only accessible and understandable through the mimetic illusions of cinema. Here again, Adorno anticipates Debord's remarks concerning the society of the spectacle, namely, that the realm of sociality is predicated on the experience of the image. As if recognizing this confusion between what is real and what is on the screen and the capacity of the one-dimensional image to capture the concrete responses of subjects, Adorno quickly adds, "Naturally, the element of introspection cannot be entirely eliminated, but by careful and critical interpretation of results it is hoped to reduce the flaws to a minimum."[77] In so saying, Adorno reveals the Institute's ultimate agenda; the presumption is that, as in the cartoon studies, the subject will *only* have the capacity to respond to the film text at one level. Introspection, that is, recourse to an interior life and critical faculties, is understood as a flaw or glitch in the expected experimental results.

The essay then goes on to describe the form such an experiment would take:

A film will be made, showing boys of twelve to fifteen at play. An argument and a fight ensue. The relation of guilt and innocence is difficult to untangle. The scene ends, however, with one boy being thrashed by the others. In one, the thrashed boy will be played by a Gentile, in the other by a Jew. Another variation will be introduced by showing each of these versions with two different dramatis personae. In one version, the thrashed boy will bear a Jewish name, and in the other a Christian name. Thus, the film will be shown in four different combinations:

1) The thrashed boy is a Gentile with a Gentile name.
2) The thrashed boy is a Gentile with a Jewish name.
3) The thrashed boy is a Jew with a Gentile name.
4) The thrashed boy is a Jew with a Jewish name.

In any one case each of these combinations will be shown to only one group of subjects, for instance to high school boys or unemployed groups, who will not be informed in advance of the aim of the experiment.[78]

While the practical elements of the film are problematic and indeed unwieldy—how, for example, the Gentile with a Jewish name was to be distinguished from the Jew with a Jewish name, and so on, and whether these differences would register with a viewing audience—the methodology of the experiment is worth noting. We see in this description an early take on the system of "indirect" questioning that would prove so important to the success of the production of the F-scale in *The Authoritarian Personality*. The film experiment can be therefore understood as an extension of Adorno's efforts to measure subjects' tendency to rationalize the irrational. Without being told that they are watching a film about prejudice, the audience is nevertheless asked to identify with and rationalize violence done in the cause of prejudice. Since the assignation of guilt or innocence is ambivalent, the audience is asked to make the case for the authority of the thrasher or the thrashee. What is interesting about the form of the experiment is that it encourages the individual audience member to perform a hermeneutic analysis of the film while assuming a general incapacity for people to penetrate beyond the surface elements of a given text. Further, it presumes, since no one will freely admit to being prejudiced, that there is an interior life to the viewer that is fundamentally at odds with the external responses he or she is either willing or able to provide. Here, Adorno and Horkheimer at once reveal their most pessimistic opinions of modern subjects, as well as their affinities with psychoanalytic techniques. The individual is assumed to lack self-awareness or to be a liar, and only through circuitous means can one hope to arrive at the kernel of truth about the subject's beliefs, terrors, and desires.

But what became of this experimental project? It would seem, based on Adorno's subsequent publications, that the filmed component of the anti-Semitism project was simply abandoned for more favorable publication prospects. However, by examining the records of the AJC, as well as Horkheimer's papers, one discovers that for the better part of the next decade, Adorno and Horkheimer actively explored getting their film made by Hollywood producers. The litany of figures involved with the project is impressive, not only in its scope but also for how closely it brings Adorno and Horkheimer into contact with both sides of the Hollywood witch hunts, those who named names and those who were blacklisted. What is more, despite their ultimate failure to see the film put on celluloid, the episode underlines just how interconnected were their lives with those of the broader Hollywood community.

It is clear, from Horkheimer's and Adorno's correspondence, as well as from the files of the AJC, that the film project was seen as an integral part of the Studies in Prejudice project and that Adorno and Horkheimer spent considerable time revising the project and seeking support (in the form of Hollywood writers and producers). While both of them were intimately involved with the project, the well-connected Horkheimer served as the initial contact to many of the celebrities involved. But Horkheimer's bicoastal responsibilities meant that Adorno was delegated much of the responsibility for developing the script and coordinating production efforts in California. Their labors took them from low-rent independent producers to personal meetings with Jack Warner at Warner Brothers. There is something both surreal and touching in the thought of Adorno and Horkheimer pitching a film project, caught in the machinery of the studio system, dealing with script doctors, consultants, high hopes, and unreturned phone calls. But it also says something about their commitment to the project—and perhaps to their European naïveté—that the two kept plugging throughout their days in Hollywood. Indeed, the history of the abortive project reads like a Hollywood story in its own right, the type that Adorno would have readily pilloried, but the fact that Adorno suffered through the vagaries of the movie-making experience ultimately helps shed light on Adorno's theory of cinematic and television images.

One of the pivotal figures in the whole episode was Leon Lewis, the Institute's attorney in Los Angeles, who seems to have been one of the primary intermediaries between the well-regarded Horkheimer and the Hollywood community. After the "Research Project in Anti-Semitism" appeared in 1941, one of the next references to the film project turned up in a memo to Lewis from April 1943.[79] In the memorandum, a substantially transformed film is described, one that is at once expressionistic and far more elegant than the plot of the alternating thrashings of Jewish and Gentile boys. In this proposed version, a beehive of statements reveals the general aggregate of the common man's opinions regarding the "Jewish Situation" and displays the overall apathy of the populace to issues concerning the Holocaust. "Since it is the general idea underlying this plan to counteract the apathy of a large part of the population," the memo says, by way of announcing its protocol, "it might be advisable to take this very apathy as the point of departure."[80] What follows are a few of the rationalizations that a disinterested public might use to militate against an active response to the Holocaust:

While it must be made plain that no average American wants to have
anything to do with Nazism or Fascism, their aversion to "atrocity
propaganda" should be made equally clear. Some of the deeper
psychological mechanisms underlying their attitudes should be brought to
the fore, e.g., the reasoning: "these things are so horrible that one cannot
believe them, and therefore they are untrue" (self protection), or: "people
who have been treated this way *must* have brought it on themselves."[81]

These responses, typical of Adorno's and Horkheimer's assessment of
how the outward response fails to mirror the inwardly held belief, are precisely what the proposed film tries to combat. The remainder of the memo
describes a utopian response to the general apathy of the citizenry in which
disinterest itself provokes a productive response at the highest levels of
government and business:

> These snatches of conversation finally reach some very prominent
> Americans who believe in probing things to the quick. They should be
> public figures whose reputation is unimpeachable like outstanding
> Congressmen, representatives of commerce and industry. They should not
> be played by actors but the personalities themselves should appear in the
> motion picture. They decide that people should learn the full, unbiased
> truth about what Nazism means to its victims and what it would mean to
> Americans in the case of a Hitler victory. . . . The skeptics shown at the
> beginning are present making embarrassing remarks, when they interrupt
> the narrators they should be answered quietly and firmly. The climax is
> reached when one of the hecklers asks: "Where are your eyewitnesses?"
> The answer is: "there are none." Then a cemetery with a fresh *Massengrab*
> [mass graves] flashes on the screen. We see how the skeptics of the
> beginning eventually are brought to the conviction: "Those devils must
> pay." They are shown, their numbers increasing, finally merging with
> a symbolic picture of the whole American nation, marching united
> against the Axis.[82]

While offering a series of powerful images, the film is problematic on
a number of levels. First, given what we now know about the Roosevelt
administration's calculated "ignorance" of the Holocaust, as well as the
outright support by certain corporate leaders of Hitler's policies regarding
the Jews (Henry Ford comes first to mind), the stern response of political
figures and industry representatives seems farcical. Second, despite its
shocking evocations of the mass graves of the extermination camps, the conclusion, in which a public outcry confronts both apathy and atrocity, is too
close to the spirit of collective consciousness that Adorno and Horkheimer

elsewhere decry and, cinematically, does nothing so much as evoke the fascist aesthetic of *Triumph of the Will, Olympia,* and other similar films.[83]

But the final problem with this version of the film project is that its usefulness is severely limited, both as a tool to test audience reaction and in its historical staying power. Its effectiveness would only last as long as the war, whatever the outcome. Thus, despite its elegance on paper, a month later, Adorno and Horkheimer together write "Notes for an Experimental Film to Be Made by the Institute of Social Research." This version is essentially similar to the one outlined in the "Research Project" protocol, except the number of variations have been reduced and the subject matter, anti-Semitism, is, in the first variant, more strongly emphasized:

> There will be two short subject scripts written. The plot of both will be identical.
>
> In one version of the script the chief protagonist is to very definitely be a Jewish boy who is imposed upon by a group of gentile boys. This script will hit as hard as possible all the juvenile prejudices and the boy will be identified as a Jew in every respect, and we will dramatize the resistance to him in terms not alone of his personality, but because he is a Jew.[84]

In the alternate version of the film, the reasons for the beating are much more ambiguous:

> In the second version of this same story the protagonist will be also imposed upon by another group, but he will not be identified either in the script or in the film as a Jew. In this second version, a different title may be used, giving him in one case the obvious name of Isidore Levy and in another version an unidentifiable name such as John Saunders. It will be that in this second version for script purposes, we will have to create a nickname such as Curley so that the name could fit either character, in other words, either Curley Saunders or Curley Levy.[85]

Along with this description, Adorno and Horkheimer include a number of questions designed to follow the films, questions that display a directness and simplicity uncharacteristic of the "indirect" questions that would be developed for the F-scale. Among them: "Did you understand the religious objections to the beating by Woody?" "Would it have been better to talk it over instead of beating up Curley?"[86]

Around the time of these two memos, Adorno and Horkheimer had begun pursuing screenwriters for their story. The first of these to give the project consideration was Dore Schary, a well-known Hollywood figure who would eventually become head of the Screen Writers Guild and ultimately the president of Metro-Goldwyn-Mayer (MGM).[87] On May 1, 1943, Hork-heimer wrote Leon Lewis about "the studies which Adorno and I intend to undertake during the months to come." With regard to the film project, he wrote, "We had a long talk with Mr. Schary on April 21st. We discussed that plan for our little motion picture and he seemed to be truly interested. We made another appointment for April 27th when he hoped to be able to spend several hours with us in order to lay the foundation for the picture. Unfortunately, he felt ill on that day and we have not heard from him since."[88]

Schary's illness could have been a case of the brush-off, and his interest in the project may well have been feigned. In July of that year Schary wrote to Lewis asking Lewis to beg off the film project for him. Still claiming illness (after more than two months), Schary explained, "I have found it impossible to do any work on the script that I have promised Dr. Horkheimer. . . . So I will have to renege on my offer to the good gentlemen and I'm writing you and asking you to take on the burden of telling them."[89]

Lewis, clearly an astute student of the Hollywood scene, recognized this as a case of "don't call us, we'll call you" on Schary's part, and in a letter later that July wrote that the problem was essentially one of institutional authority among the Hollywood establishment. Horkheimer alone had none, but had he invoked it, Lewis explained, Schary or another screenwriter would have agreed to the project:

> Am enclosing copies of letters from Dore Schary in regard to the
> Institute experimental film project, which are self-explanatory. It occurs
> to me that Dore would have found someone else in the MGM setup to do
> the job if the original contact had come through Mr. Mayer instead of
> directly from me. This suggests that in order to get someone to undertake
> the job, the approach should be made in the first instance by the AJC
> as such.[90]

In light of Schary's response, Lewis advised that if the film was going to be made, in addition to dropping the AJC name, the Institute would have to go over Schary's head to the chief of production at MGM: "In view of the understanding reached at the meeting in Harry Cohn's home, I believe that the desired result can be achieved if you will drop a note to Mr. Cohn asking for him to cooperate on the project, both in relation to the script and the actual making of the film—and then, if he expresses willingness, I will follow through directly with him on behalf of the AJC."[91]

Despite the initial glimmer of hope, after Schary dropped out of the project, the film was put on the back burner and allowed to simmer, garnering only periodic references both in the correspondence between Horkheimer and Adorno and in Horkheimer's updates to the AJC. However, a series of telegrams and letters between Horkheimer and Adorno from the fall of 1944 reveal a renewed interest in the film and a new prospect for a screenwriter. A November 14 telegram from Horkheimer to Adorno reads:

> I would like to know what kind of person the writer, Dalton Trumbo, is. Is he intelligent, does he have good relations with producers? Could he possibly be picked out as the liaison man between the Committee and the motion picture industry? Kindly try to get some information about him without mentioning to anybody why we want to know it.[92]

Nine days later, after a dinner with Salka Viertel, Adorno replied: "Yesterday evening Salka was at our place and I asked her casually about Trumbo. Although he is a top writer at MGM's Salka thinks that he is a decent man, also politically, and a much more gifted writer than, for instance, Dore Schari [*sic*]."[93] Their exchange has a number of elements worth noting. First, of course, is the assessment of the relative intelligence or the prospective merits of Trumbo and Schary, coupled with the reference to Trumbo's political "decency." There is, of course, an element of sour grapes in the exchange, but the intimations concerning the respective writing skills of Schary and Trumbo are not without merit. Trumbo, author of *Johnny Got His Gun,* was one of the top writers at MGM and ultimately the recipient of an Oscar, under the pseudonym Robert Rich, for the film *The Brave One.* Politically, however, he had been previously associated with the Communist Party and was a champion of left-wing causes. This association would, in 1948, lead Trumbo to be included among that first group of filmmakers to run afoul of HUAC and become known as the Hollywood Ten.[94] After Trumbo invoked the First Amendment and was convicted for contempt of Congress, the Hollywood Screen Writers Guild made the decision to fire those members implicated in the HUAC hearings, effectively beginning the blacklist. The person who was responsible for firing Trumbo and his colleagues was the guild's then president—none other than Dore Schary.

Recognizing that Trumbo's political affiliations might prove an obstacle and perhaps sensing the general conditions of surveillance under which they communicated, in a none-too-subtle follow-up telegram Adorno wired Horkheimer, "Writer's denomination controversial. Salka thinks it is hers but other key papers disagree. The latter advises caution because of his too well known allegiances."[95]

The second element of these cables worth mentioning is Horkheimer's insistence on secrecy. This was his frequent admonition throughout the project, and even after drafts started appearing, Horkheimer would counsel Adorno to keep their personal revisions from the scriptwriters for fear that they would make a bollix of the project, but also for fear that he and Adorno would lose control of the results. As it would transpire, these fears were not completely unfounded, but for the moment, the concern was with Trumbo's viability for the project. Ultimately, with a pun on Horkheimer's nickname, "Mammoth," as well as an acknowledgment of possible government surveillance, Adorno leaves the final decision to Horkheimer: "Meine nightmares und anderen Telegramme wegen Trumbo und Hertha Lazarsfeld hoffe ich unverstümmelt in Ihrher Hand. An Trumbo ist das beste, dass er sich auf Jumbo reimt." (My nightmares, and other telegrams regarding Trumbo and Hertha Lazarsfeld I hope [are in] your hand unmutilated. As for Trumbo, it is best that he rhymes with Jumbo.)[96]

It appears that Jumbo (Horkheimer) decided that Trumbo was out, because one of the next references to the project, in March of the following year, is a contract dated March 22, 1945, for screenwriters Gilbert Gabriel and someone identified as Major Vorhaus[97] "to write the screen play of a motion picture tentatively called *The Accident* that the American Jewish Committee is about to make for scientific purposes."[98] The writers were to receive $1,500 to take a prepared treatment of the film, supplied by Horkheimer, and return to him a completed script within a month. This treatment, probably prepared by Adorno and Horkheimer together, includes instructions for the screenwriters consistent with principles of indirect research utilized in the other AJC studies: "Audience reactions are significant only if they are expressed spontaneously, involuntarily. The purpose of this test film must therefore be veiled. The interest of the audience must be diverted from the test proper and concentrated upon something else; in this case, on the fact that the testimony of eye-witnesses is nearly always unreliable." At the same time Adorno and Horkheimer are sensitive to the problem of being too underhanded: "On the other hand, we cannot veil the purpose of the film so that the audience is completely side-tracked. It would be advisable to insert motifs which keep alive or even stimulate the more or less latent racial or religious preferences." Their overarching counsel, however, is somewhat amusing in light of their critique of fun in other circumstances. "The film should be interesting as a movie," they insist. "A dull film would weaken the interest of the audience in the problems involved, thereby reducing the value of the test."[99]

A brief outline of the film follows these admonitions, and the plot is substantially changed from the original ideas laid out in "Research Project on Anti-Semitism." To briefly summarize the action: On a crowded subway car, a one-legged peddler is pushed aside by "an obviously Jewish man."[100] Among the other passengers on the train is a woman carrying a vacuum cleaner. During the trip "for unknown reasons, a violent commotion occurs," and the woman falls out of the train onto the tracks. The lights go out, and subsequently the woman is hauled aboard and treated by a doctor "who happens to be among the passengers. She is more shocked than hurt."[101] Since the peddler, who mutters anti-Semitic slurs throughout the film, has already been pushed by the Jewish man, he tries to incite the rest of the passengers against the Jew. Factions form, and the crowd argues about the Jew's guilt or innocence. Two police officers arrive and break up the commotion. At this point in the treatment, the authors suggest two variants:

> *Variant I:* implies that one of the Gentiles is guilty: claiming indemnity, the hurt woman expresses the definite opinion that she was pushed out of the door not by the Jew, but by one of the Gentiles—the tough guy. The crowd seems to adopt her opinion. Only the one-legged man is dissatisfied.
>
> *Variant II:* implies that the Jew is guilty: the woman loudly claims indemnity, without being interested in the problems of guilt. The anti-Semitic atmosphere predominates. The one legged man remains the accepted leader.[102]

At the end, the film fades to black and a caption appears on the screen saying, "You, too, have been the eye-witness of the accident. What is your opinion?" After that questionnaires are distributed and the respondents are asked their opinions on the Jew's guilt or innocence. In a note accompanying the treatment, Adorno and Horkheimer suggest that, in addition to the Jew, there could be other variations "in which the Jew may be replaced by (a) a Negro, (b) a German, (c) an Englishman." These alternatives, they claim, would "increase the usefulness of this film as an instrument of detecting (and measuring) emotional reactions,"[103] presumably because they would illustrate the range of prejudice in regard to the given situation. An Englishman could be expected to arouse less suspicion than an African American, for example. The German would test the prevalence of people's nationalist sentiments versus their racial prejudice, and so on.

Attached to the treatment are some notes that attempt to flesh out the characters and the plot as well as some of the hypotheses of the film-makers. Among the additional characters in the crowd, the authors write, "there should be one intellectual with horn-rimmed glasses" and "two shipyard workers, but they should be dirty enough as to enable the anti-Semite to say that they look suspicious."[104] These stereotypical characters are designed to test certain attitudes that are presumed to correlate with anti-Semitism: anti-intellectualism and antilabor sentiment. Ultimately these two attitudes derive from the irrational and thus contradictory nature of anti-Semitism. "Anti-Semitism is connected with anti-intellectualism in the sense of 'sophistication.' Sophistication has a negative connotation with the anti-Semites." At the same time, they offer another hypothesis that "those of lower socio-economic level [tend] to exonerate the Jew."[105]

At first these hypotheses would seem to contradict one another, but one of the central conclusions Adorno draws in his work with AJC is that there is at once a fundamental correlation and a fundamental disconnect between class and prejudice. That is to say, anti-Semitism both takes the form of ressentiment against one's betters and at the same time expresses the wish to denigrate those inferior to oneself. The Jew is at once rentier and proletariat. This is the essential irrationality of prejudice, and one that is articulated throughout the responses to the questionnaires in *The Authoritarian Personality*. But in an unpublished introduction to Paul Massing's *Rehearsal for Destruction*, the first volume in the Studies in Prejudice series, Adorno cuts through this contradiction, revealing simultaneously the solidarity between the Jew and the working class and the awful stakes of this irrationality:

> If the struggle for a better society has, as its objective, always the lot
> of those upon whom the heaviest social pressure lasts, the fate of the Jew,
> six million of whom were murdered, can no longer be regarded as a
> mere façade of the class struggle. Quantity tilts over into quality: the
> physiognomics of a totalitarian society are revealed by the fate of those not
> included in the totality and therewith demonstrate its untruth. To repress,
> in the face of this state of affairs, the full awareness of what has happened
> and what is behind it, may itself contribute to the recurrence of the
> unspeakable at any place on earth.[106]

The hypotheses about labor and anti-intellectualism are ultimately subservient to Adorno's and Horkheimer's general hypothesis, one that apparently corresponds with Adorno's critique of the mimetic impulse of television and movies and the phantasmagoria created by the Wagnerian music drama: "The crucial question is whether the person introduces the causal relation where it does not exist. If he does, this can only be on the basis of an anti-Semitic orientation"[107] This steering question can, however, be understood in two ways. Either the film experiment assumes that people will override their literal-mindedness to "look through" to the hidden anti-Semitic agenda of the film—that is to say, they will not accept the surface meaning of the film—or, far more provocatively, it assumes that they will transform the (absent) latent content into the manifest content; that is, because the Jews are always "guilty" in some fundamental way, the anti-Semite will see what is manifestly not there and will create the coherent world in his or her own image. The latter seems to have been Adorno's and Horkheimer's presumption, and two of their secondary hypotheses speak to their belief that the spectator will create what isn't there, the guilt of the Jew. "The ambiguous events of the film will be structured in the direction of the final decision [to condemn the Jew]," they claim, and further, "upon a second showing of the film there will be a trend to maintain the verdict previously reached."[108]

The spring and summer of 1945 saw a frenzy of activity on the film project, as though the impending end of the European war had suddenly made it not only possible but also imperative to talk about anti-Semitism and its consequences. Even before Gabriel's and Vorhaus's contractual deadline, Siegfried Kracauer (perpetually short of funds and institutional support) was brought in as a consultant for the film to make suggestions for the dialogue. In addition to his suggestions in this regard, he also fleshed out a number of subsidiary characters, including an old woman with a dog, a woman in a fur coat, the peddler, and the intellectual. Importantly, into these characters' mouths he puts statements taken verbatim either from Martin Luther Thomas's radio speeches or from the "F-scale" questionnaire. Thus, the old woman, apropos of nothing, says, "Every person, I think, should have a deep faith in some supernatural force higher than himself to which he gives total allegiance and whose decisions he does not question," which is taken directly from *The Authoritarian Personality* surveys. The peddler, for his part, winds up sounding like a combination of the radio demagogue and his befuddled followers: "Human nature being what it is, there will always be war and conflict. . . . There are many important things that can never possibly be understood by the human mind."[109] Beyond providing an early rough draft of the script, Kracauer's contributions are rather unremarkable except insofar as they reveal just how much of a hand Adorno had in crafting its inflammatory dialogue, the supposed "evidence" upon which the subject was to irrationally convict the Jew of causing the accident.

Two drafts of the film exist among Max Horkheimer's papers; the first appears to have been completed sometime in June 1945; the second was definitely finished before April 1946, when it appears attached to a "Memorandum on Experimental Movie Project" that was probably written by both Adorno and Horkheimer. But it may be that the second draft was also written the previous summer. There are a number of things worth noting about the scripts. Each is substantially the same as the outline suggested in Adorno's and Horkheimer's "Project of a Test Film" from March of that year. During rush hour on a crowded subway, a woman falls out of a car and one of her fellow passengers, who had earlier pushed a peddler, is implicated. As tempers flare and epithets fly, a riot threatens until it is revealed that the woman is essentially unhurt and vague about whether she was pushed or fell. Here, too, as in Kracauer's suggestions (courtesy of Adorno), the peddler and the intellectual do a pas de deux of demagoguery. In a particularly heated moment from the first draft, the peddler once again apes Martin Luther Thomas, shouting, "Why, if I told you what I've gone through—bein' persecuted in my fight against them—my blood would boil in my veins!"[110]

However, there are a number of crucial differences between the two drafts and the original outline. In Horkheimer's and Adorno's initial conception, the guilt or innocence of the Jewish suspect was the primary difference between the films. However, in the two drafts, the screenwriters heed Horkheimer's and Adorno's note regarding the different ethnic and racial backgrounds of the accused, and those become the crucial distinction. In the memo from April 1946 that introduces the film, this variation is described: "Each version is very similar to the others with the exception of the character who is blamed for the accident. In one case it is a Jew, in another case it is a Negro, and in the third version it is a Gentile white-collar worker."[111] The scripts make the distinction between these three figures by employing broad stereotypes, most notably in the case of the "Negro" who, in one version, is described as wearing a "Harlem zoot-suit" and mouths lines like "Lawdy God!"

But the drafts also differ from the original outline in two other crucial aspects. First, in between the treatment and the draft, the title changes from *The Accident* to *Below the Surface*.[112] A second fundamental distinction between the finished scripts and Horkheimer's and Adorno's proposal is that the scripts deploy a framing narrative concerning a handsome soldier on leave and the pretty nurse he falls for while on the subway. The couple's indecision and their voice-over "will-he-or-won't-he/should-I-or-shouldn't-I" prevarication and flirtation run parallel to the film's events until the script requires them to leap into action and come to the victim's aid. The brush with someone else's death and the subsequent violence it provokes provide the requisite spark to kindle their romance. The framing device, despite its schmaltz and its somewhat clumsy exposition, serves a dual purpose as both the hook that catches the audience up in the narrative and the red herring that distracts them from the primary purpose of the "experiment." Again, the presumption is that the majority of viewers won't register the latent intent of the film and will instead presume that they are watching a romance. As the introductory memo claims:

> While any interview, even while focused or veiled, may induce the individual to think of the minorities as a problem, this motion picture is so constructed that even the audiences which view the Jewish or the Negro versions will leave the presentation mainly with impressions concerning the interesting love story and the picture as a whole. This is quite apart from the propaganda value.[113]

Why are there two drafts? It is clear, based on the meetings, memos, and consultations flying about during the summer of 1945, that there was a fair measure of dissatisfaction regarding the first draft of the film. In between the two drafts, *Below the Surface* underwent various script conferences and substantial retooling. In June of that year, Horkheimer convened a panel of social scientists, people affiliated with AJC, and members of the Institute. This group compiled a list of suggestions for revisions. Among those who got a crack at the script was Margaret Mead, who said, among other things, that "intellectuals should not be caricatured in such a typically Fascist manner."[114] For his part, Adorno held fast to the idea that the guilt or innocence of the accused should be more ambivalent than it is in the draft, and he suggested that "in the script as it is the guilt of the Jew may be too radically excluded." He therefore thought "the victim should answer a little more confusedly to the question whether she was really pushed."[115] This is consistent with Adorno's belief that the audience will work to fill in the blanks and see anti-Semitism, even when it is only implicit.

Elsewhere, however, Adorno and Horkheimer seem to take Mead's suggestions to heart and back away from using the intellectual as the mouthpiece of the fascist agitator, essentially suggesting that they make him more comically self-aware of his contradictions, that is, more like Adorno and Horkheimer themselves. Thus, in a separate memorandum, they write:

> The intellectual's speeches contain specimens of *all* the agitator's "devices" and thus sound forced. Perhaps loosen them by interpolations of self-critical nature, say "No, this wouldn't be so good," or some reference to the approach he expects to employ: "Let's rather try the anti-intellectual tune. . . ." And some cynical remark such as, "I sometimes get everything mixed up."[116]

In July, the experimental filmmaker Hans Richter, also a German émigré, was brought in as a consultant to make suggestions on the dialogue and the filming, for which he was paid a fee of $1,200.[117] Despite his shaky command of English syntax and spelling, his comments are at times graceful: "The rhythm of the rails, the moving train should influence, bind together or separate the different speeches. Then, when the train stops, the change of atmosphere will be emotionally much more felt by the audience." At other moments, he is politically incisive: "Is it right to have the Negro speak with this funny southern accent which we know so well from comedies etc. (and like so much, that is true). It might be that the 'ole good nigger' smells a little discriminating through associations."[118]

Richter's contributions suggest the potential for a film that would truly be experimental, both in form and in function. As the draft stood, however, Richter's general impression was that the film, with its new romantic angle, was "Hollywoodish." Nevertheless, while keeping Richter on retainer as a consultant, Horkheimer tried to dip back into the Hollywood trough and engaged once again in a series of correspondences trying to stir up interest in the project at the studios. In June, he received a letter from Alexander Hackenschmidt, a Hollywood agent, who wrote:

> This morning I had a talk with Mr. Elia Kazan and the practical problems of your film-project. He recommended very strongly to make the film in Hollywood and also to look there for a writer. He pointed to the fact that so many good young writers have been drawn to Hollywood in the last few years, that someone in need of a writer will find there the largest choice. Mr. Kazan suggested Albert Maltz, Alva Bessy [*sic*] or Harold Rosson. I would add the names of Irvin Shaw, Dalton Trumbo or Budd Schulberg.[119]

The letter is intriguing, not only because it reveals Horkheimer's dissatisfaction with the first draft of the film but also because it displays the way certain paths crossed in Hollywood. Elia Kazan, who would go on to direct the film version of *A Streetcar Named Desire* and *On the Waterfront*, would notoriously save his skin by naming names as a "friendly" witness in front of HUAC. Among the names he named for Horkheimer are two further members of the Hollywood Ten, Alvah Bessie and Albert Maltz.[120]

Also in June of that year, from a Judge Robert Proskauer, Horkheimer received a letter of introduction to visit Jack Warner at Warner Brothers.[121] Whether the two actually met is unclear. Perhaps it is more tantalizing to imagine it, but I can unfortunately find no record of a meeting between the German professor and the mogul.[122] Nevertheless, by the end of July, *Below the Surface* had picked up three more writers, Marvin Borowsky, Allen Rivkin, and—after all—Dore Schary.[123] That some influence was exercised to gain their participation can be gleaned from the note of thanks in the final draft's introductory memo, which claims, "These script writers volunteered to do the job of rewriting as a result of the interest of the Uptown Committee of the Los Angeles Jewish community, which includes, among its members, some of the important personalities of the motion picture industry."[124]

The final draft solves some of the problems of the first version. The first version was one script that had separate, branching pages, titled depending on the accused character ("Negro version," "Jewish version," and "White Collar version"). The second version is simply three different scripts, each called by the name of the character in question ("Johnson," "Shapiro," and "Roberts"). The intellectual disappears, and although the peddler still rants like a radio demagogue, there is less emphasis on the direct quotations from Adorno's other projects. Through his speech and dress, the "Negro" character still evokes a number of unfortunate stereotypes, but not qualitatively more so than the Jew or the businessman. Overall, there are a lot fewer instances of voice-over and interior monologue. As such, the tertiary characters are less distinctive and the romance between the soldier and the nurse plays out through flirtatious banter. Their relationship is therefore less forced and burdensome. On the other hand, since the script doesn't rely on their thoughts to convey their budding relationship, a much longer introduction is required, and the couple is forced to carry the narrative, while the accident recedes somewhat. To offer a general assessment of the final script: At twenty-five pages and fifty-seven separate shots and designed to run about twenty minutes, it is a modest, resolutely narrative exercise that bears little trace of Adorno's and Horkheimer's concerted efforts, except for the indirect character of its investigation. In its conceptualization of romance, working men, the poor, pretty nurses, and all-American boys, the film is obstinately traditional and even stereotypical. Further, because each of the characters is so distinctly a "type," the fact that any one minority was being spotlighted was bound to be obscured; rather than cathecting on one character, all characters are liable to becoming interchangeable. In many ways, therefore, *Below the Surface* formally suggests the absence of anything other than surface attributes, a fact accentuated by the loss of voice-over monologue. Indeed, the final project could be said to confirm the worst suspicions Horkheimer and Adorno shared concerning the culture industry's process of pseudo-individuation and the destruction of subjective experience.

And despite the fact that the memorandum introducing the script claims that a slow-motion trailer of the film's accident already exists, after April 1946, the film essentially disappears.[125] After nearly six years, multiple versions of the story and the script, numerous "doctors" and advisers, and a substantial outlay of time, labor, and money, Adorno and Horkheimer had been put through the Hollywood wringer with nothing to show for it except an unproduceable script, no doubt "stupider and worse" than their original idea.[126] There are a few references to Adorno's attempts to entice an independent producer to take on the project,[127] and Horkheimer's papers contain some hand-scrawled addresses of actors' studios and workshops, but after that, interest seems to have waned.

But since this is a Hollywood story, there is the inevitable denouement. Two letters from Horkheimer's papers suggest what might have happened to *Below the Surface.* In February 1946, Horkheimer wrote John Slawson regarding the status of the Studies in Prejudice research. The letter concludes with a reference to the film project that indicates there was some hesitation on the part of AJC to actually produce the script:

> With regard to the motion picture, I trust that the procedure which you indicate will lead to a situation which is satisfactory for all concerned. The Committee, of course, is not legally bound to produce the picture. On the other hand, the group of prominent writers with whom I am collaborating volunteered to prepare the script after I had explained that the American Jewish Committee had approved the project in principle and set aside the funds for the production. I made this declaration at a meeting at which members of the industry as well as of the Jewish community were present. In accordance with your suggestion, I shall carry on my preparatory work and continue to make my explorations until a stage is reached at which the project can be discussed again.[128]

While there was clearly some recalcitrance on the part of the AJC to produce *Below the Surface,* Horkheimer's presentation to a group of Hollywood personalities is likewise noteworthy. In 1946, after years of avoiding the issues of anti-Semitism and the Holocaust, the major studios had finally decided to start making films about prejudice, and by 1947 there was a critical mass of anti-Semitism films, with Kazan's *Gentleman's Agreement* (1947) winning the Best Picture Oscar, and Edward Dmytryk's *Crossfire* (also 1947) nominated for five Academy Awards, including Best Picture.

Crossfire deserves special attention, not so much for its story (a soldier, played chillingly by Robert Ryan, kills a fellow, Jewish soldier) but for the intensity of discussion the film generated among Horkheimer, Lazarsfeld, and the AJC. In July 1947, Lazarsfeld describes the situation to Horkheimer:

> Let me come back to the "Crossfire" episode which shows how bad the present confusion is. When I got your memorandum and your letter, I immediately talked with [AJC's] Flowerman. It turned out that in the meantime, the Anti-Defamation League had gotten wind of your ideas and started some "research." There resulted a little private war between the Committee and the League . . . about which you have heard. Now, from your point of view, I think the trouble was that the following question was not made clear. Was the problem what to do with "Crossfire" or was it what to do about this kind of propaganda? If the former, then you were right in raising the question, but otherwise, Flowerman's service department should have tried to get an answer. If he could not, that was his lookout.[129]

Reading between the lines of this and other documents, we may suspect that what raised Horkheimer's ire was not so much the lurid content of *Crossfire* and the potential backlash against the film but, instead, the fact that he believed that *Below the Surface* had been stolen, if not in its substance, at least in its principles. Given the belief expressed in Lazarsfeld's letter that AJC had somehow dropped the ball by letting the Anti-Defamation League poach on Horkheimer's and Adorno's research, it is easy to imagine Horkheimer's outrage and suspicion that the seeds of his project had been used to grow Dmytryk's film. If this was the case, then the worst that Adorno and Horkheimer could imagine had happened. *Crossfire* and the Anti-Defamation League had taken Adorno's and Horkheimer's "research" and had transformed it into a hit film (albeit a moderate one). And who was the producer of *Crossfire*? None other than Dore Schary.

Of course, evidence for this is all circumstantial, but should it in fact be the case that the spate of Jewish-interest Hollywood films that appeared after the war did indeed derive in part from Adorno's and Horkheimer's research, it illustrates one of the fundamental problems of narrative cinema. Since the products do function at the surface level, the individual expressions are easily interchangeable. According to the logic of cultural exchange, *Crossfire* and *Below the Surface* can be understood as essentially the same, and once one appears, the utility of the other is diminished. In terms of its viability for the studios and the AJC, the experimental film project was a failure not because it was too Hollywood but because it was not Hollywood enough. The "propaganda" of the feature film overwhelms the research value of the shorter projects envisioned by Adorno and Horkheimer.

The movies had proven a dead end for Adorno and Horkheimer, but one that suggested there was more to consider about how artworks withstand their own reification and their utilization as phantasmagoric pictures of the world. Perhaps the reason why *Below the Surface* was doomed is embedded in the title. In an increasingly administered situation, the subject is under enormous pressure to divorce himself from any elements that do not contribute to the smooth working of the machine. In the increasingly mechanized and mediated twentieth century, the Enlightenment subject with an interior life gave way to a new, posthumanist subject whose insides get in the way of efficiency and communicability. As I have suggested, the consummate transformation that movies and television shows effect is that they take the form of that exemplary bourgeois artwork, the serialized novel, and abandon what made it exceptional, the belief in a free, interior subject. What remains are the novel's surface elements, plot and stereotypical character traits. Increasingly, even those footholds for subjectivity are diminished, and all that is left is pure action. The result is that movies and television give back to their audiences the shell of a subject without the corollary free-form consciousness that stands as the last best hope for the individual's escape from mechanization and alienation.

The movies and television represent the next stage in the destruction of the shopworn individual. Instead of providing even the pretense of subjectivity, they treat the audience to a collection of interchangeable types that belie the disappearance of their individual identities. The movies are a crucial mechanism in what Giorgio Agamben calls "the historic transformations of human nature that capitalism wants to limit to the spectacle, to link together image and body in a space where they can no longer be separated, and thus to forge the whatever body."[130] This is, no doubt, an exceedingly pessimistic view of the history of cinema and its negative effects on the subject. Nevertheless, it is precisely this evolution, to the point when all types—Jew, Negro, and businessman—become interchangeable cogs in the spectacle of prejudice, upon which Adorno and Horkheimer capitalize in the crafting of *Below the Surface*. The failure of *Below the Surface*, the Mr. Biggott cartoons, and perhaps of cinema and television generally is that for the post-Fordist subject there may be nothing left other than surfaces. Adorno's and Horkheimer's pretensions to empirically register that loss seem, in retrospect, quixotic. Agamben's cautionary lament about the historical precedent of these "whatever bod[ies]" strikes a resounding tone with *Below the Surface*'s geometrical exploration of the myriad ways prejudice can manifest itself, and Agamben's inevitable conclusion about the fate of these "whatever bod[ies]" essentially confirms Adorno's and Horkheimer's worst suspicions regarding the cinema: "The glorious body," on display in cinema, television, and advertising, "has become a mask behind which the fragile, slight human body continues its precarious existence, and the geometrical splendor covers over the long lines of the naked, anonymous bodies led to their deaths in the *Lagers* (camps), or the thousands of corpses mangled in the daily slaughter on the highways."[131]

The notion that the question of subjectivity in cinema is short-circuited by the form of cinema itself invites an investigation into the texts to which Adorno turned that seemed to offer the best defense for the subject and yet that had been most denigrated by mass manipulation: literature and the written word. If the subject disappears in the cinema, it is the revolutionary potential of the most superannuated of "mass media" that offers the best hope that the exiled subject might someday find a home.

4 "IF THERE SHOULD BE A POSTERITY"
HIGH MODERNISM, HOROSCOPES, AND HEROIC SALESMEN

And I went unto the angel, and said unto him, Give me the little book.
And he said unto me, Take it, and eat it up; and it shall make thy
belly bitter, but it shall be in thy mouth sweet as honey. And I took
the little book out of the angel's hand, and ate it up; and it was
in my mouth sweet as honey: and as soon as I had eaten it, my belly
was bitter.

—Revelation 10:9-10

In the essay "The Absence of the Book," Maurice Blanchot writes, "the book (the civilization of the book) declares: there is a memory that transmits things, there is a system that arranges things; time becomes entangled in the book, where the void still belongs to a structure."[1] Blanchot's statement is provocative and exciting, for it suggests that through books one can have access to—and more, experience—history. But wait, isn't what Blanchot says somewhat obvious? Of course one reads history in books. And what he says would indeed be a simple truism were it not for Blanchot's insistence on the importance of the book's structure in the process. It is not merely historical events or the stories of individuals that the book transmits; literature's historical content alone does not afford us access to history. Rather, by virtue of its formal principles, its structural makeup, the book mirrors the workings of the social systems that arrange and condition those events and the subjects who live them. The book has a privileged relationship to civilization, Blanchot believes, because what the book does to its subjects at a formal level is analogous to what happens to individuals living in the modern world.

Adorno would have recognized in Blanchot echoes of his own literary philosophy. In a letter to Thomas Mann after the publication of Mann's *Die Betrogene* (in English, *The Black Swan*),[2] Adorno congratulates him for his success in highlighting the tension between the characters and events of the novel and the formal construction of the book: "You increase the tension between culture and the things that live beneath it to the breaking point, or better, to the point of dialectical transformation," Adorno writes, and he goes on to suggest that Mann, like the surrealist André Masson, approaches the point where the specificity of the objects of the novel are all but erased by the structure of the novel itself, a "kind of dissolution of the material in its own aura," he says.[3] The novel, like the capitalist system from which it springs, threatens to obliterate all traces of individuality. Thus, Adorno's note to Mann echoes Blanchot's statements: To be true to its historical moment the book has to do its work of transmitting "time," "memory," and "history" in conditions where, by virtue of capitalism's system of equivalences, all specificity is subsumed under the aegis of exchange value and those terms themselves are becoming meaningless. A book therefore has to do something particularly challenging. It must render the "truth" of its narrative elements as patently untrue. This was the challenge faced by the community of exiled writers, Mann and Adorno included, for whom history was, in many respects, at a standstill. At a personal level, the exiles were facing an uncertain future and the real possibility that they would never return home. In a larger context, not only had National Socialism threatened to obviate the history of Europe, and with it, the Enlightenment belief in the free-willed individual, but in America, particularly Southern California, the exiles were faced with a culture whose appetite for historical subjects threatened to transform history into kitsch.

This threat is acidly described in Aldous Huxley's corrosive 1939 Hollywood novel, *After Many a Summer Dies the Swan*. The book opens with a British antiquities professor (a stand-in for Huxley and perhaps for the rest of the émigré intellectuals) being treated to a limousine ride through Beverly Hills. On the tour, the limousine cruises through the garish Beverly Pantheon, in which all the world's architectural history is crammed together in derivative mausoleum designs. In a matter of moments the limousine passes "a full-scale reproduction of the Leaning Tower of Pisa—only this one didn't lean. . . . Then, in rapid succession, the Garden of Quiet, the Tiny Taj Mahal, the Old World Mortuary. And, reserved by the chauffeur to the last, as the final and crowning proof of his employer's glory, the Pantheon itself."[4]

If Huxley describes an architectural scene that, by virtue of its cemetery setting, spells the death of world history, an American, Nathanael West, was alert to the way this architecture of death proliferated throughout

Hollywood. "Not even the soft wash of dusk could help the houses," West's protagonist Tod, a set painter, notices. "Only dynamite would be of any use against the Mexican ranch houses, Samoan huts, Mediterranean villas, Egyptian and Japanese temples, Swiss chalets, Tudor cottages, and every possible combination of these styles that lined the slope of the canyon." But the voraciousness of Los Angeles reaches beyond architectural style and condenses all of human history—fact and fiction—into a continuous sham present. Severed from their pasts, the residents of California mold one out of pressboard and glue, and the results are even more horrifying than Huxley's mausoleums:

> On the corner of La Huerta Road was a miniature Rhine castle with tarpaper turrets pierced for archers. Next to it was a highly colored shack with domes and minarets out of the *Arabian Nights*. Again he was charitable. Both houses were comic, but he didn't laugh. Their desire to startle was so eager and guileless. It is hard to laugh at the need for beauty and romance, no matter how tasteless, even horrible, the results of that are. But it is easy to sigh. Few things are sadder than the truly monstrous.[5]

This was the milieu into which Adorno and Mann were thrust during the exile years, one that betokened a crisis in the way history, and with it the historical subject, was consumed and made legible. The rapid-fire edits of the film industry and the endless proliferation of radio "formats" seemed particularly well adapted for an era when all historical specificity could be reduced to a question of consumer choice. For literature and the printed word, however, the question of their continued adequacy to what Blanchot refers to as the "transmission" of time and memory became increasingly problematic. If the foregoing chapters have looked forward to developments in communications technologies and the increasingly globalized world of information exchange, a discussion of literature might seem retrograde, a retreat to antiquated forms long superseded by the storytelling capacities of radio, television, and the narrative film. Nevertheless, as the exile years wore on, Adorno took an increasing interest in literature, this despite Lowenthal's nominal position as the Institute's literary expert. This interest is evidenced not only by the proliferation of literary references in *Minima Moralia* (whose first aphorism is "For Marcel Proust") and the essay "Aldous Huxley and Utopia," which was crafted around 1948, but also by an increasing concern for literature as a component of his broader aesthetic theories, an interest that would see full flower in the two volumes of *Notes to Literature*. Much of what Adorno will come to say about literary works, and moreover about the social situation generally, derives both from his reading of American pulp fiction and from his exile contact with Thomas Mann, where he saw firsthand how the novel can at once liquidate the subject and yet also provide some small "hope beyond hopelessness." As Blanchot claims, the book is no less a form of transmission, of communication, and of mediation than are the radio or the cinema. But perhaps even more than in the case of radio, movies, and television, what disappears into the text has the capacity, threat, and promise of exploding into our present in unexpected and unforeseen ways.

A story written on the other side of the California exile may well be the best place to start such a consideration. *Die Betrogene,* a short book about Germany in the years following World War I, was composed by Mann after his departure from the United States to Switzerland in the early 1950s. The way these two postwar settings speak to one another of the past and present of art and the exile's ongoing dispossession is of central concern in the book. Perhaps the best way to read *Die Betrogene*'s simple story is as an allegory for the death of the novel, the end of high romanticism, and the false promise of realism. The history that this novel transmits is the history of the novel's decline as a form.

In the tale, a still-beautiful widow of fifty, Frau Rosalie von Tümmler, living in Düsseldorf during the 1920s, hires a young American to teach English to her son. Rosalie's older child, Anna, is a crippled painter who, because of an abortive love affair, has sworn herself opposed to romantic love. As a result of this incident, her intellectualism, and her disability, she has embraced asceticism and modernism in direct contradiction to her mother's joy in "beloved nature." Anna is suspicious of the hale, enthusiastic American, Ken, a veteran of World War I and a buff of all things "German," particularly trivial aspects of German history. These misgivings intensify when Rosalie falls in love with Ken and, miraculously, begins having her period again. In a fevered episode, Rosalie, ennobled by the return of her "womanhood," confesses her love to Ken while on a day trip into the country. However, before the two can consummate their union, Rosalie collapses, and the local doctor discovers that a rapidly metastasizing cancer has created the illusion of a renewed menstrual cycle. The story ends with Rosalie's elegiac salute to the nature that she has always loved and that "has been loving to her child," closing with the line, "Rosalie died a gentle death, mourned by all who knew her."[6]

The melancholy tenderness with which the novel concludes belies the cruelty done to Rosalie, both in body and in spirit. The heartrending betrayal of her hopes and the subsequent medical atrocities committed in the name of saving her evoke the terrible end of Emma Bovary after her lover leaves her. But in this echo of Flaubert, one can also hear Mann sounding the death knell for the high period of the realist novel that *Madame Bovary* inaugurated. That Eros has fled, that realism, naturalistic presentation, and romantic sentiment are no longer the benchmarks of subjective presentation, is outlined in *Die Betrogene*'s debate between Rosalie and her daughter. The loveless Anna, we are told, is a painter who has fully accepted the rigors of modernism: "She had struck out on a course of the most extreme intellectualism, which, disdaining mere imitation of nature, transfigured sensory content into the strictly cerebral, the abstractly symbolical, often the cubistically mathematical."[7] However, on their walks together, Rosalie tries to convince her daughter to paint in a representational romantic style, giving reign to the emotions and the senses. "If only you would let your art offer something to the emotions just once," Rosalie exhorts her daughter. And she naively suggests that Anna indulge in superannuated aesthetic practices: "Paint something for the heart, a beautiful still life, a fresh spray of lilac, so true to life that one would think one smelt its ravishing perfume, and a pair of delicate Meissen porcelain figures beside the vase, gentleman blowing kisses to a lady, and with everything reflected in the gleaming, polished table-top."[8]

In response, Anna tells her mother that she can't paint such things. Misunderstanding her daughter's demurral as a question of technical facility, Rosalie's motherly response is to tell her daughter that she is selling herself short, and that she could paint the natural world beautifully if she would only try. Anna, an astute student but unwilling to recognize the source of her mother's yearning for art and the beautiful to once again coincide, chides her mother's retrograde suggestions: "You misunderstand me, Mama! It's not a question of whether I can. Nobody can. The state of the times and of art no longer permits it." Rosalie's resigned reply: "So much the more regrettable for the times and art!"[9]

But while clearly sympathizing with Rosalie's desire—both for Ken and for the natural world—*Die Betrogene* nevertheless reminds us that the flip side of "O' Natura" is the nasty, brutish, and cruel, always threatening to destroy those who would only see nature as beautiful. Rosalie's walk with her daughter is cut short when the two discover a musky, stinking pile of animal and human waste, skeletons, and offal; the miraculous renewal of menstruation is revealed as a tumor; and the graceful black swans of the English title bite and hiss at Rosalie when she pretends she won't feed them. Inevitably, nature always bites back, and the subject who has sought refuge in its world finds nothing but alienation and death.

It is hard not to see this as the modernist Mann's lament for the exile's severed ties with his natural home as well as a benediction for the novelistic form itself. It is a well-known story: The novel, former refuge for the subject, proves to be inhospitable terrain, its characters cadavers, phantoms, and automata wandering through a ghost town of false storefronts and painted horizons. But that would be a strictly undialectical reading of the fate Mann sees for the novel, and perhaps a reminder of the dangers of allegorical interpretation. For if we read Rosalie's refusal to condemn nature as anything other than delusional, then it is clear that although the novel's "nature" liquidates Rosalie, in so doing and by its very violence, it more firmly cements its bond with her. As Horkheimer and Adorno write in *Dialectic of Enlightenment,* alienation from nature *is* the nature of the Enlightenment subject's existence. Rational self-preservation entails an irrevocable breach between nature and the individual, a breach that ultimately impoverishes the individual. "In class society," they claim, "the self's hostility to sacrifice included a sacrifice of the self, since it was paid for by a denial of the nature in the human being for the sake of mastery over extrahuman nature and over other human beings."[10]

On the aesthetic front, because the novel is so manifestly not an image of the subject but a representation through language, it is uniquely suited to portray the "nature" of this transformation of subjects into objects. "The reification of all relationships between individuals," Adorno claims, "which transforms their human qualities into lubricating oil for the smooth running of the machinery, the universal alienation and self-alienation, needs to be called by name, and the novel is qualified to do so as few other art forms are."[11] Mann, Adorno claims, is an exemplary case of the novelist's ability to reveal, through his attention to form, the distance between reality and its literary construction. "Mann does this most obviously, perhaps," Adorno insists, "in his late period, in the *Holy Sinner* and the *Black Swan,* where the writer, playing with a romantic motif, acknowledges the peepshow element in the narrative, the unreality of illusion, through his use of language." The twist in *Die Betrogene,* therefore, is that it is the "nature" of the novel (in terms of both its form and its content) that betrays Rosalie and kills her but by so doing reveals the truth of her character as a reified object.

As opposed to a calculated realism that pretended to innocently portray the world as it was, Mann, Adorno marvels, "returns the work of art, as he says, to the status of a sublime joke, a status it had until, with the naiveté of lack of naiveté, it presented illusion as truth in an all too unreflected way."[12] Thus, for Mann—and for Adorno—exile is always the theme of literature, since the individual "lives" within the pages but is never comfortably at home, and the writer's task is to capture the horror of this unnatural nature. The confrontation between the *Unheimlich* and the novel's subject is what Adorno identified in *Die Betrogene*. The subject, increasingly embattled by the unfreedom of the administered life, can no more live to the fullest in reality than she can in the two-dimensional, formally restrictive space of literature, but it is because the literary work is so inhospitable to the free, living individual that the memory of life is preserved. The novel flattens its subjects, but in so doing it retains the fullness of their existence. There is something of this sense in Adorno's oft-quoted statement in *Minima Moralia* that "for a man who no longer has a homeland, writing becomes a place to live."

While Mann represents the furthest limit of this unease in high European modernism, in the American context of Adorno's exile, it is pulp fiction, magazines, and the comics that best capture the reified individual. The hard-boiled fictions of the 1930s and '40s—and their affinity with the surface structure of movies and radio—perfectly illustrate this flattening of the narrative subject and suggest the heightened stakes for an individual alienated from himself. The conclusion of James M. Cain's *The Postman Always Rings Twice*, where the killer Frank thinks about his crimes, provides a particularly noteworthy example of this condition:

> There's a guy in No. 7 that murdered his brother, and says he didn't really do it, his subconscious did it. I asked him what that meant, and he says you got two selves, one that you know about and the other that you don't know about, because it's subconscious. It shook me up. Did I really do it, and not know about it?[13]

What is fascinating about Cain's texts and those of other hard-boiled writers—and perfectly in keeping with Adorno's compliments to Mann—is the sense that the characters often seem to be literally born into the book, with no history outside the confines of the text. *Postman*, for example, begins, "They threw me off the hay truck about noon," and it is as though Frank only begins to exist the moment he is flung onto the page. But without access to a past, the violence of the characters takes on an unsettling aspect of reportage, appearing all the more dehumanizing because there is no subjective reason for it. Adorno, who was clearly well aware of the conventions of hard-boiled fiction, registers the matter-of-factness of the violent subject's self-degradation in American thrillers—and hence in modernity—by quoting Ellery Queen: "Murder is so newspapery. It doesn't happen to you. You read about it in a paper, or in a detective story, and it makes you wriggle with disgust, or sympathy. But it doesn't mean anything."[14] In quoting Queen, Adorno conveys the way the thrillers operate as indexes of a situation in which all events, responses, and emotions are essentially interchangeable surface attributes divorced from their underlying meanings. Disgust and sympathy are merely affective performances for a reality no longer accessible—certainly not through the language of a novel. What Cain, West, Kenneth Fearing, Raymond Chandler, and other so-called pulp writers ultimately react against is a situation in which characters become values, exchangeable currency set adrift from history and cast to the whims of contingency—a world in which there is no "there" there.[15]

In a sense, the pulp impresarios present an image of high modernism in extremity. With their deceptively simple prose style (Chandler excepted), the hard-boiled writers of the 1940s and '50s offer a pop version of the type of subjective liquidation Mann attempts in *Die Betrogene* (whose title and hyperromanticism likewise suggest a steamy literary romp). As the camps of high modernism and literary pulp speed away from one another in their portrayal of the flattened, alienated subject, they nevertheless turn back on themselves and threaten to meet at the other end of the circle. Adorno's gift was the ability to register how both literary forms—the putatively high and the supposedly low—freeze subjects in their historical moment while at the same time animating them within the world created by the text. As Max Pensky writes, "Conceived as ruin, historical objects were not just dead but also liberated from a totalizing historical reason, and as liberated, presented themselves to the attention of the critic as the material for the construction of constellations."[16] Pensky's arguments are crucial to understanding why the distinction between high modernism and pulp may in fact be spurious for the exiled Adorno, whose *Minima Moralia* shuttles in the span of a sentence between Marcel Proust and Thomas Mann, Anatole France and King Kong, bridging the divide between "serious" and "mass" culture and always insisting that one pole is the bad conscience of the other. And Adorno's exile home no doubt played a part in these observations. California, with all its clichéd glitz, gleaming chrome, and restaurants shaped like hamburgers, was the perfect proving ground for observing the implosion of culture firsthand.

This collapse between high and low and the difficulty of distinguishing the two is the essence of what has long since come to be known as post-modernism, and evidence of the increasingly fragile nature of modernity and the modern subject is ample in Adorno's exile Hollywood. This may explain the appeal of one comic strip Adorno and Horkheimer seem to have been following during the 1940s. The strip, called *Chuck Carson*, was essentially an ad for the Chrysler Corporation, appearing every other week at the bottom of the Sunday comics page. The anonymously drawn and written strip featured square-jawed, pipe smoking Chuck Carson, "popular car dealer," and his secretary, Jerry Doyle, who would regularly pursue the perpetrators of some car-related crime.[17] In the penultimate panel, Chuck and Jerry, each still wearing their business outfits, would end up catching the bad guys, while the final panel was dedicated to Chuck dispensing some wisdom about car safety, parallel parking, and so on. For the most part, the strip was relatively devoid of sales content, except for the sporadic exclamations of "nice car" and the changing Plymouth slogan on the wall of Chuck's office. Beyond the fact that the Adornos owned a Plymouth, it is little wonder that Horkheimer and Adorno would have found this strip fascinating (and Horkheimer kept clippings of it in his files). *Chuck Carson* literalizes the notion of the bourgeois hero, but in so doing, the strip performs a telling reversal. In the traditional view of art in the Enlightenment, the artist and his or her surrogates (the protagonists of the novel, for example) escape into the totality of the fictional world created by the text and assert their individuality against the mundane conditions of existence. Although, like the bourgeois novel, *Chuck Carson* offers the reader exemplary identificatory figures, Chuck's and Jerry's heroic acts are no escape from the economic quotidian; instead, they ensure the smooth and efficient functioning of their car dealership. Further, their economic success is inevitably guaranteed by a paradoxical combination of extra-legal violence and lockstep adherence to the most trivial of laws. Chuck, after all, is essentially a vigilante with a mean right cross who nonetheless insists on the importance of following the traffic codes.

Even more than the hard-boiled pulps or Mann's *Die Betrogene,* the *Chuck Carson* comic illustrates the crisis of modernity that Adorno felt was threatening the arts at each end of the spectrum. "Telling a story means having something *special* to say," Adorno writes in "The Position of the Narrator in the Contemporary Novel," "and that is precisely what is prevented by the administered world, by standardization and eternal sameness."[18] Not only does each episode of *Chuck Carson* follow the same pattern, but the implications of the strip are that individuals should contribute to their own dissolution by transforming "their human qualities into lubricating oil for the smooth running of the machinery," even if that regularity is ensured through violence. It might seem that comparing a comic strip (and one that admittedly functions as an advertisement) with a Mann novel violates the formal specificity of each and overstates the relationship between one form of literature and another. Nevertheless, as Pensky hints, this comparison is what Adorno's insistence on the methodological use of constellations permits and the topography of Southern California perhaps even demands, so long as one understands that *Chuck Carson* and *Die Betrogene* are mediated through the same social system.

Further, during Adorno's exile years, a number of American public intellectuals and social critics—on the left and the right—were marking a crisis in print culture and a winnowing divide between modernist literature and mass-entertainment forms, and most were predicting dire consequences for citizens in a democratic society. Two of these commentators are particularly noteworthy, both because they were well known and because they run the gamut from the establishment-sanctioned academic star to the quasi-intellectual provocateur. On the former side is David Riesman, whose influential best seller *The Lonely Crowd* (1949) argues that Americans were transforming from a nation of "inner-directed," self-reliant individuals into a nation of "other-directed" creatures of the mass media and commodity culture, whose actions and beliefs were determined more by the opinions of others than by their own free choice. Symptomatic of this transformation, Riesman argues, was the development of literature under capitalism. In earlier stages, Riesman claims, the printed word helped guide the child in the complexities and richness of adult life, offering a path to eventual self-sufficiency. "One main purpose of print in the period dependent on inner-direction," he argues, "is to teach the child something about the variety of adult roles he may enter upon and to permit him to try on these roles in fantasy."[19] Riesman's emphasis here is on the "variety" of roles and on reading as the path to "the subtly individualizing traits," of adult social intercourse.[20]

In contrast to the reading practices of the inner-directed individual, however, for the child of the mass media, the model is the comic book, which encourages the child to focus not on complexity but on winners and losers. But the comic book itself is not to blame; rather, Riesman argues, the problem lies in the cultural tendency toward other-directedness that tends to promote a climate of approval-seeking and a Manichaean logic of "heroes" and "villains."²¹ This score-keeping style of reading ultimately colors the experience of reading literature altogether. "Indeed," Riesman claims, "if other-directed child comic fans read or hear stories that are not comics they will tend to focus on who won and to miss the internal complexities of the tale, of a moral sort or otherwise. If one asks them, then, how they distinguish the 'good guys' from the 'bad guys' in the mass media, it usually boils down to the fact that the former always win; they are the good guys by definition."²²

As we have seen in each of the preceding chapters, the use of comics as a marketing and testing tool is fraught with implications for the free-willed subject. Riesman's analysis of the relationship between comics and the degeneration of individuals through their reading habits speaks both to the situation of literature during the 1940s and '50s and to the importance of the comic form to the controllers of the mass media. Whether comics infantilize their readers, soften them up as consumers, or simply function as the gauge of their inability to judge the complexity of a social situation, the comic form during Adorno's American exile serves as an index of the subject in crisis. For Riesman, as for Adorno, being "other-directed" doesn't imply being community oriented or socially minded. Rather, the outwardness of the modern subject betokens a reified individual, operating only at a surface level, "lonely" because the only thing he or she shares with others is his or her function in an increasingly administered world. As a mass form, the comics, which provoke an instantaneous and uniform response among readers who "get" the joke, are a marker of this shared alienation.

Riesman's fairly measured assessment of the way that comics and literary works mirror one another is echoed in the far more vitriolic broadsides of the second commentator, Gershon Legman. Legman, perhaps best known as a folklorist and collector of ribald stories, erotica, and dirty jokes, initially gained notoriety for his 1949 publication of *Love and Death: A Study in Censorship*, which argued that the greatest challenge to the moral health of America was not sex but, rather, violence.²³ Of particular interest to Legman was the development of the "crime" comic, its influence on children, and its increasing imbrication with contemporary literature. If for Riesman, novels and comics tended to resemble one another in their reception, for Legman, the comic was making reading altogether obsolete: "The American generation born since 1930 cannot read. It has not learned. Will not learn and it does not need to. Reading ability just sufficient to spell out the advertisements is all that is demanded in our culture."²⁴ Although

Legman is hyperbolic in his assertions, he was nonetheless echoed in this assessment five years later by Rudolf Flesch in his seminal *Why Johnny Can't Read*. But whereas Flesch lays the blame for the problem on the methodological decision to abandon phonics-based reading instruction, Legman, like Riesman, roundly insists that declining literacy is part of a general cultural degradation inflicted on all the arts by popular culture.

Together, Legman and Riesman paint a far direr portrait of the debilitating effects of the mass media than Adorno does, even at his most astringent. In fact, Adorno holds out some measure of hope for the restorative power of the comics, whose frivolity would "negate the burden of labor," the seriousness of the world that "high art" tries, misguidedly, to mimic: "In some revue films, and especially in grotesque stories and 'funnies,' the possibility of this negation is momentarily glimpsed." But for Adorno, that hope is a fleeting one, precisely because of the way something like the *Chuck Carson* comic instrumentalizes amusement as a marketing tool and transforms the comic-book hero into the bourgeois businessman: "Its realization, of course, cannot be allowed. Pure amusement indulged to the full, relaxed abandon to colorful associations and merry nonsense, is cut short by amusement in its marketable form."[25]

What links Riesman and Legman, apart from their shared assessment of the degeneration of literature and the fact that their signal works appeared in the same year, is the fact that Adorno cites each of them approvingly in various writings. Riesman receives a nod in, among other places, *The Authoritarian Personality* (perhaps returning Riesman's own gracious comments about Adorno's radio essays in *The Lonely Crowd*), while Legman is cited in "How to Look at Television."[26] What the references to Riesman and Legman suggest is not only that Adorno was following American academic debates but also that his understanding of the state of literature was neither elitist nor markedly outside the currents of American intellectual life.

While it was only after the exile period that Adorno fully concentrated on the literary realm, while in America his most extended critical foray into the world of print culture, "The Stars Down to Earth," took the form of his analysis of the *Los Angeles Times* astrology column. Here, however, many of the themes addressed by Legman and especially Riesman with regard to comics are filtered through Adorno's response to magazines and newspapers. Just as children reading comic books are encouraged to identify with a one-dimensional hero, on the horoscope page, the reader becomes a bourgeois superhero in the manner of Chuck Carson:

The image presented in this area may be called, with some exaggeration, that of the *vice president*. The people spoken to are pictured as holding a superior place in life which forces them, as mentioned before, to make decisions all of the time. Much depends on them, on their reasonableness, their ability to make up their minds. . . . One may think of the well-known technique of magazines such as *Fortune* which are written to give the impression that each of their presumably very numerous readers were a big shot in some major corporation.[27]

As with Riesman's other-directed individuals, the readers of *Fortune* and of the daily horoscope are encouraged less to cultivate varied and subtle personal traits within themselves than to identify with a stock character, such as the successful businessman. "What is emphasized," Adorno continues, "is not so much the addressee's real ego power as his intellectual identification with some socialized ego ideal."[28]

Obviously comic books and horoscopes are a long way from modernist novels, but as Legman and Riesman argue, and as Adorno will ultimately conclude, the degradation of the subject in the former ultimately implicates the aesthetic and formal possibilities of the latter. Indeed, as Adorno's assessment of Mann's late work indicates, it is perhaps the business of the modernist text to map the reification of the subject that afflicts literature generally. Further, if crassly commercial literature was tending toward simplicity in order to offer a standardized and hence more marketable reading experience, in the realm of so-called high-end literature, concerted effort was also being applied to marketing modernist novels as though they were easily digestible consumer goods. As Janice Radway and Joan Shelley Rubin separately relate, from the 1920s Harry Scherman's Book-of-the-Month Club promoted the idea that literary excellence was a necessary commodity and that a library preapproved by an expert "Board of Judges" was—like a couch or dining room table—an indispensable element of the bourgeois home.[29] Hence, many critics saw in the Book-of-the-Month Club a standardization of the literary experience, the "mechanization of the American mind." The implications of this mechanization, critics argued, essentially correspond to Riesman's and Legman's pronouncements and were not unlike the veiled totalitarianism and regulation Adorno identified as being fundamental to radio broadcasts and the movies. As Rubin reports:

> The "cultural effect," the *Commonweal* argued, "is to standardize
> American reading, precisely because the selection is buttressed by
> authority. . . . Moreover, a similarity of tone pervades almost all the

selections made, so that eventually a certain kind of literature becomes the vogue."[30]

Given the Book-of-the-Month Club's ability to sway the reading populace and standardize their literary tastes, it should come as no surprise that many publishers actively courted selection by the club in addition to using a number of other methods to sell literary works, particularly challenging ones by modernist authors whose works would seem to resist such commodification. The novels of Thomas Mann and the efforts of his publisher Alfred A. Knopf provide a telling case study of this situation. In her book *Marketing Modernism between the Two World Wars*, Catherine Turner relates that Knopf, in much the same way the Book-of-the-Month Club employed a panel of experts to cultivate an aura of intellectual legitimacy, "sold books like Mann's as his personal choices and as products that could meet consumers' sense of inadequacy by reconnecting them with the sense of civilization that Knopf created around his firm."[31] Nevertheless, Turner claims that although Knopf "revered literature, . . . he never hesitated to advertise literary commodities in the same way Campbell's Soup or Listerine advertised their products."[32] Ultimately, this prickly tension between high modernism and mass culture, aesthetic object and consumer good would coalesce around Mann's most famous exile novel, *Doctor Faustus*, a book that was chosen as a Book-of-the-Month Club selection in 1947 and a book all the more interesting for my purposes because of Adorno's extensive contributions to its construction.

In *Late Marxism*, Fredric Jameson writes that "the most familiar and widely read version of Adorno's account of the crisis of art (or the emergence of modernism) we owe not to him but to Thomas Mann, who appropriated its earlier formulation (in *Philosophie der neuen Musik*) for his novel *Doktor Faustus*."[33] Jameson's statement captures the essence of the relationship, and the course of Adorno's and Mann's relationship bears some scrutiny, not so much for its biographical interest as for what it suggests about literary works, print culture, and their capacity for communicating subjectivity. In their letters and in Mann's *Story of a Novel*, which describes the genesis of *Doctor Faustus*, there emerges a portrait of the means by which literary texts can prove themselves adequate to the historical conditions that threaten the liquidation of the individual. Adorno was Mann's musical adviser on *Doctor Faustus* (1947), and he allowed Mann to read a draft of *Philosophy of New Music* (1948). Mann was so taken with Adorno's work and his lectures on musical works that he incorporated whole chunks of many of them into the novel so that Adorno appears as not just one character or idea but several. Thus, aspects of Adorno's thought appear in Kretschmar, the composer Leverkühn's early teacher, who stutters his way through a lecture on Beethoven's late style in the Piano Sonata opus 111. And one can recognize Adorno as one of the guises of the devil (the most intellectually seductive), "a member of the intelligentsia, writer on art, on music for the ordinary press, a theoretician and critic, who himself composes, so far as thinking allows him."[34]

In many ways, *Faustus* is a challenging book. A thorny, turgid tale of a modernist composer who sells his soul to the devil, it is neither Mann's most popular nor his most accessible novel. At first glance, aggressively romantic and archaic, with extended passages in mock "high German," wide-ranging digressions into philosophical debates, and long naturalistic descriptions, it reads like a late-nineteenth-century text, uncomfortably shoehorned into the middle of the next epoch. However, as Mann revealed in a 1945 letter to Adorno, the archaic impression created by the text is due in large part to Mann's technique of gratuitous textual borrowing:

> The point on which I feel I owe you an explanation concerns the principle of *montage*, which peculiarly and perhaps outrageously runs through the entire book without any attempt at concealment. I was struck by it again in a recent passage where it occurs in half amusing, half uncanny fashion; I was describing the hero's critical illness, and I included Nietzsche's symptoms word for word as they are set forth in his letters, along with the prescribed menus, etc. I pasted them in, so to speak, for anyone to recognize. . . . To plead Molière's "*Je prends mon bien où je le trouve*" strikes me as an insufficient excuse for this conduct. It might be said that I have developed an inclination in old age to regard life as a cultural product, hence a set of mythic clichés which I prefer, in my calcified dignity, to "independent" invention.[35]

Mann's protestations of old age and obviousness are perhaps too coy. What his letter to Adorno reveals is that *Faustus*, far from being a throwback to an earlier period, is instead a radically conceived attempt to express, formally, the impossibility of "'independent' invention" by smuggling into this apparently "straight" novel all manner of disparate sources and seamlessly weaving them together. This stylistic experiment, it should be noted, mirrors the parts of the novel where Leverkühn, disillusioned by late-romantic music, "solves" the problem of composition by collapsing all of musical history into a piece that ultimately proves to be a grand pastiche and parody of music's development toward romanticism.

Just how extensive was Mann's use of what he calls "montage" is explored in an exceptional, if ultimately pedantic, piece of detective work by Gunilla Bergsten. Setting herself the unenviable task of tracking down as many of Mann's sources as possible, Bergsten reveals the breadth and depth of Mann's borrowings, the diversity of his sources, and the facility with which he shuttles between them. Bergsten then makes the somewhat obvious argument that Mann's innovations are in line with those of other modernist literary giants and reflect a dilemma for the novel as a literary form. "The art of fiction experiences a crisis in the twentieth century," she writes. "Unfettered imagination, spontaneous invention of characters and plots is impeded by reflection and by the paralyzing feeling that everything the conventional novel can express has already been said."[36] Adorno would describe this crisis differently, not as a crisis of the novel but as one of the diminished subjectivity of administered existence. Novels haven't run out of things to say; human beings have bumped up against the limits of their capacity for experience. Nevertheless, Bergsten's description of Mann's solution to the challenge posed to the writer essentially corresponds to Adorno's critique of aesthetic construction and technique. Mann, she claims, "seeks to overcome the crisis by accepting the sense of sterility and finding his way to a consciously 'constructed' (in contrast to 'invented') novel. The main task of the novelist now becomes that of arranging his material. But if inspiration is completely eliminated, the writer becomes something of an engineer."[37]

Bergsten rightly suggests that Mann differs from his more pyrotechnic modernist contemporaries like James Joyce and John Dos Passos in that his constructions are less self-evident and seem more natural,[38] and that seeming straightforwardness can be traced all the way back to the success of Mann's *Buddenbrooks,* which many take to be the realist novel par excellence. But, as Mann tells Adorno, even that youthful novel bore the seeds of a full-flowering practice of construction:

> I know only too well that quite early in life I went in for a kind of higher copying: i.e., in describing Hanno Buddenbrook's typhoid fever, the details of which I unabashedly lifted from an encyclopedia article and then "versified," as it were. The chapter has become famous. But its merit consists only in a certain poeticization of mechanically appropriated material.[39]

As Bergsten's diggings reveal, *Faustus* is to be the novel that most fully expresses this "higher copying." But as the novel's narrator, the teacher

Serenus Zeitblom, indicates, such copying is not without its own rigors and labor: "To copy, understandingly and critically, is in fact, an occupation as intensive and time-consuming as putting down one's own thoughts."[40] In their correspondence, Mann extended the younger Adorno the courtesy of specifically asking his permission to use sections of *Philosophy of New Music* in *Faustus*. After explaining his conception of montage and his methodology, Mann writes:

> The case is more difficult—not to say more scandalous—when it is a matter of appropriating materials that are themselves already poetic—that is, when a real literary borrowing is involved, performed with an air that what has been filched is just good enough to serve one's own pattern of ideas. You rightly presume that when I say this, I have in mind the brazen—and I do hope not altogether doltish—snatches at certain parts of your essays on the philosophy of music. These borrowings cry out all the more for apology since for the time being the reader cannot be made aware of them; there is no way to call his attention to them without breaking the illusion.[41]

Mann's request displays certain noteworthy elements. First, there is the obvious appeal to Adorno's vanity, calling his writing poetic immediately after claiming that Mann's own prose was merely versified mechanics. Second, there is a reference to the deferred time in which Adorno will receive his due reward. Mann continues in this vein in his next lines, using flattery as a wedge for his request:

> Scholarship is wanted, and that I simply lack. Which is one reason I was determined from the start, since the book in any case is based on the principle of montage, to shrink from no borrowing, no appropriation of other men's property. I trust that the borrowings will serve as an independent function within the pattern of the whole, will acquire a symbolic life of their own—while at the same time continuing to exist *intact in their original places* in works of criticism.[42]

Mann's request implies that Adorno should willingly submit his work to a certain bifurcation and self-exile. This deferral, however, becomes increasingly theoretically problematic both in the context of the novel's own mechanics and in the sense that *Faustus* contains, as if hibernating, an Adorno ready to awaken in another era. There will be, Mann claims, the coherent words "intact in their original places," but so too will there be the alienated work—as Mann himself says, "property"—appropriated labor, which takes on a life of its own. Mann's request fairly echoes with Marxian and post-Marxian descriptions of value formation and classical interpretations of commodity fetishism and reification in which labor divorces itself from its owner and enters into independent relations. By suggesting that Adorno's reward will have to be deferred, Mann describes the crucial biphasic mechanism of subjective desire in conditions of objective domination that Adorno identifies in his study of the *Los Angeles Times* astrology column:

> *The problem how to disperse with contradictory requirements of life is*
> *solved by the simple device of distributing these requirements over different*
> *periods*. . . . This again feeds on realistic elements: the order of everyday
> life takes care of a number of antinomies of existence, such as that of work
> and leisure or of public functions and private existence. . . . Everything
> can be solved, so runs the implicit argument, if one only chooses the right
> time, and if one fails, this is merely due to a lack of understanding of some
> supposedly cosmic rhythm.[43]

Mann's request therefore requires Adorno to capitulate to an exploitative temporal mode. The Adorno in *Faustus* diverges from the Adorno of *Philosophy of New Music* in a fashion analogous to that of the putative split between public life and private existence. Adorno the devil and Adorno as Kretschmar cannot exist simultaneously with the historical Adorno. Instead, Adorno's words become commodities within the microeconomy that is *Faustus*'s world. As Jameson's comments about the public's familiarity with Adorno suggest, the real Adorno must always defer to the public image presented by Mann. Mann's closing lines to Adorno illustrate the temporal imperative of the novel's political economy. Thus, when Mann writes, "Let [this letter] be the groundwork for our conversation, as well as a record for posterity, if there should be a posterity,"[44] he somewhat cannily consigns Adorno's contribution to the background but at the same time lays the groundwork for Adorno's reemergence from the text at a later date.

There is, in Mann's subsequent descriptions of the project, a strange effort to both confess and conceal his debts. It is well known that *Doctor Faustus* so thoroughly enraged Schoenberg that Mann felt he had to mollify the composer and acknowledge him in a postscript that accompanied later printings of the novel. However, his acknowledgment of other sources is somewhat more paradoxical. In *The Story of a Novel*, Mann's description of a reading of Hermann Hesse's *Magister Ludi* is especially illuminating. Upon finishing his friend's manuscript, Mann expresses a certain discomfort in the thematic similarities between *Magister Ludi* and *Doctor Faustus* and describes the awkwardness of seeing one's own ideas expressed by another. He refers to his diary entry on *Magister Ludi* to describe his anxiety: "'To be reminded that one is not alone in the world—always unpleasant,' bluntly renders this aspect of my feelings. It is another version of the question in Goethe's *Westöstlicher Diwan:* 'Do we then live if others live?'"[45]

This question resonates with a sustained preoccupation in *Faustus* and expresses one of the fundamental paradoxes of modernity: The subject is made profoundly uncomfortable by the insistent presence of the other and must therefore reduce the experience of the other to a function of his own experience. In so doing, however, the subject gives over to the other, essentially becoming a patchwork of identities. This is, it would seem, the dark flip side of Riesman's other-directed individual. If an individual acts in a stereotypical fashion so as to garner the approval of others, others exist so as to affirm that individual. Each becomes a function of the other. This system of exchange coincides with that of the political economy generally. Capitalism cannot bear to have anything outside the relations of production and thus colonizes and commodifies all alterity. But once everything is exchangeable, each individual loses any core or kernel of personal identity. This is, essentially, the postmodern, posthumanist condition, in which capitalism has made everything into an infinitely proliferating market, where everything is part of its identity, but nothing is an identity as such.

Mann, whose novels are both fictions and philosophical exercises, represents a heightened case of the incapacity of the subject to identify the other as anything other than expression of the self. His remarks on his discovery of Adorno are especially enlightening in this regard: "What could fit better into my world of the 'magic square'? I discovered in myself, or, rather, rediscovered as a long familiar element in myself, a mental alacrity for appropriating what I felt to be my own, what belonged to me, that is to say, to the 'subject.'" Here Mann updates Walt Whitman's child who goes forth each day and becomes whatever he observes. The subject makes the objective world an expression of itself. Then, after acknowledging that much of the musical dialogue, including Kretschmar's stuttering lecture on Beethoven's Piano Sonata opus 111, is taken verbatim from Adorno and his writings, Mann makes the following, curious, nonconfession:

> As for the—what word should I use?—serenity with which I put my
> version of them into the mouth of my stammerer, I have only this to say:
> after prolonged activity of the mind it frequently happens that things which
> we once upon a time threw upon the waters return to us recast by another's

hand and put into different relationships but still reminding us of what was once our own. Ideas about death and form, the self and the objective world, may well be regarded by the author of a Venetian novel of some thirty-five years ago as recollections of himself. They could well have their place in the younger man's musicological essay and at the same time serve me in my canvas of persons and an epoch. An idea as such will never possess much personal and proprietary value in the eyes of an artist. The thing that matters is the way it functions within the framework of his creation.[46]

As James Schmidt writes in his fine essay on the relationship among Adorno, Mann, and Schoenberg, Mann believed that there were a set of "mythic clichés," truths floating in the air, waiting to be organized and actualized by the artist. "Art mined life," Schmidt writes, "constructing a fictional world composed of these same mythic clichés but rearranged to suit the purpose of the artist."[47] Thus, the subtext of Mann's pseudo-confession is that Adorno's *Philosophy of New Music* was really Mann's all along, just waiting to be recoded by Mann for the purpose of his novel. Conversely, *Death in Venice* was merely the rough draft for Adorno's text, which in turn could now be refined and completed in *Doctor Faustus*.

Mann's compulsion to confess what he had taken from others is coupled with his attempts to obscure their contributions or to claim that, in Adorno's case, they were really his to begin with. Thus, in a letter to his daughter Erika, he writes:

> I'd really like to hear nothing more about the *Confessions* [the working title for *The Story of a Novel*], and let them lie for an indefinite time. But I suppose it won't be feasible and would also be unjust, since I have given Schoenberg so much credit in the postscript. But then, I have made too much of my indebtedness to Adorno. These matters can be abridged, eliminated, and generalized, I should think.[48]

It would be easy to attribute Mann's words to mere bad faith, were it not that *Faustus*, like the later *Die Betrogene*, is so self-consciously concerned with the inevitable bad faith of the task of writing. Zeitblom the narrator is often ill at ease with the project he has undertaken. Beethoven, the novel claims, may have written his compositions first in words and then in musical notation, but Zeitblom is no Beethoven. How is one truly to convey the magnitude of a musical piece in prose? How, for that matter, can the human being be captured in words? "How many writers before me," Zeitblom asks, "have bemoaned the inadequacy of language to arrive at the visualization or produce an exact portrait of an individual!"[49]

Hence, the modernist novel is indeed limited in the same ways as the comic book or the horoscope page—perhaps even more so, because while the comic book operates in a continuous present and the horoscope seeks to capture a fungible future, the novel tries to describe past, present, and future simultaneously, portraying not only characters but the history they move through. Zeitblom's problems are compounded by time, and he continually reminds the readers of the overlapping temporalities the novel hopes to reach. It is something of the genius of *Doctor Faustus* that the text foregrounds the way modernity provokes the collapse not only of subjectivity but also of temporality into one all-encompassing moment poised on the brink of an uncertain history. From the very outset of the novel, the past threatens to spill into the present in violent and unforeseen ways. In describing the town of his youth, Zeitblom remarks on the way certain figures, such as a witchlike old woman, seemed to be throwbacks to earlier periods in German history and yet, at the same time, predicted the future:

> Our time itself tends, secretly—or rather anything but secretly; indeed, quite consciously, with a strangely complacent consciousness, which makes one doubt the genuineness and simplicity of life itself and which may perhaps evoke an entirely false, unblest historicity—it tends, I say, to return to those earlier epochs; it enthusiastically re-enacts symbolic deeds of sinister significance, deeds that strike in the face of the spirit of the modern age, such, for instance, as the burning of the books and other things of which I prefer not to speak.[50]

The time of *Doctor Faustus*, the history described in the novel, is proceeding to a standstill where all epochs will be present simultaneously: The burning of witches, the torching of books, and the incineration of Jews will become one. This is the worst nightmare of postmodern consciousness, where everything is homologous, interchangeable, and hence equivalent.

If, as Adorno claims, the novel takes "as its own criterion the highest norms of bourgeois art, the individual and his psychology, thereby helping to reveal the objective structure of a life space which tries of its own accord to dissolve all objectivity into subjectivity,"[51] then Mann represents the reversal of that agenda. *Faustus* is nothing if not about the subject: the artistic genius and his retreat from the world. Here however, the subjective presentation, the heroic bourgeois, is only possible through an overwritten assemblage of preexisting objects and prefabricated temporalities. Georg Lukács, in his effort to claim Mann as an opponent to modernism, is forced to reimagine these conflicting temporalities as consistent with the regulated passage of history. "Both in reality and in the novel they form one unified time sequence," he writes.[52] Lukács, transparently eager to bully Mann into the Communist Party's anti-avant-garde aesthetics,[53] ignores what Mann calls the obviousness of his montage technique and insists that Mann is in fact a realist: "The great writer has his heart in the right place; he is sensitive to new impressions, but can always tell the difference between reality and appearance, between the objective character of the world and its distorted reflection."[54] Lukács then goes on to claim that even when time appears discontinuous in *Faustus,* Mann is ultimately confirming the coherence of history: "Thus Thomas Mann's apparent use of a modern 'multiple time' only reinforces (though in a complicated, roundabout way) the 'traditional' realist treatment of time as a social and historical unity."[55] I would suggest however, that here Lukács fundamentally misses the point and indulges in the brand of "extorted realism" Adorno identifies in his later writings.

Instead of restoring a continuous historical process, *Faustus* reveals an imploding history. With all epochs and temporalities simultaneously accessible, no time has a claim on independence or alterity, and there can therefore be no subjective temporal experience. Since every temporal moment in the novel is essentially equivalent, *Faustus* brings us to the brink of capital's fondest dream, a state in which all time can be actualized as productive time. This is the bad faith of literature revealed: Literature claims to offer an escape into timelessness and the private sphere of leisure but instead trains the reader to accept the homogeneity of time in public and private sphere alike.[56] Mann's novel combats this predicament through an act of subterfuge. It resembles the high bourgeois text with its romantic hero, but it dissolves back into an objective system devoid of affect, in which its protagonist is damned to know no love or human warmth at all. This is precisely the implication of Adorno's pronouncements on the failure both of the funnies and of art: Neither the comics nor art has the capacity to "negate the burden of labor." The funnies become marketing, and the modernist novel, with its formal rigor and difficulty, mirrors the working life.

Thus, the historical setting of the novel, with the bombs falling down around Zeitblom's Germany, is extraordinarily important. The future eats all and yet holds no promise of coming to fruition. *Faustus* is a book written in exile and sent into exile. Toward the end, Zeitblom despairs of finding a German publisher and imagines that his tale might appear in America. But he wonders whether his biography could ever find a satisfactory translator,

as if confirming the perpetual homelessness of his text whatever its des-
tination. The one hope for the future that Zeitblom holds out is the one
beyond death. But his plaint—"would that it were so!"—holds little promise, except perhaps the promise half-suggested in Zeitblom's own name
that hope will bear a flower (*Blume*) in time (*Zeit*). What merits Mann for-
giveness for his treatment of his borrowed texts is that *Faustus* allows for
itself the same promise Mann offers to Adorno, an uncertain redemption
in a time no one can tell. As Blanchot writes, "The book rolls up time,
unrolls time, and contains this unrolling as the continuity of a presence in
which present, past, and future become actual."[57] There is something of
this at work within the text of *Faustus* itself, but perhaps negatively so, for
Faustus describes the foreboding that there may well be no future to actu-
alize, at least not in Germany, or in the German language.

This potential for the artwork to perform an act of destruction is the sal-
vational element to which *Faustus* clings and to which Adorno made perhaps his most salient contribution. The climactic scenes of Mann's novel
include a description of Leverkühn's final work, "The Lamentation of Dr.
Faustus." After the death of his beloved nephew, Nepomuk/Echo, Leverkühn declares that with this, his final work, he is going to "take everything
back" that Beethoven's Ninth Symphony gave to the world, "the good and
the noble," joy, freedom, individuality, and subjective experience itself.
The cantata he composes is a cry of desolation, seeking to negate not only
all of music, but history itself. Only by keeping his bargain with the devil
and pursuing annihilation can Leverkühn's Faust neutralize the meaning-
lessness of the world. In the composition, and in the character of Leverkühn, "Faust rejects as temptation the thought of being saved: not only out
of formal loyalty to the pact and because it is 'too late,' but because with
his whole soul he despises the positivism of the world for which one would
save him, the lie of its godliness."[58] But in the final bars of the cantata,
where "the uttermost accents of mourning are reached, the final despair
achieves a voice," and the work pushes beyond that destruction, not into
positivism but into the determinate negation that would save some memory of subjective freedom, if only by virtue of its utterly cataclysmic fate.

For its uncanny articulation of the negative dialectical process, Zeitblom's description of the negation of Faust's negation is worth repeating at
length:

I will not say it, it would mean to disparage the uncompromising character
of the work, its irremediable anguish to say that it affords, down to its very

last note, any other consolation than what lies in voicing it, in simply
giving sorrow words; in the fact, that is, that a voice is given the creature
for its woe. No, this dark tone-poem permits up to the very end no
consolation, appeasement, transfiguration. But take our artist paradox:
grant that expressiveness—expression as lament—is the issue of the
whole construction: then may we not parallel with it another, a religious
one, and say too (though only in the lowest whisper) that out of the sheerly
irremediable hope might germinate? It would be but a hope beyond
hopelessness, the transcendence of despair—not betrayal to her, but the
miracle that passes belief.[59]

In Mann's original conception of the novel, Leverkühn was to have
only written fragments of the finished work. However, as both Mann and
Adorno relate, Adorno convinced Mann that Leverkühn should be allowed
to complete his *Lamentations*. Nevertheless, when Mann read to Adorno
an original draft of the sequence, the result was too firmly redemptive,
the resolution too neat, the formal issues too heavily in favor of subjective
transfiguration. Adorno's description sheds light on the problem, as well
as on the success of Mann's ultimate solution. "I found the heavily laden
passages too positive," Adorno explains, "too unbrokenly theological in
relation to the structure not only of the Lamentation of *Dr. Faustus* but
of the novel as a whole. They seemed to lack what the crucial passage required, the power of determinate negation as the only permissible figure of
the Other."[60]

This evocation of the other is important, for even if narratives are, like
Riesman's social subject, "other-directed," the other is precisely what literature gives lip service to but is unable to completely acknowledge.
Alterity is always reduced to a function of the self. Nonidentity is transformed into an identity. What the *Faustus* episode and Adorno's comments
on *Die Betrogene* reveal is the way literature offers—even in its debased
forms—a possible avenue of escape for the subject. But that escape is only
possible through an experience of exile. By consigning itself to its own
dissolution, the subject remains nonidentical through the process of its
liquidation. That which dies in the novel betokens rebirth.

Of *Die Betrogene* Adorno writes, "Bourgeois civilization has suppressed
the 'fiese' [disgusting] quality of death and either ennobled death or fenced
it off with hygiene. People do not want to take cognizance of the futility of
the false life; they do not want to endure the fact that something lowly and
vile is revealed in death, that death is an insult to the human being and
ought to be abolished rather than celebrated in the name of the tragic."[61]

To read beyond this statement somewhat, it is not simply that literature must acknowledge death but, rather, that it must admit to its complicity in the killing, to the way art takes the subjective and alive and renders it lifeless, dead, and mangled. *Faustus* ultimately rescues itself from the sterility of the romantic novel by killing off the romantic and redeems the violence of comic books and pulp fiction through its cataclysmic violence. The task of literature should be to preserve history and the memory of the heroic subject by cutting off all avenues to their existence. Mann's technique, whatever its taint of bourgeois consumerist ethics, survives as the best possible system of the novel as it shoots for the reanimation of life beyond that death.

This is a dangerous game, for, as we have seen in other texts from the exile period, literary *and* popular, as well as in Adorno's own American writings, there is a narrow line between a literary sublation—a destruction of the subject that preserves the subject—and a laying waste to history altogether. Thus, I would like to argue that *Doctor Faustus* is, in many respects, the book that most completely captures the precariousness of Adorno's exile experience. Not only does Mann, through his wholesale copying of Adorno's writings, threaten to devour Adorno whole and condemn him to perpetual homelessness, but so too does *Faustus,* through its formal technique, suggest that the only way out is by passing through that mutilating/mediating experience. What comes out on the other end of this exile may well be "damaged life," the place from which Adorno claimed his reflections in *Minima Moralia* came, but it is life nonetheless.

Thus, after the exile years end, it may be that we should recognize, in Adorno's long letter to Mann about the uneasy temporal and spatial anachronisms of *Die Betrogene*'s characters, some reflection about his own continued existence:

> If I am not mistaken, the figure of Ken has all the earmarks of an American from the late forties or the fifties and not from the decade following the First World War; naturally, you would know better than I. . . . The attempt to distance what is closest to hand is probably involved, to transpose it magically to a prehistoric world. . . . One would almost think that there is not a simple opposition between the permeation of the work with subjectivity and the demands of realism which in a certain sense resound through the whole of your *oeuvre*, such as our education and history would lead us to think—but that instead the greater the precision one maintains with the regard to the historical details, including those regarding types of human beings, the more likely one is to achieve spiritualization and attain

the world of the *imago*. . . . At the moment it seems to me as though this kind of precision can atone for some of the burden of sin under which every artistic fiction labors; it is as though that fiction could be healed of itself through exact imagination.[62]

The term "exact imagination," which appears a number of times in Adorno's work, is crucial here and is the subject of a book by Shierry Weber Nicholsen. Exact imagination, she writes, marks the "conjunction of knowledge, experience, and aesthetic form."[63] It is the way rigorous observation and the mimetic impulse on the part of the artist transcend themselves to become something imaginative, the way respect for the object transforms into freedom for the subject. In trying to do right by objects in a given historical situation, the artist finds the literary form best suited to expressing their condition. "The primacy of the object—the material at hand—produces, as it were, the need for configurational form."[64] For Nicholsen, exact imagination is the positive spin on Mann's montage. In *Die Betrogene*, the various historical elements are held in tension with each other until their incommensurability becomes untenable. The atonement of fiction's sins, Adorno would have it, takes place through this acknowledgment—not through the knowing and showy irony of postmodern texts but through the humble awareness of the text's inadequacy to historical and social reality.

In *Faustus* Mann solves the problem of "untimeliness" in part by heightening the tension between the fictional world and the "truth" exiled in the space of the book.[65] This is, essentially, what J. M. Bernstein argues in a far more sophisticated and theoretically nuanced account of *Doctor Faustus* than I am providing here. He claims, ultimately, that the novel, through its formal acrobatics, effectively jump-starts history by bringing its narrative elements to the brink of their obliteration:

> Mann, in a work of sustained duration, was able to overcome "the negation of narrative in German history" through and by means of a humane narrative. He can remain within narrative and offer us a fiction, with all of fiction's traditional play and pretence, only by realizing within the text both its fictionality and its essential interpretative function. *Doctor Faustus* is both an interpretation of history and self-consciously an interpretation *in history*. Writing is revealed as a moral act, authoritative where one least expects it: in its interpretative function rather than in its mimetic function.[66]

Thus, the most brazen act of imagination is performed not by Leverkühn, who is content to explore the permutations of his own technique, but by the narrator Zeitblom, who, faced with the limits of his perception, invents crucial scenes. To excuse himself, he writes that because he has been so faithful to the historical events at all other times, he is entitled to bend the rules when it suits him. "I know, let the objection be raised that I could not know it because I was not there. No, I was not there, but today it is a psychological fact that I was there, for whoever has lived a story like this, lived it through, as I have lived this one, that frightful intimacy makes him an eye- and ear-witness even to its hidden phases."[67]

But once the rule of strict fidelity to the facts has been broken, Zeitblom gives himself leave to do the same thing again in the very next chapter. But this time, the righteous entitlement of the bourgeoisie—I have worked for it, I have earned it—slips over into the monomania of the dictator who can impose his will unfettered and create his own history: "Does anyone doubt," he asks, "that I could tell what happened between Rudolf and Marie Godeau, just as I knew the whole course of the dialogue between him and Adrian in Pfeiffering? Does anyone doubt that I was 'there'? I think not. But I also think that a precise account is no longer useful or desirable."[68] Hence Zeitblom illustrates the razor-thin edge of the morality of writing, so sure of his authority and command of raw materials that he takes upon himself their manipulation and ultimately their destruction in hopes of their eventual resurrection. This is the moral gamble Mann takes in his "higher copying," and Bernstein's nod toward the ethical dimension of writing is in keeping with the rigors of the "exact imagination" on which Adorno congratulates Mann as well as with Adorno's assessment of "morality and style" in *Minima Moralia*. In that aphorism, Adorno again makes the case that the ethical dimension of writing shares affinities with the lot of the exile: "Rigorous formulation demands unequivocal comprehension, conceptual effort, to which people are deliberately disencouraged, and imposes on them in advance of any content a suspension of all received opinions, and thus an isolation, that they violently resist."[69] The writer, therefore, in choosing to do right by his material, becomes something of a resistance fighter, battling against the material's capitulation to the reifying logic of commerce and facile communicability. In the sentences that follow, Adorno then proclaims what could be both the summation of his exile dealings with the representatives of the culture industry and the rallying cry for the word in its struggle on behalf of the individual: "Only what they do not first need to understand, they consider understandable; only the word coined by commerce, and already alienated, touches them as familiar. Few things contribute so much to the demoralization of intellectuals.

Those who would escape it must recognize the advocates of communicability as traitors to what they communicate."[70]

Adorno's willingness to cede himself to Mann, to impose exile on his words, to put them in the mouth of the devil, reflects a trust that Mann will behave ethically toward the material. But for Adorno, the morality of the gesture lies in willingly choosing exile within the text of *Faustus*, without hope of reward, and where the journey out finds no certain homecoming. The journey undertaken without guaranteed return is a fundamentally ethical gesture, for it requires the subject to look forward to a posterity in which the self is no longer present. The work—and I would suggest that this is true of the "work" Mann takes from Adorno even more than of the work that bears Adorno's name—offers the potential for the subject's actualization in its absence. Thus, as Adorno suggests in his letter to Mann, it is only by facing up to the violence of death, by facing liquidation and dissolution, that the subject is able to withstand its negation, to remain nonidentical within administered existence.

Adorno's capitulation to reification and the reification of subjects generally is the history that can be read in the book and that offers us a reason to still read the novel, to still read Adorno, to still read. It is a paradoxical and dangerous time for the word. Pundits and pedants insist that we have lost the capacity to read and write, and yet most of our information comes from a rapid-fire engagement with written text via the Internet, scrolling tickers, and CNN updates. The art of written correspondence is said to have been superseded by mass communications, but more people write e-mail as part of their daily activity than ever wrote letters. Our world is in an increasingly textual one, but those texts are heavily regulated and administered, commercialized and sanitized. Adorno reminds us that we should be alert to what texts contain, no matter how facile they seem or how quickly they scroll by. Since the negation of the texts' subjects is contained in the work, the only ethical response we have to history is to rescue those exiles who have consigned themselves to the work. Only by rediscovering what has been killed by the book, the magazine, or the comic strip, by rediscovering the way they go about their murderous work, can we also discover the life they breathe.

In *Faustus*, one of Leverkühn's last, great works is the *Apocalypse of John the Divine*, based on the sixteen Albrecht Dürer engravings from the book of Revelation. Of central importance to the composition is the image of "Saint John Commanded to Swallow the Book." The idea that a book could be sweet yet bitter in the belly is particularly appropriate to Mann's late work, which looks natural but reveals itself to be synthetic. But Adorno, both Adorno the writer and the Adorno who appears within the pages of *Faustus*, engenders a somewhat different type of indigestion. Adorno's works ask that we consume them, but then they disgorge themselves in gristly aphorisms and unpalatable negations, irreducible and not easily digestible. Adorno always cautioned against a gustatory approach to artworks, and the challenge readers face today is not to swallow texts whole but to let the inassimilable remain undigested.

But in feeling ill or ill at ease, we should also recognize the generosity of the other whose history remains in the text. If Blanchot wants us to remember "the civilization of the book," the memory it transmits to us and the structures to which those memories adhere, Mann's *Faustus* transmits Adorno's exile experience to us, as do Adorno's own works. He does not come to us undamaged, or unaltered. He gives himself over to objectification, so that therein we may read which structures he shared with us and which are our own. What Adorno offers us is himself as exile in the text, perpetually but not permanently. It is each successive generation's job to return his generosity and give him a home.

CODA: THEODOR ADORNO, AMERICAN

In 1938, an alien from a Jewish background landed in America. His name having been changed, and with his origins thus somewhat obscured, he nevertheless had talents that set him apart from others and marked him as exceptional, different. Still, as he went about his daily business in thick spectacles, many of his colleagues mistook his physical myopia for a deeper spiritual and intellectual one, and many more dismissed him as uptight and something of a wet blanket. When he did exercise his prodigious gifts, his actions tended to frighten his peers and did little to endear him to the authorities. As a result, these same government authorities initiated investigations into his activities and his whereabouts, and although they ultimately concluded he posed no threat to this country, a certain measure of suspicion continued to follow him. Initially, at least, his efforts on behalf of his new home seemed haughty and perhaps even a little cruel. But even those who thought they knew him would have been surprised by how committed he was to America and the concepts of justice and truth. Despite the misgivings of others, at heart, the alien was an ardent defender of his adoptive country and the democratic ideals it represented.

As this book hurtles toward its close, I hope that readers will recognize this as the story of Theodor Adorno and his years in America. It is also, of course, the tale of another famous alien who also first appeared in the

United States in 1938: Kal-El of Krypton—Clark Kent—Superman. Created by young Jewish illustrators from Cleveland, Jerry Siegel and Joe Shuster, Superman took his comic-book bow in June, four months after Adorno landed in New York. Almost from his inception, critics have noted that Superman embodies much of the 1930s immigrant and exile experience in America: the flight from cataclysmic destruction, the awkward efforts to assimilate, the identity obscured by a changed name, and the xenophobia of suspicious native-born citizens. And we should remember that in his early years, before he was "anglicized" and began socking caricatured Hitlers and Tojos, Superman was a far more problematic character than the paragon of white, middle-class, manly virtue that he would become. While Clark Kent still represents the superannuated stereotype of the ineffectual intellectual wimp (complete with glasses), in the early stories (beginning with Action Comics number 1), Superman is all but a vigilante, battling police officers, sadistically twisting a woman's arm to gain information, and terrorizing his unnamed state's governor in the middle of the night to secure a last-second pardon for a wrongfully convicted man. In certain panels, Superman even tends to look vaguely Semitic, partly because he has dark hair and a pronounced brow, but also because the forward momentum of his muscled torso often gives him the hunched posture of the Old World peddler. In these early issues, Superman does not so much represent the ideal of heroic patriotism as he does the dark threat of immigrant strength, the possibility that the exile would overwhelm the country.

There is a poignant resonance between the exile experience of the German scholar Adorno and the serialized life of the Man of Steel, a poignance that becomes more pronounced when one considers that, despite the fact that both Superman and Adorno were committed to the notions of "truth, justice, and the American way," Americans ultimately embraced the superhero as a populist icon, while Adorno has been dogged for years by charges of elitism and anti-Americanism. Hence, the fears that initially attached themselves to Superman followed Adorno through his American years—and beyond. Initially, Siegel's and Shuster's conception of Superman was much more threatening. They portrayed the character as an evil genius, using his advanced powers to take over the Earth, and it seems that at times the U.S. government suspected Adorno and his colleagues of exactly the same grandiose ambitions. In fact, one of the FBI's informants, an associate professor of medicine at UCLA, expressed concerns that Institute members, including Adorno, were hatching a vast conspiracy, a belief the informant held solely on the basis of the Institute's air of intellectual superiority. As the special agent on the case writes of his information regarding the Frankfurt School:

> [Informant] reported that he believes that all of these individuals are extremely close in their work and their views and that they think alike and stand for the same concepts. [Informant] reported that he expects that any one or all of these men might, like Klaus Fuchs, the recently convicted scientist, regard themselves as so intellectually ahead of everyone else that they might take it upon themselves to decide what is best for the world.[1]

Obviously, that this suspicion was even entertained, and that the members of the Institute might be compared to Fuchs, the German-born British physicist who passed Manhattan Project secrets to the Soviets, reflects the paranoia of the then-newborn Cold War. Nevertheless, it is well worth noting the way the language of the FBI report mirrors that of the Rockefeller Foundation memo I cite in chapter 1, in which Louis Wirth issued "warnings . . . about Horkheimer, Adorno & Company" and their use of "UN, UNESCO, the German Government, American occupying forces, foundations, and everybody else" in order to stake out a claim as the final word on the social sciences in Germany.[2] Despite the fact that in the years following the exile the influence of the Frankfurt School in and on America has generally been minimized, it is clear that, in official circles at least, people took Adorno and his colleagues very seriously. Further, these suspicions the government harbored about the Frankfurt School were, if indeed without merit, not completely without reason. We should remember that while Adorno and his colleagues were in the United States, they were, because of their German refugee status, classed as wartime "enemy aliens" by virtue of a number of congressional acts and presidential decrees, including the Alien Enemies Act of 1918, and President Roosevelt's Proclamation 2526 of December 8, 1941 (the day after the attacks on Pearl Harbor), which specifically designated German-born residents of the United States as "alien enemies" and which stated, in part:

> All alien enemies are enjoined to preserve the peace toward the United States and to refrain from crime against public safety, and from violating the laws of the United States and of the States and Territories thereof; and to refrain from actual hostility or giving information, aid or comfort to the enemies of the United States or interfering by word or deed with the defense of the United States or political processes and public opinions thereof; and to comply strictly with the regulations which are hereby or which may be from time to time promulgated by the President.[3]

Read broadly, the various enemy alien acts and decrees had wide-ranging implications for the Frankfurt School members, who, even after their expedited citizenship, faced constant surveillance, were required to register and update their whereabouts, and, under the technical provisions of the law, were essentially barred from being critical of America "by word or deed." And while German-born citizens were rarely dealt with as shabbily as Japanese Americans, the laws that governed both groups—and that legitimated the forced internment of thousands of Japanese—were essentially the same. Further, the government had a vested interest in the continuing loyalty of the Frankfurt School because a number of its members were working on sensitive government research projects. Marcuse and Neumann were working for the OSS, and Lowenthal was the research director for Voice of America. Indeed, perhaps as many of the documents in Adorno's FBI files concern the tabs being kept on the essentially loyal Marcuse and Lowenthal as concern Adorno's contacts with the potentially "subversive" Hanns Eisler.

To say, therefore, that the U.S. government unambivalently regarded the Institute as a threat would be to wildly misstate the nature of the government's response to Adorno and company, suspicious though the FBI and other state agencies were. As Andrew Rubin richly details in his essay "The Adorno Files," and as I indicated in the introduction, Adorno and the Frankfurt School were more or less continuously under surveillance by the FBI during their stay in the United States.[4] Adorno shows up on the Censorship Daily Reports (CDR), the list of people whom the FBI was watching, at least as early as July 22, 1942, when the FBI decided to monitor all the associates of the Institute of Social Research. Citing the Institute's history and the substance of its writings, the CDR notes that "in view of the subject's general background, it is felt that cable traffic should be watched."[5] But the portrait painted by the documents gleaned during the course of Adorno's surveillance may come as a shock to Adorno's supporters, not because the government discovered Adorno engaged in clandestine and illicit activities but rather because Adorno emerges as someone who, despite his reservations about his exile home, deeply and genuinely loved America.

Perhaps it will be equally surprising, and certainly saddening, to note that some of the information the FBI had regarding Adorno was supplied courtesy of an informant within the Institute of Social Research itself. In January 1951, the FBI logged a statement concerning the Institute and many of its members by a figure—I won't speculate as to his or her identity—who, according to the affidavit, joined the Institute at Columbia in

1942 and worked with the Institute for many years. After a lengthy general statement, the informant provides a detailed summary of each of the Institute's members. The informant's assessment of Adorno, I believe, captures the essence of Adorno's paradoxical position within the United States. "He surpasses Horkheimer in egocentrism, is extremely tense, vain, and so over-intellectualized that it is very hard to be relaxed in his presence," the informant writes, confirming the standard picture of the intellectual who knows better than everyone what is best. But regarding Adorno's political affiliations, the informant has this to say:

> To the best of my knowledge, Adorno never was politically active and during the years I have known him he was very clear in his appraisal of Communism, and was interested in analyzing similarities of the National Socialist and Soviet systems with regard to the treatment of the individual.
> The impression and the factual knowledge I have of Adorno with regard to his loyalty may be summed up as follows:
> As far as I know, he was neither in Europe nor in the United States politically active within the Communist Party or any of its affiliates. I have never heard of him being connected with any front organization in this country. I have no reason to believe that he is not loyal to this country, and I know that he cherishes his American citizenship.[6]

For those readers of Adorno who still hope to find some concrete evidence of radical political practice, his FBI and State Department files are not the places to look. Instead, time and again, the same refrain is sounded: Adorno may have been prickly and even dilettantish, but he did, in fact, deeply care about America and appreciated the promise it represented for the development of a living democracy. Indeed, what evolves over the course of the official documentation of Adorno's life in the United States is the idea that it is precisely his exacting intellectual character that separates him from the chumminess of America while at the same time marking him as potentially useful for the U.S. government's reconstruction of Germany. Thus, in 1953, when his tenure in America was more or less at an end, Adorno fought to keep the privileges associated with the U.S. citizenship conferred on him in 1943. Thus, along with Horkheimer and a number of officials associated with the High Commission for Germany (HICOG), the organization responsible, in large part, for reconstructing Germany after World War II, Adorno sought to keep his U.S. passport while he worked at the Johann Wolfgang Goethe–Universität in Frankfurt. The language of these documents and testimonials is in keeping with the image of Adorno as a dedicated defender of democracy. Thus, Horkheimer's statement on Adorno's behalf argues that "Dr. Adorno's expert knowledge and his vast experience both in the United States and in Germany are invaluable for the Institute's development and the furtherance of the aims pursued by U.S. cultural policies in Germany."[7] At roughly the same time, Shepard Stone, the influential director of public affairs at HICOG, wrote a personal note to the State Department also claiming that Adorno's passport should be extended because he was helping spread freedom in the wake of the European war: "The Institute of Frankfurt is helping to train German leaders who will know something of democratic techniques. I believe it is important for our over-all democratic objectives in Germany that such men as Professor Adorno have an opportunity to work in that country."[8]

As for Adorno himself, he doesn't shy from waving his own patriotic flag in this instance, not to mention touting his intellectual credentials. In his affidavit, he writes:

> The Institute of Social Research at Frankfort [sic] University was founded with the support of HICOG and largely supported by American means. It is the aim of this Institution to develop an integration of American and German research methods and to help in the education of German students in the spirit of American democracy. Having been connected with this Institution for a long time and being equally well acquainted with German and American Social Sciences, I am considered as particularly well qualified for performing this task. I regard it as my patriotic duty to take up once again my work with this institution.[9]

The spelling mistakes and the curious gloss on the Institute's history—intimating that it was essentially an American-financed arm of HICOG instead of predating the American exile—suggest not only that the statement was typed by someone other than Adorno but also that we should take its sentiments with a very large grain of salt. After all, we would be wise to recognize that not everyone tells the whole truth when speaking to government functionaries. Still, the consistency with which these documents attest to Adorno's patriotism and democratic feelings are noteworthy and perhaps should not be lightly dismissed. If indeed Adorno did feel the sentiments about America that the government documents record, it would certainly be a strange irony, but one I believe in keeping with Adorno's overall dialectical trajectory. Whereas Adorno was certainly Teutonic in his opposition to the American culture industry, in order to be at his most American, he had to return to Germany. In the "Scientific Experiences" piece, which was initially broadcast over the radio, Adorno reflects on how

America forced him to stand outside culture, to criticize it as though he was both a part of it and apart from it. This experience was liberating, but even more so, he claims, was that promise of freedom that America offered its subjects, a promise whose materiality and human qualities he praises in a charming and arresting note of affection:

> More important and more gratifying was my experience of the substantiality of democratic forms: that in America they have seeped into life itself, whereas at least in Germany they were, and I fear still are, nothing more than formal rules of the game. Over there I became acquainted with a potential for real humanitarianism that is hardly to be found in old Europe. The political form of democracy is infinitely closer to the people. American everyday life, despite the oft lamented hustle and bustle, has an inherent element of peaceableness, good naturedness and generosity, in sharpest contrast to the pent-up malice and envy that exploded in Germany between 1933 and 1945. Surely America is no longer the land of unlimited possibilities, but one still has the feeling that anything could be possible.[10]

It is a breathtaking passage, modulating peace and malice, hope for the future and nostalgia for a past that might be foreclosed, and so much of what is conveyed in the official language of Adorno's government files finds poetic confirmation here. Democracy has a substance; it seeps into the life of its subjects, but as such it also has a weight; it must be borne, and the heartbreaking final line of the passage hints that although increasingly Americans might be shirking that load, it is not too late to bear it once again.

As I have demonstrated, Adorno's ongoing engagement with the material practices and cultural institutions of America make the case that his commitment to his exile home was deeper and more complicated than the bureaucratic necessity and official convenience that the conferral of wartime citizenship implies. Although many defenders of Adorno have worked to minimize the impression, the reputation Adorno has always had is of the barbed intellectual who held America at arm's length. Even among the members of the Left who might embrace Adorno as a model of intellectual—if not political—resistance, that misperception persists. To take just one example, Mark Greif, in an *American Prospect* essay on the current state of critical theory, claims that one of the challenges confronting theory in America has always been that European theorists "like Sartre and Theodor Adorno, had been anti-American, both temperamentally and politically."[11]

But Greif's claims of Adorno's anti-Americanism and others like them hardly seem fair or even particularly well motivated, and what I have tried to do in this book is demonstrate that, contrary to the widely held belief that Adorno criticized American cultural practices from afar, he was in fact deeply enmeshed in those practices—he really did know the American radio industry; he knew the television industry; he knew Hollywood. And he was also hardly the first or most vitriolic of European critics of America. Indeed, as Simon Schama has written in a series of articles, the trope of the European in America, passing (perhaps deserved) judgment on our perceived vulgarity and arrogance, has a long if not entirely noble tradition. "By the end of the nineteenth century," he writes, "the stereotype of the ugly American—voracious, preachy, mercenary, and bombastically chauvinist—was firmly in place in Europe. Even the claim that the United States was built on a foundation stone of liberty was seen as a fraud."[12]

As Schama relates, the trend would really get under way with Frances Trollope, who in 1832 published *Domestic Manners of the Americans,* in which she lamented Americans' stubbornness, recalcitrance, anti-intellectualism, and rabid patriotism. "If the citizens of the United States were indeed the devoted patriots they call themselves," she wrote, "they would surely not thus encrust themselves in the hard, dry, stubborn persuasion, that they are the first and best of the human race, that nothing is to be learnt, but what they are able to teach, and that nothing is worth having, which they do not possess."[13] Trollope was scarcely the last to voice such sentiments. Perhaps the most famous European visitor to take a crack at America was Charles Dickens, who in both *American Notes for General Circulation* (1843) and *The Life and Adventures of Martin Chuzzlewit* (1844) lambastes an America he found coarse, greedy, and rife with the contradictions of slavery. On describing eating habits onboard a steamboat in *American Notes,* he complains, "There is no conversation, no laughter, no cheerfulness, no sociality, except in spitting; and that is done in silent fellowship round the stove, when the meal is over."[14] However, in *Martin Chuzzlewit,* while still maintaining an overall impression of dismay, Dickens includes the following exchange between his two main characters as they travel by a steamboat, an exchange that resonates with Adorno's hopeful ambivalence:

"Why, Cook! what are you thinking of so steadily?" said Martin.
    "Why, I was a-thinking, sir," returned Mark, "that if I was a painter and was called upon to paint the American Eagle, how should I do it?"

"Paint it as like an Eagle as you could, I suppose."

"No," said Mark. "That wouldn't do for me, sir. I should want to draw it like a Bat, for its short-sightedness; like a Bantam, for its bragging; like a Magpie, for its honesty; like a Peacock, for its vanity; like an Ostrich, for its putting its head in the mud, and thinking nobody sees it—"

"And like a Phoenix, for its power of springing from the ashes of its faults and vices, and soaring up anew into the sky!" said Martin. "Well, Mark. Let us hope so."[15]

Trollope and Dickens were by no means anomalous in their criticism of America, and Schama by no means milks all the venom European visitors have had for the United States. Even among Adorno's contemporaries, many of whom owed their life to the extension of the safe haven America offered, the criticism ranged from the constructive to the extreme. In an essay for *Life* magazine from 1949, Evelyn Waugh uncannily—and most probably unknowingly—parses Adorno's 1945 predictions in "What National Socialism Has Done to the Arts" to explain Europe's trepidation about the increasing power of America on the world stage. Just as Adorno feared that the rest of the world would inevitably adopt American aesthetic practices and that "the arts . . . as far as they have contact with the broad masses, above all moving pictures, radio, and popular literature, will indulge in a kind of streamlining in order to please the customer, a sort of pseudo-Americanization,"[16] Waugh too diagnosed a growing trepidation about American cultural hegemony. Compare to Adorno, therefore, Waugh: "The peoples of other continents look to America half in hope and half in alarm. They see that their own future is inextricably involved with it and their judgment is based on what they see in the cinema, what they read in the popular magazines, what they hear from the loudest advertiser. Gratitude for the enormous material benefits received is tempered with distaste for what they believe is the spiritual poverty of the benefactor."[17]

Even Schoenberg, one of Adorno's musical heroes, who initially felt that he was "driven into paradise" when he was exiled to Southern California, would eventually carp, "You complain of lack of culture in this amusement-arcade world, I wonder what you would say to the world in which I nearly die of disgust."[18] Hence, charges of Adorno's anti-Americanism strike me as unjust and as acutely unaware of the massive din of criticism shouted at America almost from its origins. This dismissal of Adorno has as little to do with his actual feelings about culture as it does with his uncompromising intellectual rigor and dedication to theory. After all, Adorno was hardly even the first to castigate the American tendency to forgo theoretical or abstract thinking in favor of a more pragmatic, stolid mode of thought. That honor goes, not surprisingly, to Alexis de Tocqueville, who noted this as a defining characteristic of the American mind in *Democracy in America*, where he writes (in a chapter entitled "Why the Americans Are More Addicted to a Practical Than a Theoretical Science"):

> In America the purely practical part of science is admirably understood, and careful attention is paid to the theoretical portion which is immediately requisite to application. On this head the Americans always display a clear, free, original, and inventive power of mind. But hardly anyone in the United States devotes himself to the essentially theoretical and abstract portion of human knowledge. In this respect the Americans carry to excess a tendency that is, I think, discernible, though in a less degree, among all democratic nations.[19]

Compared to this history, therefore, Adorno's critique of America is certainly benevolent and measured, if not at times downright loving. If I am allowed then, at this point, the hazarding of a modest proposal, I would suggest that what makes Adorno so threatening and difficult, even to those who profess to agree with his intellectual project, is that his criticisms of America are inseparable from his genuine *love* for it. It is easy, if one were inclined to blindly defend America and American exceptionalism, to dismiss Adorno simply as an anti-American elitist. But it is equally easy—and perhaps more tragic—for those who would defend Adorno to defend him solely as scornful of his exile home. This assumption that the strength of his critique lies in its pure negativity, misses, I think, the complexity and depth of Adorno's relationship with America.

I should be clear: By stating that Adorno was, in some of his sensitivities and at a certain legal level, American, I do not want to suggest that he was not also thoroughly and completely German and European. After all, Adorno himself raised strong objections to the notion that he might have "adjusted" completely to the American scene. "I have never denied," he claims in "Scientific Experiences of a European Scholar in America," "that I considered myself a European from the first to the last. That I would maintain this intellectual continuity seemed self-evident to me as I fully realized quickly enough in America."[20] Adorno's European credentials are hardly in doubt, but such an unalloyed assertion of *identity* by Adorno should not go uninterrogated. This, after all, is the theorist who most forcefully insists on the nearly sacred powers of negation and nonidentity with prevailing social conditions. Much of what makes Adorno "Adorno" is this insistence on nonidentity, the notion that one could mediate between conceptual poles and span the space between, thereby resisting being pinned down in any one camp or other, and his response to America is characterized by seemingly irreconcilable contradictions that he nonetheless manages to bridge. For Adorno, empirical social science research is antidemocratic, but at the same time he feels that, methodologically reformulated, it could help us intellectually defend against totalitarianism. The radio voice is authoritarian, and yet its "physiognomy" could be reanimated to give humanity back its voice. Every visit to the movies left Adorno "stupider and worse," and yet he tried to make a movie. Literature told a lie about the interior life of the bourgeois subject, but literature could be made to tell the truth about the subject's violent death, and out of that carnage, a memory of life could again arise. One of the frustrations faced by students, both those new to Adorno and those reading him for the 101st time, is that he is so contradictory. But this quicksilver inability to firmly occupy a single position is what makes Adorno so exciting, and what makes him potentially useful to contemporary readers. The insider FBI informant at the Institute testified that "he is a philosopher but belongs to those ingenious scholars who are pretty much at home in a good many fields." And as if to drive home the bicontinental nature of Adorno's interests, the informant concluded that he was "quite familiar with European and American history" alike. As such, instead of thinking of Adorno as anti-American, we might instead consider how Adorno offers those of us who might still naively believe in the democratic promise of this country a model for how to be engaged citizens.

In a recent issue of *Telos*, Michael Werz agitates for the power of ambivalence as part of an engaged response to political conditions in the United States, but in so doing, he singles out Adorno as a practitioner of a bad politics of negative critique, "for," he says, "ambivalence toward the US is interwoven with justified criticism, and is not identical with the paranoid worldview that Theodor Adorno and Max Horkheimer characterized as the 'dark side of knowing and perception.'"[21] While I agree with Werz's overall assessment, it seems to me that, given Adorno's intimate knowledge of American cultural practices, not only was he more than "justified" in his criticisms of America, but he was also, I would strongly argue, the very embodiment of that ambivalence that Werz claims should be interwoven with those criticisms. For Adorno, the essence of freedom is the ability to maintain ambivalence despite all the pressures to shackle oneself to a side. Hence, perhaps the most assertive passage of *Minima Moralia* insists on the abandonment of all assertions. "Freedom," he claims, "would be not to choose between black and white but to abjure such prescribed choices."[22] Adorno's response to America, his intermingled love and critique, his horror and his attraction, should be understood in terms of this embrace of ambivalence. And the freedom he claims for ambivalence is a freedom we ourselves might well celebrate. Now, perhaps even more than when he was an American citizen, Americans need Adorno and the type of freedom he espoused.

Adorno was born on September 11, 1903. It is of course only a biographical accident that he shares a birthday with the 9/11 attacks. Nonetheless, in the political aftermath of our September 11, it is my belief that by embracing Adorno and his complicated relationship to the United States, Americans stand the best hope of defending the "substantive democracy" Adorno himself so cherished. After all, we are faced with a moment, when, much as in Adorno's time, the U.S. government seems willing, even eager, to deny citizens their democratic rights and—very literally—their freedom, under the pretense of national defense. The USA Patriot Act has, for all intents and purposes, expanded the "alien enemies" acts and decrees. Since we are at war, not with a nation but with "terrorism," virtually any foreign national can be indefinitely detained for no verifiable reason other than that the Justice Department determines that the alien vaguely and broadly "is engaged in any other activity that endangers the national security of the United States."[23] Xenophobia is on the rise. Further, and perhaps more frighteningly, as Adorno himself experienced, we once again find ourselves at a moment when our law enforcement officials are subjecting citizens, even law-abiding ones, to increasing levels of surveillance. Not only are foreign nationals subject, under provisions of the Patriot Act, to an increased possibility of secret wire-tapping, but so too are American citizens. As David Cole writes in his book about the winnowing of constitutional rights in the wake of 9/11:

> The PATRIOT Act's most controversial intelligence-gathering amendment potentially affects citizens and foreign nationals alike. . . . It authorizes secret searches and wiretaps in criminal investigations without probable cause to believe that the target is engaged in criminal conduct or that evidence of a crime will be found. The constitutional protection of privacy found in the Fourth Amendment generally forbids searches or wiretaps unless the government has probable cause. In addition, federal law generally requires notification of the targets of searches and wiretaps, either before or after the search or tap. The PATRIOT Act allows the

government to evade these requirements in criminal investigations wherever it also has a significant "foreign intelligence" purpose.[24]

Thus, the America in which Adorno lived bears a certain queasy resemblance to our own, and as we have discovered in the fallout of 9/11, the FBI is all too willing to label legal organizations who deign to protest against U.S. policies as "radical" or "subversive," thereby justifying the unfettered collection of thousands of pages of documents about civil rights organizations and such antiwar organizations as Greenpeace and the American Civil Liberties Union.[25]

At an official level, ambivalence, and the freedom to choose that comes with it, is in preciously short supply. Famously, during his speech to Congress immediately following the 9/11 attacks, President George W. Bush announced, "Every nation, in every region, now has a decision to make. Either you are with us, or you are with the terrorists." Further, shortly after September 11, Defense Secretary Donald Rumsfeld claimed, "We have two choices, either to change the way we live, which is unacceptable, or change the way they live." While it is now a cliché to argue that the president's policies display an implacable moral certainty, one that precludes moral ambiguity and betokens a Manichaean view of good and evil in keeping with the president's evangelicalism, it is nevertheless worth noting that in real political terms, the current administration refuses to recognize ambivalence either as an ethical position or as a state policy and metes out serious consequences for a refusal to take sides.

This difficulty, in today's political climate, to "abjure such prescribed choices" returns us to Adorno. Beyond his tendentious embrace of America, and beyond the fact that he was subject to a level of state surveillance similar to what we see today, it is Adorno's ambivalence, an ambivalence that gestures toward freedom, that stands as his great contribution to America. To compare Adorno to Superman, as I did at the outset of this coda, may have seemed childish. But in his own way, Adorno was a heroic figure; one we might do well to emulate. Today, for any of us trying to hold on to the awesome burden of subjective freedom and substantive democracy he defended in his time, Adorno can help us bear the weight.

NOTES

Introduction

1. Jay, "Adorno in America," 120.

2. Horkheimer, "Telegram to Friedrich Pollock," April 19, 1941, Federal Bureau of Investigation, file 61-7421-5.

3. For example, Juliane Favez was the Institute of Social Research's secretary in Geneva, where, after 1933, the Institute had initially reconstituted to escape the economic and political privations of the Nazi regime.

4. J. Edgar Hoover to Special Agent in Charge, El Paso, Texas, July 18, 1941, Federal Bureau of Investigation, file 61-7421-4.

5. See chapter 3 for a description of Walter Winchell's "information" regarding Institute members.

6. The pervasiveness of the FBI surveillance of exiles has been well documented by Alexander Stephan in *Communazis*.

7. These dates might cause some confusion. Although Adorno did return to Frankfurt for extended stays and teaching duties from 1949 to 1951, he returned, albeit reluctantly, to California in 1952–1953 to serve as research director for an institute run by the psychologist William F. Hacker. In that capacity, he performed the studies on television that resulted in "How to Look at Television" and the study of the *Los Angeles Times* astrology column, published as "The Stars Down to Earth." After 1953, however, he never returned to the United States. Given that finality and the importance of these two studies to Adorno's overall conception of

the "culture industry," I have made 1953 the terminal date in Adorno's American sojourn.

8. His birth date was September 11, 1903, a fact I learned on September 11, 2002, the one-year anniversary of the World Trade Center and Pentagon attacks, while I was visiting the Institut für Sozialforschung in Frankfurt. While sirens were blaring to test the readiness of the American consulate's security systems, the Institute's delightful secretary informed me of this strange coincidence with a mixture of bemusement and sadness that Adorno's birth date should be linked with a day now so infamous.

9. I should also acknowledge that, at that time in musicology, the pioneering work of Rose Subotnik was instrumental in bringing Adorno to American readers.

10. On the last of these, see Apostolidis, *Stations of the Cross*, as well as my review of that book, "Stations of the Cross: Adorno and Christian Right Radio."

11. Adorno received his expedited citizenship on November 26, 1943. He was renaturalized as a citizen of the Federal Republic of Germany, after protracted wrangling about his U.S. visa and passport status, on October 26, 1954.

12. He did, however, at times, write in English, and these texts are often looser and more mordantly funny than his German writings.

13. Shils, "Daydreams and Nightmares," 600.

14. Adorno, "Scientific Experiences of a European Scholar in America," 241.

15. Jay, *Adorno*, 16–17.

16. Adorno, "Commitment," 80.

17. MacRae, "Frankfurters," 786.

18. Jameson, *Marxism and Form*, xiii.

19. In subsequent chapters I discuss Agamben's relationship with Adorno's work and the uneasy alliance they form.

20. In addition to Apostolidis's work on Christian right radio, see also Witkin, *Adorno on Popular Culture.*

21. See chapter 2 for a fuller explanation of this concept.

22. While I was writing this book, it came to my attention that similar work on Adorno's "American experience" has been attempted, in a far more "German" context, in one of the new biographies of Adorno, that written by Detlev Claussen, *Theodor W. Adorno.*

23. Adorno and Horkheimer were rigorous in their use of the phrase "culture industry," preferring it to the terms "mass culture" or "popular culture" because they did not want to convey the impression that the products of the entertainment conglomerates were in any way expressions of the popular will. I must confess that I have not been so rigorous and have used these terms interchangeably. In part, however, this decision derives from what I perceive as a certain inelegance in using mouthfuls like "culture-industrial" and "cultural-industrial" as modifiers for nouns like "texts," "products," "broadcasts," and so on.

24. Fearing, *The Big Clock*, 27.

25. Quoted in Jay, "The Frankfurt School in Exile," 41.

26. Adorno, untitled list, November 1, 1939, Max Horkheimer-Archiv, VI, 1A, 41.

27. Müller-Doohm, *Adorno*, 262.

28. Demirovic, *Der nonkoformistische Intellektuelle*. See also Pensky, "Beyond the Message in the Bottle." I am grateful to Professor Pensky for pointing me toward Demirovic's work.

29. Until recently, Jay's *Permanent Exiles* was one of the few texts to acknowledge the crucial influence of the Frankfurt School's American exile on Adorno's subsequent writings.

30. Adorno, *Minima Moralia*, 15–16.

31. Ibid.

32. Ibid., 47.

33. For the source of these statistics as well as a description of the development, see especially Davis, *City of Quartz*.

34. Adorno, *Minima Moralia*, 40.

35. Davis, *City of Quartz*, 20.

36. Said, "Reflections on Exile," 184–85.

37. Adorno's "Träume in Amerika: Drei Protokole" appears, without a date, in the Max Horkheimer-Archiv (VI, 1B, 5–7). The protocols were subsequently published in *Aufbau* in October 1942. The full collection of his "Traumprotokolle" appears in the *Gesammelte Schriften*, 20.2:572–82. The dreams have recently been translated by Anne Halley and published in English as "Theodor W. Adorno's Dream Transcripts." In the quotation above, I have very slightly modified Halley's wonderful translation, based on the original version, which ends with the emphasized word for things, "*Dinge.*"

38. Adorno, "Aldous Huxley and Utopia," 97–98.

39. Said, "The Future of Criticism," 168.

40. Adorno, *Minima Moralia*, 87.

41. Kracauer, *Theory of Film*.

42. Theodor W. Adorno, "The Experiential Content of Hegel's Philosophy," 59.

43. Ibid., 58.

44. Adorno, *Negative Dialectics*, 79, my emphasis.

45. Ibid., 99.

46. Adorno, "What National Socialism Has Done to the Arts," 385–86.

47. Adorno, "The Experiential Content of Hegel's Philosophy," 69.

48. Adorno, "Analytical Study of NBC's *Music Appreciation Hour*."

49. Adorno, "Memorandum: Music in Radio," June 26, 1938, Lazarsfeld Papers, Columbia University Archives, 1.

50. Kracauer, *Theory of Film*, xlvii.

1. The Monster under the Stone

1. Adorno, "Procrustes," in "Minima Moralia," 1945, Max Horkheimer-Archiv. This and the other aphorisms excised from the final version of *Minima Moralia* have been published as Adorno's "Message in a Bottle."

2. Adorno, "Procrustes."

3. Ibid.

4. Interviews: LCD, April 13, 1951, p. 25, folder 155, box 15, series 7175, Record Group (RG) 1.2, Rockefeller Foundation Archives, Rockefeller Archive Center, Sleepy Hollow, New York (hereafter designated RAC).

5. This assessment comes from the British communications scholar David Morrison, whose work on Paul Lazarsfeld will be discussed in some detail in this chapter. See Morrison, "*Kultur* and Culture," 332.

6. Adorno, "On the Fetish-Character in Music and the Regression of Listening," 288.

7. The Vienna Circle was, from the 1920s, a group of philosophers and social scientists dedicated to the ideas of logical positivism. Among the better-known figures associated with the Vienna Circle were Rudolf Carnap, Kurt Gödel, and Otto Neurath. Like Lazarsfeld, many of the members of the group fled into exile in the 1930s.

8. Lazarsfeld, "Some Remarks on the Typological Procedures in Social Research," 129.

9. Ibid.

10. This is a term Adorno uses throughout his writings. See particularly "The Schema of Mass Culture."

11. Adorno and Benjamin, *The Complete Correspondence*, 180.

12. Adorno's remarks about Lazarsfeld (and Neurath) come as Adorno is confiding in Benjamin about his feelings regarding Herbert Marcuse and Leo Lowenthal and what Adorno believed was their inadequacy as members of the Institute. At the time—and well into the exile period—Adorno, Marcuse, and Lowenthal jockeyed for position with Horkheimer, each one sending confidential memos and letters to Horkheimer about why he was the best one to lead a certain project or collaborate with Horkheimer on a manuscript. When, ultimately, Horkheimer moved to California, asking Adorno to accompany him while leaving Marcuse and Lowenthal behind on the East Coast to work for the Office of Strategic Services (OSS) (Marcuse) and the Office of War Information and Voice of America (Lowenthal), Marcuse and Lowenthal each separately expressed his dismay and disappointment that Teddie was now Horkheimer's chosen collaborator. Adorno's letter in 1937 to Benjamin registered some of the pettiness of this infighting. "With young men like this," Adorno writes, "one has the feeling that they have had no further aesthetic experience since the time they first began to resent their senior German teacher at primary school. And in that respect, they naturally find it rather easier to liquidate art than we do" (Adorno and Benjamin, *The Complete Correspondence*,

180). It should definitely be noted that these "young men," Lowenthal (born in 1900) and Marcuse (born in 1898), were Adorno's senior by three and five years, respectively.

13. The journal, formerly *Zeitschrift für Sozialforschung*, had changed its name the year before (in issue 3 of volume 8). The decision to publish in English was occasioned by the loss of the European publisher and printer of the *Zeitschrift* as well as by the Institute's stated gratitude to their exile home. "America," Horkheimer writes in issue 3 of the volume, "especially the United States, is the only continent in which the continuation of scientific life is possible. Within the framework of this country's democratic institutions, culture still enjoys the freedom without which, we believe, it is unable to exist. In publishing our journal in its new form we wish to give this belief its concrete expression" (321).

14. Horkheimer, "Preface," 1.

15. Ibid.

16. Institut für Sozialforschung, *Authority and the Family*.

17. Morrison, *The Search for a Method*, 77.

18. Lazarsfeld, "Introduction by the Guest Editor."

19. Morrison, *The Search for a Method*, 80.

20. Much to Lux's dismay, Lazarsfeld discovered that Lux's ad campaign was having unintended effects: "Lux worried that the ad might create the idea in the mind of the listeners that use of their cosmetics was harmful. Lazarsfeld's study confirmed Lux's worst fears: 'Thirty-eight percent of the women, when they were asked directly, replied that they thought the advertisement meant that cosmetics are harmful.' In a related and even more surprising result, Lazarsfeld asked the women respondents to agree or disagree with the statement, 'Nowadays, the consumer needs legal protection against the manufacturers of cosmetics,' and discovered that more than three-quarters of women, or 76 percent, agreed that consumers 'definitely' or 'probably' needed protection against cosmetics manufacturers" (Newman, *Radio Active*, 17).

21. Newman, *Radio Active*, 18.

22. In addition to Lazarsfeld's lead essay, the mass-communications volume also contains the essay "On Borrowed Experience: An Analysis of Listening to Daytime Sketches" by Herta Herzog who was, at that time, Lazarsfeld's wife. (My suggestion of nepotism should not be taken as a criticism of Herzog's essay, which by all standards is an influential classic of communications research.) Further, Lazarsfeld was listed in the Institute's roster of volume 8 of the *Zeitschrift* as a research associate, although his name did not appear on Institute letterhead. Walter Benjamin, however, who was, according to most sources, never officially a member of the Frankfurt School, did have his name listed on the letterhead, on the roster, and on most of the Institute's introductory materials as a full member. According to letters exchanged between Benjamin and Adorno, this was done to help guarantee Benjamin's visa to the United States. That the ploy failed is made

even more heartbreaking and eerie by the fact that Benjamin's name can still be found on Institute letterhead *five years* after Benjamin's suicide (various correspondences, central files, 1891–1971, Institute of Social Research Files, box 549, folders 7–8, University Archives and Columbiana Library, Columbia University).

23. Morrison, "*Kultur* and Culture," 334.

24. Lazarsfeld, "An Episode in the History of Social Research," 322.

25. Memorandum to Dr. [Hadley] Cantril and Dr. [Frank] Stanton, April 27, 1938. Lazarsfeld Papers, Columbia University Archives.

26. MacRae, "Frankfurters," 786.

27. Lazarsfeld to Adorno, n.d., Lazarsfeld Papers, Columbia University Archives, 2, 5.

28. Adorno, "Memorandum: Music in Radio," June 26, 1938, Lazarsfeld Papers, Columbia University Archives.

29. Adorno, "Scientific Experiences of a European Scholar in America," 224.

30. Lazarsfeld to Adorno, n.d., Lazarsfeld Papers, Columbia University Archives, 5, 1.

31. Adorno's original name was Theodor Adorno Wiesengrund. "Adorno" was his mother's maiden name and reflected her Corsican heritage. Adorno's Jewish identity and the name "Wiesengrund" derived from his father. Around the time of his emigration, Adorno changed the order of these parental names to the formation we know today.

32. Lazarsfeld, "Memorandum to Dr. [Hadley] Cantril and Dr. [Frank] Stanton," April 27, 1938, Lazarsfeld Papers, Columbia University Archives.

33. Lazarsfeld, "Remarks on Administrative and Critical Communications Research," 3.

34. Ibid., 3–5.

35. Ibid., 5–7.

36. Ibid., 7.

37. Ibid., 8, his emphasis.

38. Ibid., 9.

39. Ibid., 9–10.

40. Horkheimer and Adorno, *Dialectic of Enlightenment*, Jephcott translation, 97.

41. Lazarsfeld, "Remarks on Administrative and Critical Communications Research," 12–13.

42. Ibid., 2.

43. Lazarsfeld to Adorno, n.d., Lazarsfeld Papers, Columbia University Archives, 3.

44. Ibid., 2.

45. Ibid.

46. Adorno, "Procrustes," 41–42.

47. Wakeman, *The Hucksters*, 68–69.

48. See Shils, "Daydreams and Nightmares," 587–608.

49. "At one time," Habermas writes, "the process of making proceedings public was intended to subject persons or affairs to public reason, and to make political decisions subject to appeal before the court of public opinion. But often enough today the process of making public simply serves the arcane politics of special interests; in the form of 'publicity' it wins public prestige for people or affairs, thus making them worthy of acclamation in a climate of non-public opinion" (Habermas, "The Public Sphere," 55).

50. National Public Radio, "Music Testing," my transcription.

51. Ibid.

52. Simonet, "Industry," 72.

53. "However," Simonet continues, "the way someone like [David O.] Selznick would use the resultant graphs was simplistic, Gallup thinks. 'Selznick used to just put a ruler on this graph and then have his people cut out the valleys'— editing out every scene that registered below the line" (ibid., 72).

54. Simonet, "Industry," 72.

55. Levy, "The Lazarsfeld-Stanton Program Analyzer," 32.

56. Ibid., 34.

57. Ibid., 33.

58. Nielsen, *How You Can Get the Ideal Radio Research Service*, 3.

59. Ibid., 32, 33.

60. Ibid., 35.

61. National Broadcasting Company, *Broadcast Advertising: A Study of the Radio Medium*, 5.

62. Columbia Broadcasting System, *Broadcast Advertising: The Sales Voice of America*, 5.

63. It is worth noting that both of these manuals were the victims of very bad timing. Both were released in September 1929, thus rendering their exponential progressions of advertising sales and new listeners somewhat pathetically moot.

64. Columbia Broadcasting System, *Broadcast Advertising: The Sales Voice of America*, 17.

65. National Broadcasting Company, *Broadcast Advertising: A Study of the Radio Medium*, 109.

66. Ibid., 110.

67. See Barnard, *The Great Depression and the Culture of Abundance*.

68. Columbia Broadcasting System, *The Very Rich*, 1–2.

69. Ibid., 3–4.

70. Ibid., 9.

71. Ibid.

72. Hardt, *Critical Communication Studies*, 14.

73. Ibid.

74. Asimov, *Foundation*, 28.

75. Actually, there are two flip sides: One can naturally compare the preservationist psychohistorians to J. Robert Oppenheimer and his secret clan of scientists working on the Manhattan Project.

76. Adorno, "The Schema of Mass Culture," 58.

77. Ibid, 60.

78. Arendt, "Society and Culture," 48.

79. Ibid.

80. See the introduction for the substance of Shils's accusations.

81. Morrison, *The Search for a Method*, 80.

82. Ibid.

83. Morrison claims that "Adorno's gift for misunderstanding the world around him was truly remarkable." However, he seems to miss Adorno's fundamental objection to positivist protocols—namely, that they refused to acknowledge the vital importance of the dialectic, the complex relation that governs fact and value. Although Morrison has spent many years studying the tempestuous relationship between Lazarsfeld and Adorno, here as elsewhere he betrays a certain myopia about critical theory. For example, while he criticizes Adorno for not understanding his American hosts while in exile and for resisting his new academic surroundings, Morrison's insistence that "the writings of the Frankfurt School do not form the key texts of cultural studies" reveal a scholar who seems unable to see beyond the shadow of the Birmingham School and comprehend the broader influence of Adorno in the American academy. Nevertheless, those who study Adorno owe a definite debt to Morrison for his archival work to unearth the facts of Adorno's relationship with Lazarsfeld on the PRRP. His essay "*Kultur* and Culture" is necessary reading for those interested in Frankfurt School exile or in the rise of mass-communications research. But just as Adorno claims that "theoretical reflections upon society as a whole cannot be completely realized by empirical findings," so too it seems to be the case that the "facts" Morrison discovers about the PRRP might miss the fundamental importance of that period to the understanding of the modern subject. Only an understanding of the entire system of assumptions, opinions, and values of a society would be able to make sense of answers given by subjects caught up in that system ("*Kultur* and Culture," 104).

84. Adorno, "On the Logic of the Social Sciences," 114.

85. Adorno et al., *The Positivist Dispute in German Sociology*. The book bills the exchange between Adorno and Popper as a debate, but Popper argued after its publication that he had been ambushed by the pro-Adorno camp. Having been asked to provide an introductory lecture on positivism, his seemingly straightforward and at times simplified account was easily demolished by Adorno. Popper's positivism, if it can be called that, is substantially more sophisticated than he himself makes it appear.

86. Adorno, "Sociology and Empirical Research," 68.

87. Nietszche, *Beyond Good and Evil*, 21.

88. Adorno, "Sociology and Empirical Research," 68.

89. Joyce, *Ulysses*, 28.

90. Adorno, *Minima Moralia*, 81.

91. "Scientific Experiences of a European Scholar in America," 234.

92. Adorno et al., *The Authoritarian Personality*, 15.

93. Adorno, "Memorandum to: Berkeley Group," October 2, 1946, American Jewish Committee Papers, Gen 12, YIVO Center for Jewish Research Archives.

94. Horkheimer to Adorno, November 2, 1944, Max Horkheimer-Archiv, VI, 1B, 200; also Adorno and Horkheimer, *Briefwechsel, 1927–1969*, vol. 2, *1938–1944*, 345. In the time between my researching this book and its publication, Suhrkamp has published nearly all the correspondence between Adorno and Horkheimer. At the kindly request of Henri Lonitz of the Adorno Archive, I have indicated where these letters appear in the published *Briefwechsel*, but I have also retained references to where I found these documents among Horkheimer's papers.

95. Gorer, an extremely influential sociologist in his own right, was the author of *The Life and Ideas of the Marquis de Sade* (1953) and *The American People: A Study in National Character* (1948).

96. Adorno, "Memorandum to Dr. Lazarsfeld from T. W. Adorno Re: Reply to Dr. Gora's [*sic*] Letter," n.d, Lazarsfeld Papers, Columbia University Archives, 1.

97. Adorno, "Scientific Experiences of a European Scholar in America," 221.

98. Ibid.

2. Adorno in Sponsor-Land

1. Charles E. Mitchell (1877–1955) was the president of National City Bank (later Citigroup) from 1921 to 1929 and is often made one of the scapegoats for the stock market collapse that led to the Great Depression. Elizabeth Mitchell was an ardent supporter of modernist music, belonging to the Auxiliary of the League of Composers, which had, in 1930, sponsored a New York production of Arnold Schoenberg's *Die glückliche Hand*. See Oja, "Women Patrons and Activists for Modernist Music."

2. Letter to Mrs. Charles E. Mitchell, n.d., Max Horkheimer-Archiv, VI, 1A, 29–30.

3. See Lazarsfeld, "An Episode in the History of Social Research"; Adorno, "Scientific Experiences of a European Scholar in America"; Morrison, "*Kultur* and Culture"; and Morrison, *The Search for a Method*.

4. Lohr, quoted in National Broadcasting Company, *The Place of Radio in Education*, 4.

5. Adorno [with George Simpson], "On a Social Critique of Radio Music: Paper Read at the Princeton Radio Research Project," October 26, 1939, 19 pages, folder 3274, box 273, series 200, RG 1.1, RAC.

6. Ibid.

7. This nineteen-page talk serves as a methodological and theoretical introduction to Adorno's radio work and incorporates many of the themes and examples that subsequently reappear in the essay "A Social Critique of Radio Music,"
published in the *Kenyon Review* in 1945. One of the assertions Adorno makes in
the presentation (and one that notably raised eyebrows at the gathering) that
famously reappears in the later article is that "an important group of problems
connected with this [the question of radio's effect on social consciousness] concerns radio's promotion of the idea of universal participation in culture by the radio
population through radio music. It would appear that the illusion is furthered that
the best is just good enough for the man on the street" (ibid., 8). Given that Arturo
Toscanini was, at that time, the conductor of the NBC Symphony Orchestra, it is
understandable that Adorno's paper provoked ire. This unwillingness to pull his
punches is precisely what Lazarsfeld laments about Adorno in his memoirs.

8. W[alter] G. Preston Jr. to John Marshall, December 18, 1939, p. 1, folder
3242, box 272, series 200R, RG 1.1, RAC.

9. Marshall to Preston, December 20, 1939, p. 1, folder 3242, box 272,
series 200R, RG 1.1, RAC.

10. Marshall, "Discussion of the Columbia University Request for a Grant
toward the Expenses of Lazarsfeld's Research in Radio Listening," pp. 1–2, folder
3243, box 272, series 200, RG 1.1, FAC.

11. Ibid.

12. Ibid.

13. Marshall did, however, waver quite a bit on this decision. On June 19,
1941, Marshall met with Adorno to "explain as tactfully as possible to Adorno the
administrative reasons which prevented a consideration to Lazarsfeld's request for
a further grant-in-aid to enable Adorno to continue his work." But even after this
meeting, Marshall had second thoughts. "The grounds given Adorno undoubtedly
justify declining further aid," Marshall writes, "but this talk left JM rather unhappy
about that decision. He is convinced now that Adorno's work has substantial value
and this view is fully confirmed by [renowned music critic Virgil] Thomson, who
is to JM's mind both a hard-boiled and competent critic. Adorno clearly has something to say about the social position of music in this country. . . . JM has suggested
to Lazarsfeld that he discuss Adorno's work with [Charles] Dollard of the Carnegie
Corporation. If DHS agrees, JM would like to leave the possibility open of considering a smaller grant-in-aid than Lazarsfeld asked ($1,000 or $1,500) toward
Adorno's further work with Lazarsfeld, if funds for it cannot be found elsewhere."
These funds, however, were not forthcoming. (Marshall, diary entry June 19, 1941,
p. 1, folder 3243, box 272, series 200, RG 1.1, RAC.)

14. Ibid.

15. Adorno to Horkheimer, July 4, 1940, Max Horkheimer-Archiv, Stadt- und
Universitätsbibliothek, Frankfurt am Main, VI, 1A, 28; also Adorno and Horkheimer, *Briefwechsel, 1927–1969*, vol. 2, *1938–1944*, 68–69.

16. These are "On Popular Music," "The Radio Symphony," and "A Social Critique of Radio Music."

17. Levin, with von der Linn, "Elements of a Radio Theory."

18. Adorno, "Memorandum: Music in Radio," June 26, 1938, Lazarsfeld Papers, Columbia University Archives, 3.

19. Adorno, *Current of Music*, 504. I am greatly indebted to Bob Hullot-Kentor for allowing me to see the advance page proofs of this manuscript. Without such access, much of what follows could not have been written.

20. Adorno, *Current of Music*, 671.

21. Adorno, "On a Social Critique of Radio Music," 2.

22. Ibid.

23. Ibid.

24. Adorno, "A Social Critique of Radio Music," 209–10.

25. "Watch what we say; watch what we do" was the somewhat sinister expression used by press secretary Ari Fleischer to warn George W. Bush's critics (specifically Bill Maher) in the wake of the attacks of September 11, 2001.

26. National Broadcasting Company, [*Musical Leadership Maintained by NBC*], 24.

27. As Michelle Hilmes writes, NBC's programming during the months leading up to World War II had an unofficial yet extensive bias in favor of U.S. intervention: "NBC's records indicate how widespread were the as-yet uncoordinated efforts toward interventionist programming by 1941 in an in-house report titled 'In Defense of America: A Nation Listens.' The report tallied up 'defense broadcasts' from January to July 1941—months before Pearl Harbor—and arrived at a total of 627 separate broadcasts on NBC's two networks, in cooperation with the Treasury Department, the War Department, the U.S. Navy, the 'US Govt. Administration,' and special organizations and service groups. Of the subject matter of the programs, the largest category by far was 'civilian defense and morale,' with 233 programs, followed by 'production for defense and morale,' with 153 and 'general defense talks' with 142. The programs ranged from weekly series to special one-time reports and discussions" (*Radio Voices*, 233).

28. See the discussion of his speech "What National Socialism Has Done to the Arts" in the introduction to this book.

29. Adorno, "A Social Critique of Radio Music," 212.

30. In addition to Marshall, who worried that Adorno's tone would alienate industry representatives, Lazarsfeld too, in his memoirs of the period, writes of his constant fear that Adorno would sour the privileged relationship PRRP had with NBC and CBS.

31. National Broadcasting Company, [*Musical Leadership Maintained by NBC*], 16, and quoted in Adorno, "Memorandum: Music in Radio," 89, and in Adorno, *Current of Music*, 668.

32. Adorno, "Memorandum: Music in Radio," 89.

33. Adorno is profoundly suspicious of this supposedly "natural" aspect of folk music and claims in *Current of Music:* "Of course, according to European standards the actual oral tradition of music does not play any important role at all and it seems to me most unlikely that things in America should be different. The assertion of the 'oral tradition' serves only the purpose of making this music appear something reverent and near to the community of people" (*Current of Music,* 669).

34. Ibid., 117.

35. Adorno, "On the Fetish-Character in Music and the Regression of Listening" and "The Culture Industry."

36. Adorno, *Introduction to the Sociology of Music,* 1–20. Among other places, "A typology of musical listening" shows up as a stand-alone text in the Max Horkheimer-Archiv and in Paul Lazarsfeld's papers, as well as in an extremely long footnote in *Current of Music,* 371–78.

37. To name just one, however, Richard Leppert's edited collection of Adorno's musical essays offers incisive commentary on the various aspects of Adorno's musicological thought and provides an exemplary introduction to the body of writing on Adorno. It also gives the reader an indispensable bibliography of Adorno's writing and subsequent scholarship. See Adorno, *Essays on Music,* ed. Richard Leppert.

38. Attali, *Noise,* 37.

39. Adorno, *Current of Music,* 118–19.

40. See Beller, "Capital/Cinema," 86–87, as well as my analysis of the problems with Beller's claim vis-à-vis Adorno's cinematic writings in "The Hole Is the True."

41. Adorno, *Current of Music,* 81. As Adorno writes of this phenomenon: "This illusion of closeness makes the listener feel that he is actually present at the place where the broadcast originates—or purports to originate."

42. Ibid., 19.

43. National Broadcasting Company, *The Word of God,* 1.

44. During the 1940s and '50s, Fulton J. Sheen (1895–1979) was, in many ways, the voice and face of U.S. Catholicism. A former philosophy professor at Catholic University, in 1930 he became the first host of NBC's *The Catholic Hour,* which was to evolve into television's *Life Is Worth Living.* At their heights the radio and television shows reached nearly 10 million viewers per week.

45. National Broadcasting Company, *The Word of God,* 3.

46. Adorno, *Current of Music,* 19.

47. Kittler, *Gramophone, Film, Typewriter,* 37.

48. Cantril, with Gaudet and Herzog, *The Invasion from Mars,* 203.

49. Quoted in Shirer, *The Rise and Fall of the Third Reich,* 693.

50. Inspired by events like the Naujocks raid and Welles's *War of the Worlds,* Kenneth Fearing's 1942 novel, *Clark Gifford's Body,* provides another variation on

the theme of radio's capacity to create reality. In the novel, a band of revolution-aries and radio engineers organize the takeover of strategically located radio trans-mitters and convince the populace of an unnamed country that an armed revolt is being waged against an authoritarian regime. However, the force of these amateur broadcasts is nothing compared to the might of the institutional culture machin-ery that drowns out the guerrillas in a wave of newspaper reports, press releases, counterbroadcasts, and clever propaganda.

51. Stern, "Spuk und Radio," 65. Quoted by Adorno in *Current of Music*, 77.

52. Adorno, *Current of Music*, 139.

53. Ibid., 139–40.

54. Ibid., 140.

55. Adorno and Benjamin, *The Complete Correspondence*, 282–83.

56. Agamben, "The Prince and the Frog," 116.

57. Adorno, *Current of Music*, 148.

58. Adorno, "A Social Critique of Radio Music," 210–11.

59. Ibid.

60. Ibid.

61. Quoted in National Broadcasting Company, *Broadcasting in the Public Interest*, 10.

62. Adorno, "A Social Critique of Radio Music," 212.

63. Fearing, "Radio Blues," 49.

64. Kittler, *Gramophone, Film, Typewriter*, 45.

65. Adorno, "The Form of the Phonograph Record," 59.

66. Beethoven's works have always been at the vanguard of musical record-ing—if only as its guinea pig. As Attali notes in *Noise*, "It was not until 1914 that the first symphony was recorded (Beethoven's Fifth, directed by Artyr Nikish)." And when CDs were first marketed, each disc was limited to seventy-four minutes of material, the length of time it took to perform Beethoven's Ninth Symphony.

67. Adorno, "The Radio Symphony," 122–23.

68. Specifically, Adorno repeats this critique about the mutilation of sym-phonic music in *Composing for the Films*. In movies, as on the radio, the broad band of sonic resources is reduced to an underwhelming middle ground. "The dif-ferent degrees of strength are leveled and blurred to a general mezzoforte," Adorno insists. And here he draws specific attention to the fact that, "incidentally, this practice is quite analogous to the habits of the mixer in radio broadcasting" (Eisler and Adorno, *Composing for the Films*, 18).

69. McClary, "The Blasphemy of Talking Politics during Bach Year," 58.

70. Attali, *Noise*, 64–65.

71. Adorno, "The Radio Symphony," 116–17.

72. Kant, *Critique of Judgment*, 116, emphasis added.

73. Ibid.

74. Ibid.

75. Quoted in Attali, *Noise*, 112.

76. Columbia Broadcasting System, *"Seems Radio Is Here to Stay,"* 36–37.

77. Ibid., 38.

78. Ibid., 16.

79. Ibid., 12.

80. Director Victor Fleming's *The Wizard of Oz* premiered on June 6, 1939, nearly six weeks later. The similarities between the floating head of Oz in the movie and that of Beethoven in *"Seems Radio Is Here to Stay"* are too striking to go unmentioned.

81. Columbia Broadcasting System, *"Seems Radio Is Here to Stay,"* 12–13.

82. Bradley, *Appearance and Reality*, x.

83. National Broadcasting Company, *Broadcasting in the Public Interest*, 18.

84. Jäger, *Adorno*, 10.

85. Adorno, "Looking Back on Surrealism," 88.

86. Adorno, "Memorandum: Music in Radio," 128.

87. Ibid.

88. Adorno, "Analytical Study of NBC's *Music Appreciation Hour*," 326.

89. Ibid., 328.

90. Ibid., 344.

91. Ibid., 358.

92. Ibid., 355.

93. National Broadcasting Company, *"Music Appreciation Hour" Instructor's Manual*, 23.

94. Adorno, "Analytical Study of NBC's *Music Appreciation Hour*," 358.

95. Attali, *Noise*, 66.

96. National Broadcasting Company, *What Goes On behind Your Radio Dial?* 3.

97. Ibid., 3–4.

98. Ibid.

99. Ibid.

100. Adorno, *The Psychological Technique of Martin Luther Thomas' Radio Addresses*, 55–56.

101. Ibid.

102. National Broadcasting Company, *What Goes On behind Your Radio Dial?* 16.

103. Ibid., 17.

104. Ibid., 18.

105. As a result of an anticompetitive-practices lawsuit, NBC was ordered to split up the network into two separate entities, NBC Red and NBC Blue. Damrosch and the *NBC Music Appreciation Hour* were on Blue.

106. National Broadcasting Company, *Alice in Sponsor-Land*, 6.

107. Ibid., 42.

108. Ibid., 39.

109. Ibid., 40.

110. Columbia Broadcasting System, *We Don't Know Why They Listen (so much!)*, 9, 12.

111. Adorno, *Minima Moralia*, 49.

112. Adorno, "Memorandum: Music in Radio," 39.

113. Jay, *Adorno*, 46.

114. Adorno, "Freudian Theory and the Pattern of Fascist Propaganda," 117.

115. Ibid., 129.

116. National Broadcasting Company, *Alice in Sponsor-Land*, 38–39. One should, of course, note the sexual innuendo in the Queen's exclamation, itself a "psychological moment" of some importance.

117. National Broadcasting Company, *It's Not Done with Mirrors*, 1.

118. It is from one of Arno's cartoons (an image of military brass watching an airplane crash to the ground) that we get the phrase "Looks like it's back to the old drawing board."

119. National Broadcasting Company, *It's Not Done with Mirrors*, 3. In *The Psychological Technique of Martin Luther Thomas' Radio Addresses*, Adorno cites demagogues' use of "magic words," such as "serious crisis," that stand in for and activate the prejudices of the listener.

120. National Broadcasting Company, *It's Not Done with Mirrors*, 3.

121. Ibid., 4.

122. Ibid., 13.

123. Ibid., 12.

124. To take just one example, and hardly the most inflammatory: On September 1, 2005, on his radio show, Rush Limbaugh responded thus to the human tragedy of Hurricane Katrina, which left perhaps as many as 100,000 people, mostly poor and predominately black, without food and water in a situation of dire chaos: "The non-black population was *just* as devastated, but apparently they were able to get out, and the black population wasn't able to get out. Maybe New Orleans has a half decent mass transit people and some of these people don't need cars."

125. Krane, "FCC's Powell Declares TiVo 'God's machine.'"

126. Marshall, "Discussion of the Columbia University Request for a Grant toward the Expenses of Lazarsfeld's Research in Radio Listening."

127. See chapter 1 for specific examples of his outlandish suggestions.

128. Adorno, "Memorandum: Music in Radio," 153–54. "Mr. Kramer" is probably the architect Ferdinand Kramer, a minor Bauhaus figure who, like Adorno, emigrated from Frankfurt to the United States in the 1930s. After returning to Frankfurt in the '50s, he designed many of the buildings at the Johann Wolfgang Goethe–Universität, including the famous Stadt- und Universitätsbibliothek, a wonderful example of late-modernist/functionalist space.

129. Adorno, "Memorandum: Music in Radio," 151.

130. For an overview of the history and uses of the instrument, see Theremin, "The Design of a Musical Instrument Based on Cathode Relays"; Montague, "Rediscovering Leon Theremin"; and Kavina, "My Experience with the Theremin."

131. "The first orchestral work with a solo electronic instrument was [Andrey] Paschenko's *Sinfonicheskaya misteriya* ('Symphonic Mystery') for theremin and orchestra, which received its first performance in Leningrad on May 2, 1924, with Termen [Theremin] as soloist. In the same year it was also prominent in Valentin Yakovlevich Kruchinin's score for the science fiction film *Aelita.* Later composers for the instrument include Joseph Schillinger, with the *First Airphonic Suite* (1929) for theremin and orchestra, [Edgard] Varèse, Anis Fuleihan, [Ron] Grainer, [Bohuslav] Martin, and [Alfred] Schnittke. The fingerboard theremin was used by [Leopold] Stokowski to reinforce the double basses in the Philadelphia Orchestra at the end of 1930" (Orton and Davies, "Theremin," 25:386–87).

132. The U.S. public first heard a performance of the theremin at the Metropolitan Opera House on January 31, 1928. It was billed as "Music from the Ether" and opened, somewhat portentously, with Franz Schubert's "Ave Maria."

133. Adorno, "Memorandum: Music in Radio," 152.

134. Ibid.

135. Ibid.

3. Below the Surface

1. Friedrich, *City of Nets,* 222.

2. An interesting aside: According to Friedrich, among the various medical and mental-health personnel who were paid by the studios to attend the fragile Garland in the inevitable event of a crisis was Dr. Fredrick Hacker. This was the same Hacker whose psychoanalytic institute sponsored Adorno's work on television and the *Los Angeles Times* astrology column. Whatever its actual influence in Hollywood, there were very few degrees of separation between the Institute and the studios. The Hollywood net was very tight indeed, and Adorno and Horkheimer were certainly caught up in it.

3. To consider the legacy of just one of these, Thomas Pepper, in his book *Singularities,* writes of *Minima Moralia* that "few would deny that the book is one of the masterpieces of twentieth-century prose overall" (Pepper, *Singularities,* 20).

4. Jay, "Adorno in America," 131.

5. See Jay, *Adorno,* throughout.

6. Gorbman, "Hanns Eisler in Hollywood," 274.

7. Gross, "Adorno in Los Angeles," 343.

8. Kluge, interview by Liebman, "On New German Cinema, Art, Enlightenment, and the Public Sphere," 42.

9. See Hansen, "Introduction to Adorno," "Of Mice and Ducks," "Benjamin, Cinema, and Experience," "Mass Culture as Hieroglyphic Writing," and "Kracauer's Early Writings on Film and Mass Culture."

10. Hansen, "Introduction to Adorno," 197.

11. Ibid, 197.

12. Hansen, "Mass Culture as Hieroglyphic Writing," 83.

13. Huyssen, "Adorno in Reverse," 21.

14. Adorno, "Commitment," 80.

15. Adorno, *Aesthetic Theory*, 226–27.

16. Adorno, *Minima Moralia*, 25.

17. Gorbman, "Hanns Eisler in Hollywood," 274.

18. "New School for Social Research Music in Film Production," January 19, 1940, box 259, folder: New School/Music Filming, series 200, RG 1.1, RAC.

19. Eisler and Adorno to Marshall, July 27, 1946, box 260, folder: New School/Music Filming, series 200, RG 1.1, RAC.

20. The Adornos, it seems, were providing a slightly different form of hospitality for Eisler's wife. As Eisler's and Adorno's FBI files report, "It is known to [the Los Angeles] office that Louise Eisler, wife of Hanns Eisler, has used the address of Adorno for correspondence with ——, New York, in order to hide from Hanns Eisler a clandestine relationship between herself [and] ——" (n.d., Federal Bureau of Investigation, file L.A.100-6133; obtained through the Freedom of Information Privacy Act).

21. Adorno to Horkheimer, August 10, 1941, Max Horkheimer-Archiv, VI, 1B; also Adorno and Horkheimer, *Briefwechsel, 1927–1969*, vol. 2, *1938–1944*, 184.

22. This incident is described in a short essay from 1964 occasioned by Chaplin's seventy-fifth birthday. In the piece Adorno confirms his acquaintance with Chaplin, saying, "Only because I knew him many years ago would I stress, without any philosophical pretensions, two or three observations which might contribute to a descriptive account of his image" ("Chaplin Times Two," 59).

23. Walter Winchell (1897–1972), who once said that "the way to become a famous person is to throw a brick at a famous person," was the template for the modern gossip columnist. He was also a red-baiting reactionary who maintained a decades-long correspondence with J. Edgar Hoover. Winchell's FBI file, consisting mainly of tips he sent to the director, runs to 3,900 pages.

24. Telegram to Winchell, September 29, 1948, Federal Bureau of Investigation, file 61-7421-15.

25. On this, see Adorno and Horkheimer, *Briefwechsel*, vol. 2, *1938–1944*, and vol. 3, *1944–1949*.

26. I have not been able to view the finished version of *Syncopation*, which is long out of print. However, based on critical accounts, this film is by any lights a very minor work, even in Dieterle's frequently spotty résumé. Since the film is

currently unavailable in any video formats, I am basing my description of it on Adorno's letter, as well as on the skimpy plot summary available on the Internet Movie Database Web site (http://www.imdb.com/title/tt0035405/) and the reviews of the film in *Variety* (May 6, 1942) and *Harrison's Reports* (May 9, 1942). In the finished version, starring Adolphe Menjou, Jackie Cooper, and Bonita Granville, a number of "jazz" notables, including Gene Krupa and Benny Goodman, appear as themselves in something called the "All American Dance Band." Given the withering comments about Goodman and Lombardo elsewhere in Adorno's work (especially "The Culture Industry"), this clearly is not the film that Adorno would have wished.

27. Adorno to Horkheimer, October 18, 1941, Max Horkheimer-Archiv, VI, 1B, 20; also Adorno and Horkheimer, *Briefwechsel, 1927–1969,* vol. 2, *1938– 1944,* 269–70.

28. Adorno, telegram to Horkheimer, October 20, 1941, Max Horkheimer-Archiv, VI, 1B, 17; also Adorno and Horkheimer, *Briefwechsel, 1927–1969,* vol. 2, *1938–1944,* 271.

29. Ibid.

30. See Adorno, "On Jazz" and "Jazz, Hot and Hybrid." Also, for an interesting, if ultimately unsatisfying, take on Adorno's use of race in his critique of jazz, see Gabbard, "Signifyin(g) the Phallus."

31. I am of the opinion that most critics of Adorno's jazz essays approach his arguments undialectically, focusing on the elements of the essays that denigrate jazz's capitulation to the logic of standardization rather than taking full measure of how jazz represents a certain exemplary culmination of the history of bourgeois music and thus of the bourgeois subject.

32. Adorno, telegram to Horkheimer, October 20, 1941; also Adorno and Horkheimer, *Briefwechsel, 1927–1969,* vol. 2, *1938–1944,* 271. Compare this scene to the sonic experiments by the band the Flaming Lips, whose 1997 album *Zaireeka* consists of four separate compact discs designed to be played on different players simultaneously.

33. It is with no little amusement that one reads in the *Harrison's Reports* review that *Syncopation* "appears to have encountered script trouble."

34. Adorno, "Transparencies on Film," 156.

35. Ibid.

36. Curiously, Bertolt Brecht cites the finished version of *Syncopation* as unsuccessful precisely because it fails to do what Adorno suggests in his telegram and instead makes the visual images preeminent: "In Dieterle's film *Syncopation,* a presentation of the history of jazz, one sequence, which showed the trip of its heroine, a musician, from New Orleans to Chicago, failed in its effect. Traveling through various cities, she hears certain characteristic songs associated with them. The idea of a journey through various jazz forms was not understood by the audience. The reason was that, at the beginning of the film, scenes were accompanied

by music in such a way as to emphasize not the music but the scene. The audience did not comprehend that now the scene (the girl's journey) was meant to be less important than the music. The audience had grown accustomed to hear the accompaniment with only one ear and to consider it to be without meaning" (Brecht, *Brecht on Film and Radio*, 18).

37. Hansen, "Mass Culture as Hieroglyphic Writing," 91.

38. Adorno, "Transparencies on Film," 160.

39. Adorno, *In Search of Wagner*, 90.

40. Marx, *Capital*, 1:165, his emphasis.

41. Adorno, *In Search of Wagner*, 85.

42. Ibid., 90.

43. Ibid.

44. "As an instance of the progressive reification of aesthetic expression, the notion of mass-cultural hieroglyphics merely elaborates for film and television what Adorno had stressed earlier in his critique of popular music, in particular his writings on jazz and his essay on Wagner" (Hansen, "Mass Culture as Hieroglyphic Writing," 88).

45. Horkheimer and Adorno, *Dialectic of Enlightenment*, Cumming translation, 127.

46. Adorno, "The Culture Industry," 126.

47. Adorno, *In Search of Wagner*, 91.

48. Stemmrich, "Dan Graham's 'Cinema' and Film Theory."

49. Horkheimer and Adorno, *Dialectic of Enlightenment*, Cumming translation, 127.

50. See particularly Jonathan Crary, "Techniques of the Observer," chapter 4 in *Techniques of the Observer*, 97–136.

51. Nietzsche, quoted in ibid., 97.

52. Merleau-Ponty, *Phenomenology of Perception*, 5.

53. Ibid., 9.

54. Ibid., 7.

55. Ibid.

56. Adorno, *Negative Dialectics*, 149. I expand on this argument and on this quotation in an essay that strives to link Adorno's *Negative Dialectics* with Gilles Deleuze's *Cinema* books; see my "The Hole Is the True."

57. Gertrud Koch, in her essay "Mimesis and *Bilderverbot*," argues that there is a dialectical relationship between the mimetic impulse—"the compulsion in the culture industry to conform to a false image"—and the concept of *Bilderverbot*, the ban on graven images. At first glance, she argues, it would seem that the two were mutually exclusive. However, when thought of in terms of Adorno's insistence on "determinate negation," one can understand that the mimetic impulse could be rescued from the culture industry and employed in revealing what is not pictured, the fissures in the system where the subject achieves nonidentity. Koch

writes, "Adorno speaks of such a ban on graven images in terms of its constituting a boundary in human cultural history which we cannot cross back over. This seems surprising not least because at first glance the primacy of the *Bilderverbot* and a stringent interpretation of the concept of mimesis would appear to be mutually exclusive; after all, the ban prohibits precisely the production of likeness on which the mimetic impulse rests. The enigmatic image is, however, that image which does not rely on mirror-like similarity, whereas the culture industry produces images which mirror the second nature of society and thus assert a positive similarity. In this manner, such images contravene the *Bilderverbot* just as positivism violates immanent negation" (215).

58. Adorno, *Minima Moralia*, 15.

59. Debord, *The Society of the Spectacle*, 12.

60. Ibid., 15.

61. Adorno, *Minima Moralia*, 15.

62. Adorno, "How to Look at Television," 139.

63. Ibid., 141–42.

64. One such experiment, for example, featured a series of photographs of groups of businesspeople standing in an elevator. In each grouping, two figures stand, affectless, in the foreground, while in the background, their fellow passengers are scowling. One of the two foreground figures is marked as a racial or ethnic minority (either by his skin color, dress, or, in the case of one figure, by his Star of David lapel pin). The other figure is blandly Caucasian, but, among the properly dressed passengers, he is the only one not wearing a hat. Presumably, the series of photos was designed to test whether racial or ethnic difference was more offensive than the sartorial faux pas.

65. Since Horkheimer was the director of research for AJC and Adorno was listed as codirector of the Research Study on Social Discrimination and de facto head of the so-called Berkeley Group at work on *The Authoritarian Personality*, there is a strong probability that both men were familiar with these experiments, a fact to which the next example testifies.

66. The Mr. Biggott cartoons were drawn by Carl Rose, a well-known cartoonist and contributor for the *New Yorker*. Rose was responsible for one of that publication's most famous cartoons from 1928. In the panel, a well-dressed mother and her child are sitting at the dinner table. The caption reads:

MOTHER: It's broccoli dear.

CHILD: I say it's spinach, and I say the hell with it!

67. American Jewish Committee Department of Scientific Research, "Summary Report of Study of Mr. Biggott Cartoon," January 11, 1946, American Jewish Committee Papers, gen 10, box 14, YIVO Center for Jewish Research Archives.

68. American Jewish Committee Department of Scientific Research, "A Research Study of a Cartoon . . . *Biggott and the Minister*," June 1946, YIVO Center for Jewish Research Archives.

69. Lazarsfeld, memorandum to Slawson, August 28, 1945, Max Horkheimer-Archiv, II. 10, 298–99.

70. Ibid., 298.

71. One of them is distinguished with the abbreviation "org." which, given the fact that the list is both in English and in German, could mean a variety of things, from "original" to "*organisiert*," implying that Adorno was the administrative agent behind the project.

72. Despite insisting to the Rockefeller Foundation that he was politically neutral and that it was merely a coincidence that many of his compositions were turned into proletarian anthems, in 1948, partly as a result of his brother Gerhardt's espionage trial, Eisler became one of the most recalcitrant and unrepentant witnesses before HUAC. Greeting his interrogators with an admixture of bemused disdain and European civility, Eisler delivered some of the most incisive testimony of the sordid era. When asked the inevitable question about his membership in the Communist Party, Eisler claimed, "I would be a swindler if I called myself a Communist. I have no right. The Communist underground workers in every country have proven that they are heroes. I am not a hero. I am a composer" (quoted in Friedrich, *City of Nets*, 303). Were it not for the unfortunate taint of his brother's trial, Eisler could well have served as a shining model for all those who named names to follow.

73. While in England, he had dabbled in dramatic writing, penning the libretto for a *Singspiel* based on Mark Twain's *The Adventures of Tom Sawyer*, a text he discussed at some length with Benjamin in their correspondence. But a libretto and a film script are two very different species.

74. Adorno and Horkheimer had worked since 1939 on "Research Project on Anti-Semitism," which was published anonymously in volume 9 of *Studies in Philosophy and Social Science*. Adorno was particularly keen on the project and was primarily responsible for the final draft (with help from Neumann and Lowenthal).

75. Adorno, "Research Project on Anti-Semitism," 135.

76. Ibid., 158.

77. Ibid.

78. Ibid., 159.

79. While the memo was sent to Lewis under Horkheimer's cover letter, it is unclear whether Horkheimer or Adorno wrote this description. Horkheimer's letter claims that it is based on notes "we had jutted down [*sic*]," but based on the typewriter print, which resembles that normally used by Adorno, and the style of the description, I would guess that Adorno was responsible for crafting the memo. In the absence of further evidence, I cannot be sure.

80. Memorandum on a motion picture project, April 27, 1943, Max Horkheimer-Archiv, II, 10, 397.

81. Ibid.

82. Ibid., 398–99.

83. A short film somewhat similar to the one described in this memorandum was in fact made through the auspices of the AJC under the title *Don't Be a Sucker* (1944). The film starred Paul Lukas, one of the actors from *Watch on the Rhine*.

84. [Horkheimer and Adorno], "Notes for an Experimental Film to Be Made by the Institute of Social Research," May 28, 1943, Max Horkheimer-Archiv, II, 10, 386.

85. Ibid.

86. Ibid.

87. Schary (1905–1980) has a long, if not particularly impressive, list of credits, both as a producer and as a screenwriter. He was perhaps most famous—outside of his work as head of MGM—for his script for *Sunrise at Campobello* (1960) based on his play, as well as *Lonelyhearts* (1958), an interesting, if flawed, adaptation of Nathanael West's novel *Miss Lonelyhearts*.

88. Horkheimer to Lewis, May 1, 1943, Max Horkheimer-Archiv II, 10, 395.

89. Schary to Lewis, July 7, 1943, Max Horkheimer-Archiv, II, 10, 385.

90. Lewis to Rosenblum, July 19, 1943, Max Horkheimer-Archiv, II, 10, 283.

91. Ibid.

92. Horkheimer, telegram to Adorno, November 14, 1944, Max Horkheimer-Archiv, VI, 1B, 191; also Adorno and Horkheimer, *Briefwechsel, 1927–1969*, vol. 2, *1938–1944*, 356.

93. Adorno to Horkheimer, November 23, 1944, Max Horkheimer-Archiv, VI, 1B, 182; also Adorno and Horkheimer, *Briefwechsel, 1927–1969*, vol. 2, *1938–1944*, 367–68. Adorno pointedly adds "Please Destroy" to the end of this letter.

94. As is now well known, the Hollywood Ten could have easily been the Hollywood Eleven, except for the fact that, following his evasive testimony in front of Congress, Bertolt Brecht fled the country rather than face the fate of the other witnesses.

95. Adorno, telegram to Horkheimer, November 29, 1944, Max Horkheimer-Archiv, VI, 1B, 182; Adorno and Horkheimer, *Briefwechsel, 1927–1969*, vol. 2, *1938–1944*, 372.

96. Adorno to Horkheimer, December 2, 1944, Max Horkheimer-Archiv, VI, 1B, 172; also Adorno and Horkheimer, *Briefwechsel, 1927–1969*, vol. 2, *1938–1944*, 375. Note the sensitivity Adorno displays to the fact that his correspondences were being watched by the censors.

97. Gabriel (1890–1952) was decidedly "ein B film" writer, with only three produced scripts to his credit. Among these is a potboiler called *This Woman Is Mine* (1941) with Franchot Tone and Walter Brennan. The identity of Major Vorhaus is somewhat more ambiguous. This may be Bernard Vorhaus (1904–2000), the blacklisted writer whom David Lean once described as "the greatest influence" of his life. If so, his career is markedly more interesting then Gabriel's, since he worked on films from the remake of D. W. Griffith's *Broken Blossoms* (1919; remake 1936) to the John Wayne oater *Three Faces West* (1940).

98. Slawson to Gabriel, March 22, 1945, Max Horkheimer-Archiv, VI, 10, 17.

99. [Horkheimer and Adorno], "Project of a Test Film," March 1945, Max Horkheimer-Archiv, IX, 150, 11a.

100. Ibid.

101. Ibid.

102. Ibid.

103. Ibid.

104. [Horkheimer and Adorno], "Motion Picture," March 1945, Max Horkheimer-Archiv, IX, 150, 10.

105. Ibid.

106. Adorno, unpublished introduction to *Rehearsal for Destruction* [1948?], Max Horkheimer-Archiv, VI, 1D, 119.

107. [Horkheimer and Adorno], "Motion Picture," 10.

108. Ibid.

109. Kracauer, "Suggestions for the Dialogue," April 4, 1945, Max Horkheimer-Archiv, IX, 150, 10.

110. "Below the Surface," Max Horkheimer-Archiv, IX, 150, 1.

111. [Horkheimer and Adorno], "Memorandum on an Experimental Motion Picture," April 18, 1946, Max Horkheimer-Archiv, IX, 150, 2.

112. I can discover no record saying who thought of the title, but it seems particularly appropriate to Adorno's analysis of the one-dimensional elements of cinema spectatorship and the consequent belief in the hollow character and phantasmic externality cultivated by motion picture texts.

113. [Horkheimer and Adorno], "Memorandum on an Experimental Motion Picture."

114. "Notes and Suggestions re Experimental Motion Picture," June 1945, Max Horkheimer-Archiv, IX, 150, 8.

115. Ibid.

116. [Adorno and Horkheimer], "Memorandum re: *Below the Surface*," July 1945, Max Horkheimer-Archiv, IX, 150.4. Although this memorandum is unsigned, two identical versions of it appear in the files (IX, 150, 12a, 12b) with corrections almost certainly written by Adorno. It is more than likely that Horkheimer and Adorno both contributed to the final memorandum. And this is confirmed by the memorandum's inclusion in the recently published collection of Adorno's and Horkheimer's correspondence (Adorno and Horkheimer, *Briefwechsel, 1927–1969*, vol. 3, *1945–1949*, 527–29).

117. Richter (1888–1976) was well known in modernist art circles and was an extremely important figure in the development of experimental cinema. Richter's "Dadascope I, II" (1956–1957), created with Marcel Duchamp, Jean Arp, Man Ray, and others, is at once a comprehensive portrait of the dadaists and a formal exploration of many of their key themes. He had emigrated to the United States in

1941, and many of his films, whimsical, irrational, and nonnarrative, concentrate on the rhythm and movement of objects.

118. Richter, "Report about the Film Script *Below the Surface*," July 7 and 8, 1945, Max Horkheimer-Archiv, IX, 150, 6 (spelling corrected).

119. Hackenschmidt to Horkheimer, June 19, 1945, Max Horkheimer-Archiv, IX, 150, 16.

120. In addition to Dalton Trumbo, Hackenschmidt's choice of Schulberg bears noting. A well-known Hollywood writer (he collaborated with Kazan on *On the Waterfront*), he gained notoriety for his novel *What Makes Sammy Run*, a bracing satire of the Hollywood film industry published in 1939.

121. The letter, scrawled on notepaper, reads as follows:

Dear Dr. Horkheimer,
I have no stenograph here and this makeshift does not permit much leeway. When you get to L.A. call up Jack Warner's secretary and say you have this letter of introduction from me and wish to see J.W. Use this as your letter of introduction. It is for his eyes, and I am here asking him to give earnest consideration to what you ask. If he should be away, call up Walter Hillborn, lawyer (of Loeb and Loeb) and ask him to get you in touch with some of the others.
Best regards,
Faithfully Yours,
Judge Joseph M. Proskauer. (Proskauer to Horkheimer, [July?] 1945, Max Horkheimer-Archiv, IX 150, 15)

122. For his part, Adorno was working on questions of casting and production. In a letter to Horkheimer from May of that year, while waiting for the first draft of the script, he writes: "Mit Lewis werde ich nochmals reden—alles, was Ihr Brief enthält, hatte ich ihm im wesentlichen bereits gesagt. Den Film ohne professional Schauspieler herzustellen hatte ich ihm sogleich vorgeschlagen, er meinte aber, es ginge nicht. Wenn ich das neue Skript erhielte, wäre is es natürlich gut." (I will once again discuss everything with Lewis; I had already told him essentially what your letter contains. I had immediately explained to him that the film should be delivered without professional actors, but he believes that wouldn't work. It would of course be good were I to receive the new script.) (Adorno to Horkheimer, May 23, 1945, Max Horkheimer-Archiv, VI, 1C, 58; also Adorno and Horkheimer, *Briefwechsel, 1927–1969*, vol. 3, *1945–1949*, 117).

123. Borowsky (1907–1969) was a Hollywood screenwriter whose script credits include the Delmer Daves–directed John Garfield vehicle *Pride of the Marines* (1945) and the Joseph L. Mankiewicz film noir *Somewhere in the Night* (1946). The more prolific Rivkin (1903–1990) includes among his credits the Humphrey Bogart classic *Dead Reckoning* (1947) and *Joe Smith, American* (1941), which, despite the title, has nothing to do with the founder of the Mormon church.

124. [Horkheimer and Adorno], "Memorandum on an Experimental Motion Picture," April 18, 1946, Max Horkheimer-Archiv, box IX, folder 150, 2.

125. I could find no further references to it in Horkheimer's papers, the AJC archives, the YIVO Center for Jewish Research, or Dore Schary's papers at the University of Wisconsin.

126. The parallels to *Barton Fink* (1991)—a film about the travails of a Jewish filmmaker trying to get his "honest" ode to the common man produced during the 1940s—are almost irresistible.

127. Two telegrams from October 1945, written to Horkheimer while he was in New York, indicate that Adorno was pursuing Eddie Golden, an Irish actor and independent producer. In the first he writes, "Leon Lewis informed me that independent producer Eddie Golden is strongly interested in production of picture we shall see him next week love Teddie." A second followed soon thereafter, indicating that the final draft was nearing completion: "Negotiations with Golden proceeding favorably next meeting scheduled for Sunday. Lewis most cooperative makes project his own. Golden seems genuinely interested. Promises having ready all details for final decision at your arrival. Suggest we settle ultimate write up" (Adorno telegrams to Horkheimer, October 1945, Max Horkheimer-Archiv, IX, 150, 14; also Adorno and Horkheimer, *Briefwechsel, 1927–1969*, vol. 3, *1945–1949*, 152, 163).

128. Horkheimer to Slawson, February 14, 1946, Max Horkheimer-Archiv, II, 14, 42–43.

129. Lazarsfeld to Horkheimer, July 14, 1947, Max Horkheimer-Archiv, II, 10, 291.

130. Agamben, "Dim Stockings," 50.

131. Ibid., 50.

4. "If There Should Be a Posterity"

1. Blanchot, "The Absence of the Book," 385–86.

2. A literal translation of the German title would be "The Betrayed."

3. Adorno, "From a Letter to Thomas Mann on His *Die Betrogene*," 319.

4. Huxley, *After Many a Summer Dies the Swan*, 13–15.

5. West, *The Day of the Locust*, 60–61.

6. Mann, *The Black Swan*, 139.

7. Ibid., 8.

8. Ibid., 9.

9. Ibid., 10.

10. Horkheimer and Adorno, *Dialectic of Enlightenment*, Jephcott translation, 42.

11. Adorno, "The Position of the Narrator in the Contemporary Novel," 32.

12. Ibid., 34.

13. Cain, *The Postman Always Rings Twice*, 116.

14. Ellery Queen, quoted in Adorno, *Minima Moralia*, 180–81.

15. For an excellent account of the relationship between American cultural consciousness and pulp fiction, see Rabinowitz, *Black and White and Noir*. In addition, these themes are addressed in Barnard, *The Great Depression and the Culture of Abundance*, as well as in Jenemann and Knighton, "Time, Transmission, Autonomy."

16. Pensky, "Editor's Introduction" to *The Actuality of Adorno*, 9.

17. Information about the history and development of the strip is notably scant. When I spoke to Bruce Thomas, senior archivist at the Chrysler Historical Collection in Detroit, he claimed that he had never heard of the strip, partly because, for the most part, the collection did not start gathering marketing material until 1962.

18. Adorno, "The Position of the Narrator in the Contemporary Novel," 31.

19. Riesman, with Glazer and Denny, *The Lonely Crowd*, 91.

20. Ibid., 93.

21. To quote the words of just one contemporary public figure who was a child at the time Riesman's book appeared: "Every nation, in every region, now has a decision to make. Either you are with us, or you are with the terrorists" (George W. Bush, "Address to a Joint Session of Congress and the American People," September 20, 2001). See my discussion of ambivalence in the coda.

22. Riesman, with Glazer and Denny, *The Lonely Crowd*, 100.

23. For an account of Legman's fascinating if ultimately somewhat sad career, see Holt, "Punch Line."

24. Legman, *Love and Death.*

25. Horkheimer and Adorno, *Dialectic of Enlightenment*, Jephcott translation, 113–14.

26. Sadly, Adorno didn't live long enough to find a reason to cite Legman's *Oragenitalism: Oral Techniques in Genital Excitation.*

27. Adorno, "The Stars Down to Earth," 62.

28. Ibid., 63.

29. See Radway, *A Feeling for Books,* and Rubin, *The Making of Middlebrow Culture.* On the whole, Radway's book, which deals entirely with the Book-of-the-Month Club, is much more even-handed and conciliatory to the club and its effects on the reading public.

30. Rubin, *The Making of Middlebrow Culture,* 97.

31. Turner, *Marketing Modernism between the Two World Wars,* 82.

32. Ibid., 81–82.

33. Jameson, *Late Marxism,* 165.

34. Mann, *Doctor Faustus,* 338.

35. Mann to Adorno, December 30, 1945, in *Letters of Thomas Mann, 1889–1955,* vol. 2, *1942–1955,* 493–96.

36. Bergsten, *Thomas Mann's "Doctor Faustus,"* 99–100.

37. Ibid., 101.

38. Here we risk running aground on the very rocks that the novel sets before us; namely, even the naturalist novel is a construction, albeit a more cohesive, less self-conscious one than its so-called new or postmodern heirs. That is its ideological ruse—and one that cinema capitalizes upon expertly: It presents to the reader a false life that seems real.

39. Mann to Adorno, *Letters of Thomas Mann*, vol. 2, *1942–1955*, 493–96.

40. Mann, *Doctor Faustus*, 251.

41. Mann to Adorno, *Letters of Thomas Mann*, vol. 2, *1942–1955*, 493–96.

42. Ibid.

43. Adorno, "The Stars Down to Earth," 67.

44. Mann to Adorno, *Letters of Thomas Mann*, vol. 2, *1942–1955*, 496.

45. Mann, *The Story of a Novel*, 74–75.

46. Ibid., 45–46.

47. Schmidt, "Mephistopheles in Hollywood," 155.

48. Thomas Mann to Erika Mann, November 6, 1948, *Letters of Thomas Mann*, vol. 2, *1942–1955*, 564.

49. Mann, *Doctor Faustus*, 462.

50. Ibid., 37–38.

51. Adorno, "On Dickens' *The Old Curiosity Shop*," 172.

52. Lukács, "The Tragedy of Modern Art," 84.

53. "By a remarkable coincidence (if coincidence it be) I had just finished reading *Dr. Faustus* when the Central Committee of the Communist Party of the Soviet Union published its decree on modern music. In Thomas Mann's novel this decree finds its fullest intellectual and artistic confirmation, particularly in those parts which so brilliantly describe modern music as such" (ibid., 71–72). One wonders what Lukács—a vocal opponent of the Frankfurt School and of Adorno— would have said had he known who actually wrote those descriptions.

54. Ibid., 82.

55. Ibid., 84.

56. For a fuller explanation of this argument, see Virno, "The Ambivalence of Disenchantment."

57. Blanchot, "The Absence of the Book," 383.

58. Mann, *Doctor Faustus*, 490.

59. Ibid., 491.

60. Adorno, "Toward a Portrait of Thomas Mann," 17–18.

61. Adorno, "From a Letter to Thomas Mann on His *Die Betrogene*," 319.

62. Ibid., 321.

63. Nicholsen, *Exact Imagination, Late Work*, 4.

64. Ibid., 4–5.

65. Bernstein, *The Philosophy of the Novel*, 219.

66. Ibid.

67. Mann, *Doctor Faustus*, 434.

68. Ibid., 442–43.

69. Adorno, *Minima Moralia*, 101.

70. Ibid.

Coda

1. Federal Bureau of Investigation, Los Angeles Bureau Report, September 25, 1950, LA123-436, obtained through the Freedom of Information Privacy Act (FOIA).

2. Interviews: LCD, April 13, 1951, p. 25, folder 155, box 15, series 7175, RG 1.2, RAC. See chapter 1 for the full quotation.

3. Roosevelt, Proclamation, "Aliens, Proclamation 2526, Alien Enemies—German," December 8, 1941, Freedom of Information Times, http://www.foitimes.com/internment/Proc2526.html.

4. Obtaining documents through the Freedom of Information Act (FOIA) is an at times aggravating and difficult process, in part because of the slowness with which this "free" information is disseminated, but also because documents about a specific individual might be spread throughout hundreds of files without necessarily being placed in the individual's own file. The FOIA staffs of the various government agencies I contacted have been extraordinarily helpful, but it should also be noted that I have asked for information regarding Adorno three separate times, and each time I have received widely different documents (and in one case, no documents at all). Thus, some of what I cite appears in Rubin's fine essay; some documents he has, I have yet to receive; and, I believe, some of what I will cite would be new to him.

5. Federal Bureau of Investigation, "Censorship Daily Reports," July 22, 1942, document 62-62736-1138 (obtained through FOIA).

6. Federal Bureau of Investigation, January 27, 1951, document 100-106126 (obtained through FOIA).

7. Horkheimer to U.S. Department of State Passport Divisions, June 9, 1953, United States Department of State, Theodor Adorno files (obtained through FOIA).

8. Stone to U.S. Department of State Passport Divisions, November 3, 1952, United States Department of State, Theodor Adorno files (obtained through FOIA).

9. "Affidavit by Native or Naturalized American to Explain Protracted Foreign Residence," October 28, 1953, United States Department of State, Theodor Adorno files (obtained through FOIA).

10. Adorno, "Scientific Experiences of a European Scholar in America," 239–40.

11. Greif, "Life after Theory."

12. Schama, "The Unloved American," *New Yorker*, March 10, 2003, http://www.newyorker.com/fact/content/articles/030310fa_fact.

13. Ibid.

14. Dickens, *American Notes for General Circulation* in *American Notes and Pictures from Italy,* 164.

15. Dickens, *The Life and Adventures of Martin Chuzzlewit,* 547.

16. Adorno, "What National Socialism Has Done to the Arts," 385–86.

17. Waugh, "The American Epoch in the Catholic Church," 152.

18. Quoted in Schmidt, "Mephistopheles in Hollywood," 150.

19. Tocqueville, *Democracy in America,* 2:43.

20. Adorno, "Scientific Experiences of a European Scholar in America," 213.

21. Werz, "Anti-Americanism and Ambivalence," 78.

22. Adorno, *Minima Moralia,* 132.

23. *USA Patriot Act,* HR 3162, 107th Cong., 1st sess., October 24, 2001, Sec. 412, Mandatory Detention of Suspected Terrorists; Habeas Corpus; Judicial Review, http://thomas.loc.gov/cgi-bin/query/F?c107:4:./temp/~c107CpUP6I:e258114:. As Georgetown University law professor David Cole writes of these provisions in the act: "Preventive detention is constitutional only in very limited circumstances, where there is demonstrated need for the detention—because of current dangerousness or risk of flight. Where an individual does not pose a threat to the community or a risk of flight, there is no justification for preventive detention, for there is literally nothing to prevent. Detention in such circumstances violates substantive due process. Yet it is authorized under the PATRIOT Act" (Cole, *Enemy Aliens,* 66).

24. Cole, *Enemy Aliens,* 66–67.

25. Lichtblau, "Large Volume of F.B.I. Files Alarms Activist Groups."

WORKS CITED

Archival Sources

American Jewish Committee Archives, New York.

American Jewish Committee Papers. YIVO Center for Jewish Research Archives, New York.

Federal Bureau of Investigation files, information received in response to Freedom of Information Act requests. Files consulted: Institute of Social Research; Theodor W. Adorno; Bertolt Brecht; Hanns Eisler; Max Horkheimer; Leo Lowenthal; Friedrich Pollock.

Institute of Social Research Files. University Archives and Columbiana Library. Columbia University, New York.

Lazarsfeld, Paul Felix. Papers. Columbia University Archives, New York.

Max Horkheimer-Archiv. Stadt- und Universitätsbibliothek, Frankfurt am Main.

Horkheimer/Pollock Archiv. Frankfurt am Main.

Rockefeller Foundation Archives. Rockefeller Archive Center, Sleepy Hollow, New York.

Published Works

Adorno, Theodor W. *Aesthetic Theory.* Edited by Gretl Adorno and Rolf Tiedemann. Translated by Robert Hullot-Kentor. Minneapolis: University of Minnesota Press, 1997.

————. "Aldous Huxley and Utopia." In *Prisms*, trans. Samuel and Shierry Weber, 95–118. Cambridge, Mass.: MIT Press, 1981.

————. "Analytical Study of NBC's *Music Appreciation Hour*." *Musical Quarterly* 78, no. 2 (Summer 1994): 325–77.

————. "Chaplin Times Two." Translated by John MacKay. *Yale Journal of Criticism* 9, no. 1 (1996): 57–61.

————. "Commitment." In *Notes to Literature*, trans. Shierry Weber Nicholsen, 2:76–94. New York: Columbia University Press, 1992.

————. *Critical Models: Interventions and Catchwords*. Translated by Henry W. Pickford. New York: Columbia University Press, 1998.

————. "The Culture Industry: Enlightenment as Mass Deception." In Max Horkheimer and Theodor W. Adorno, *Dialectic of Enlightenment*, trans. John Cumming, 120–67. New York: Continuum, 1986.

————. *Current of Music: Elements of a Radio Theory*. Edited by Robert Hullot-Kentor. Frankfurt am Main: Suhrkamp, 2006.

————. *Essays on Music*. Edited by Richard Leppert. Berkeley and Los Angeles: University of California Press, 2002.

————. "The Experiential Content of Hegel's Philosophy." In *Hegel: Three Studies*, trans. Shierry Weber Nicholsen, 53–88. Cambridge: MIT Press, 1993.

————. "The Form of the Phonograph Record." In *Essays on Music*, ed. Richard Leppert, 277–82. Berkeley and Los Angeles: University of California Press, 2002.

————. "Freudian Theory and the Pattern of Fascist Propaganda." In *The Culture Industry: Selected Essays on Mass Culture*, ed. J. M. Bernstein, 114–35. London: Routledge, 1991.

————. "From a Letter to Thomas Mann on His *Die Betrogene*." In *Notes to Literature*, trans. Shierry Weber Nicholsen, 2:318–21. New York: Columbia University Press, 1992.

————. *Hegel: Three Studies*. Translated by Shierry Weber Nicholsen. Cambridge: MIT Press, 1993.

————. "How to Look at Television." In *The Culture Industry: Selected Essays on Mass Culture*, ed. J. M. Bernstein, 136–53. London: Routledge, 1991.

————. *In Search of Wagner*. Translated by Rodney Livingstone. London: Verso, 1991.

————. *Introduction to the Sociology of Music*. Translated by E. B. Ashton. New York: Continuum, 1988.

————. "Jazz, Hot and Hybrid." *Studies in Philosophy and Social Science* 9, no. 1 (1941): 167–78.

————. "Looking Back on Surrealism." In *Notes to Literature*, trans. Shierry Weber Nicholsen, 1:86–90. New York: Columbia University Press, 1992.

————. "Message in a Bottle." In *Mapping Ideology*, ed. Slavoj Žižek, 34–45. New York: Verso, 1994.

———. *Minima Moralia: Reflections from Damaged Life.* Translated by E. F. N. Jephcott. London: Verso, 1974.

———. *Negative Dialectics.* Translated by E. B. Ashton. New York: Continuum, 1973.

———. *Notes to Literature.* 2 vols. Translated by Shierry Weber Nicholsen. New York: Columbia University Press, 1991–92.

———. "On Dickens' *The Old Curiosity Shop.*" In *Notes to Literature*, trans. Shierry Weber Nicholsen, 2:171–77. New York: Columbia University Press, 1992.

———. "On Jazz." In *Essays on Music*, ed. Richard Leppert, 470–95. Berkeley and Los Angeles: University of California Press, 2002.

———. "On Popular Music." With George Simpson. *Studies in Philosophy and Social Science* 9, no. 1 (1941): 17–48.

———. "On the Fetish-Character in Music and the Regression of Listening." In *Essays on Music*, ed. Richard Leppert, 288–317. Berkeley and Los Angeles: University of California Press, 2002.

———. "On the Logic of the Social Sciences." In Theodor W. Adorno, Hans Albert, Ralf Dahrendorf, Jürgen Habermas, Harald Pilot, and Karl Popper, *The Positivist Dispute in German Sociology*, 105–22. New York: Harper and Row, 1976.

———. "The Position of the Narrator in the Contemporary Novel." In *Notes to Literature*, trans. Shierry Weber Nicholsen, 1:30–36. New York: Columbia University Press, 1992.

———. *Prisms.* Translated by Samuel and Shierry Weber. Cambridge: MIT Press, 1981.

———. *The Psychological Technique of Martin Luther Thomas' Radio Addresses.* Stanford, Calif.: Stanford University Press, 2000.

———. "The Radio Symphony." In *Radio Research, 1941*, ed. Paul F. Lazarsfeld and Frank Stanton, 110–39. New York: Duell, Sloan and Pearce, 1941.

———. "Research Project on Anti-Semitism: Idea of the Project." In *"The Stars Down to Earth" and Other Essays on the Irrational in Culture*, ed. Stephen Crook, 135–61. London: Routledge, 1994.

———. Reviews of *American Jazz Music* and *Jazz, Hot and Hybrid. Studies in Philosophy and Social Science* 9, no. 1 (1941): 167–78.

———. "The Schema of Mass Culture." In *The Culture Industry: Selected Essays on Mass Culture*, ed. J. M. Bernstein, 53–84. London: Routledge, 1991.

———. "Scientific Experiences of a European Scholar in America." In *Critical Models: Catchwords and Interventions*, trans. Henry Pickford, 215–42. New York: Columbia University Press, 1998.

———. "A Social Critique of Radio Music." *Kenyon Review* 7, no. 2 (Spring 1945): 208–17.

———. "Sociology and Empirical Research." In Theodor W. Adorno, Hans Albert, Ralf Dahrendorf, Jürgen Habermas, Harald Pilot, and Karl Popper,

The Positivist Dispute in German Sociology, 68–86. New York: Harper and Row, 1976.

———. "The Stars Down to Earth." In *"The Stars Down to Earth" and Other Essays on the Irrational in Culture*, ed. Stephen Crook, 34–127. London: Routledge, 1994.

———. *"The Stars Down to Earth" and Other Essays on the Irrational in Culture*. Edited by Stephen Crook. London: Routledge, 1994.

———. "Theodor W. Adorno's Dream Transcripts." Introduced and translated by Anne Halley. *Antioch Review* 55, no. 1 (Winter 1997): 57–95.

———. "Toward a Portrait of Thomas Mann." In *Notes to Literature*, trans. Shierry Weber Nicholsen, 2:12–19. New York: Columbia University Press, 1992.

———. "Transparencies on Film." In *The Culture Industry: Selected Essays on Mass Culture*, ed. J. M. Bernstein, 154–61. London: Routledge, 1991.

———. "Traumprotokolle." In *Gesammelte Schriften*, 20.2. Edited by Rolf Tiedemann, 572–82. Frankfurt am Main: Suhrkamp, 1997.

———. "What National Socialism Has Done to the Arts." In *Essays on Music*, ed. Richard Leppert, 373–90. Berkeley: University of California Press, 2002.

Adorno, Theodor W., Hans Albert, Ralf Dahrendorf, Jürgen Habermas, Harald Pilot, and Karl Popper. *The Positivist Dispute in German Sociology*. New York: Harper and Row, 1976.

Adorno, Theodor W., and Walter Benjamin. *The Complete Correspondence, 1928–1940*. Edited by Henri Lonitz. Translated by Nicholas Walker. Cambridge, Mass.: Harvard University Press, 1999.

Adorno, T. W., Else Frenkel-Brunswik, Daniel J. Levinson, and R. Nevitt Sanford. *The Authoritarian Personality*. New York: Norton, 1969. (Orig. pub. 1950.)

Adorno, Theodor W., and Max Horkheimer. *Briefwechsel, 1927–1969*. 4 vols. Frankfurt am Main: Suhrkamp, 2003–2006.

Agamben, Giorgio. "Dim Stockings." In *The Coming Community*, trans. Michael Hardt, 47–50. Minneapolis: University of Minnesota Press, 1993.

———. "The Prince and the Frog: The Question of Method in Adorno and Benjamin." In *Infancy and History: The Destruction of Experience*, trans. Liz Heron, 107–24. London: Verso, 1993.

Apostolidis, Paul. *Stations of the Cross: Adorno and Christian Right Radio*. Durham, N.C.: Duke University Press, 2000.

Arendt, Hannah. "Society and Culture." In *Culture for the Millions? Mass Media in Modern Society*, ed. Norman Jacobs, 43–58. Boston: Beacon Press, 1961.

Asimov, Isaac. *Foundation*. New York: Ballantine Books, 1951.

Attali, Jacques. *Noise: The Political Economy of Music*. Translated by Brian Massumi. Minneapolis: University of Minnesota Press, 1985.

Barnard, Rita. *The Great Depression and the Culture of Abundance*. Cambridge: Cambridge University Press, 1995.

Beller, Jonathan L. "Capital/Cinema." In *Deleuze and Guattari: New Mappings in Politics, Philosophy, and Culture*, ed. Eleanor Kaufman and Kevin Jon Heller, 77–95. Minneapolis: University of Minnesota Press, 1998.

Bergsten, Gunilla. *Thomas Mann's "Doctor Faustus": The Sources and Structure of the Novel*. Translated by Krishna Winston. Chicago: University of Chicago Press, 1969.

Bernstein, J. M. *The Philosophy of the Novel: Lukács, Marxism, and the Dialectics of Form*. Minneapolis: University of Minnesota Press, 1984.

Blanchot, Maurice. "The Absence of the Book." Translated by Lydia Davis. In *Deconstruction in Context*, ed. Mark Taylor, 382–95. Chicago: University of Chicago Press, 1986.

Bradley, Francis H. *Appearance and Reality: A Metaphysical Essay*. Oxford: Clarendon Press, 1930.

Brecht, Bertolt. *Brecht on Film and Radio*. Translated and edited by Marc Silberman. London: Methuen, 2000.

Cain, James M. *Double Indemnity*. New York: Vintage, 1936.

———. *The Postman Always Rings Twice*. New York: Vintage, 1934.

Cantril, Hadley. With Hazel Gaudet and Herta Herzog. *The Invasion from Mars: A Study in the Psychology of Panic*. New York: Harper Torchbooks, 1966. (Orig. pub. 1940.)

Claussen, Detlev. *Theodor W. Adorno: Ein Letztes Genie*. Frankfurt am Main: Fischer, 2003.

Cole, David. *Enemy Aliens: Double Standards and Constitutional Freedoms in the War on Terrorism*. New York: New Press, 2003.

Columbia Broadcasting System. *Broadcast Advertising: The Sales Voice of America*. New York: Columbia Broadcasting System, 1929.

———. *"Seems Radio Is Here to Stay": A Columbia Workshop Production by Norman Corwin*. Illustrations by Rudolph Charles von Ripper. New York: Columbia Broadcasting System, 1939.

———. *The Very Rich: An Unsentimental Journey into Homes We Often Read About but So Seldom See (Their Gates Are Too High)*. New York: Columbia Broadcasting System, [1937].

———. *We Don't Know Why They Listen (so much!)*. New York: Columbia Broadcasting System, 1949.

Crary, Jonathan. *Techniques of the Observer: On Vision and Modernity in the Nineteenth Century*. Cambridge: MIT Press, 1992.

Davis, Mike. *City of Quartz: Excavating the Future in Los Angeles*. New York: Vintage, 1992.

Debord, Guy. *The Society of the Spectacle*. Translated by Donald Nicholson-Smith. New York: Zone Books, 1995.

Demirovic, Alex. *Der nonkoformistische Intellektuelle: Die Entwicklung der Kritischen Theorie zur Frankfurter Schule*. Frankfurt am Main: Suhrkamp, 1999.

Dickens, Charles. *American Notes and Pictures from Italy.* London: Everyman, 1997.

———. *The Life and Adventures of Martin Chuzzlewit* (1844). London: Oxford University Press, 1951.

Eisenstein, Sergei M. "Our 'October': Beyond the Played and the Non-Played." In *Selected Works,* vol. 1, *1922–34,* ed. and trans. Richard Taylor, 100–105. London: BFI Press, 1988.

Eisler, Hanns, and Theodor W. Adorno. *Composing for the Films.* Atlantic Highlands, N.J.: Athlone Press, 1994.

Fearing, Kenneth. *The Big Clock.* New York: Harper and Row, 1946.

———. *Clark Gifford's Body.* New York: Random House, 1942.

———. "Radio Blues." In *Dead Reckoning,* 49. New York: Random House, 1938.

———. "U.S. Writers in War." *Poetry: A Magazine of Verse* 56, no. 6 (September 1940): 318–23.

Friedrich, Otto. *City of Nets: A Portrait of Hollywood in the 1940s.* Berkeley and Los Angeles: University of California Press, 1986.

Gabbard, Krin. "Signifyin(g) the Phallus: Mo' Better Blues and Representations of the Jazz Trumpet." *Cinema Journal* 32, no. 1 (Fall 1992): 43–62.

Gorbman, Claudia. "Hanns Eisler in Hollywood." *Screen* 32, no. 3 (Autumn 1991): 272–85.

Greif, Mark. "Life after Theory." *The American Prospect Online,* August 1, 2004. http://www.prospect.org/web/page.ww?section=root&name=ViewPrint&articleId=8138.

Gross, Harvey. "Adorno in Los Angeles: The Intellectual in Emigration." *Humanities in Society* 2, no. 4 (Fall 1979): 339–51.

Habermas, Jürgen. "The Public Sphere: An Encyclopedia Article (1964)," *New German Critique* 3 (Fall 1974): 49–55.

Hansen, Miriam. "Benjamin, Cinema, and Experience: 'The Blue Flower in the Land of Technology.'" *New German Critique* 40 (Winter 1987): 179–224.

———. "Introduction to Adorno, 'Transparencies on Film' (1966)." *New German Critique* 24–25 (Fall–Winter 1981–82): 199–205.

———. "Kracauer's Early Writings on Film and Mass Culture." *New German Critique* 54 (Fall 1991): 47–76.

———. "Mass Culture as Hieroglyphic Writing: Adorno, Derrida, Kracauer." In *The Actuality of Adorno: Critical Essays on Adorno and the Postmodern,* ed. Max Pensky, 83–111. Albany: SUNY Press, 1997.

———. "Of Mice and Ducks: Benjamin and Adorno on Disney." *South Atlantic Quarterly* 92, no. 1 (Winter 1993): 27–61.

Hardt, Hanno. *Critical Communication Studies: Communication, History, and Theory in America.* London: Routledge, 1992.

Harrison's Reports. Review of *Syncopation,* May 9, 1942.

Hilmes, Michelle. *Radio Voices: American Broadcasting, 1922–1952.* Minneapolis: University of Minnesota Press, 1997.

Holt, Jim. "Punch Line: The History of Dirty Jokes and Those Who Collect Them." *New Yorker*, April 19 and 26, 2004. http://www.newyorker.com/critics/books/ ?040419crbo_books.

Horkheimer, Max. "Preface." *Studies in Philosophy and Social Science* 9, no. 3 (April 1941): 365–88.

Horkheimer, Max, and Theodor W. Adorno. *Dialectic of Enlightenment.* Translated by John Cumming. New York: Continuum, 1986.

———. *Dialectic of Enlightenment: Philosophical Fragments.* Edited by Gunzelin Schmid Noerr. Translated by Edmund Jephcott. Stanford, Calif.: Stanford University Press, 2002.

Huxley, Aldous. *After Many a Summer Dies the Swan.* Chicago: Ivan R. Dee, 1993.

Huyssen, Andreas. "Adorno in Reverse: From Hollywood to Richard Wagner." *New German Critique* 29 (Spring–Summer 1983): 8–38.

Institut für Sozialforschung. *Authority and the Family.* Translated by A. Lissance. New York: State Department of Social Welfare, 1937.

Jäger, Lorenz. *Adorno: A Political Biography.* Translated by Stewart Spencer. New Haven, Conn.: Yale University Press, 2004.

Jameson, Fredric. *Late Marxism: Adorno, or The Persistence of the Dialectic.* London: Verso, 1990.

———. *Marxism and Form.* Princeton, N.J.: Princeton University Press, 1971.

Jay, Martin. *Adorno.* Cambridge, Mass.: Harvard University Press, 1984.

———. "Adorno in America," in *Permanent Exiles: Essays on the Intellectual Migration from Germany to America.* New York: Columbia University Press, 1986.

———. *The Dialectical Imagination: A History of the Frankfurt School and the Institute of Social Research, 1923–1950.* Boston: Little, Brown, 1973.

———. "The Frankfurt School in Exile." In *Permanent Exiles: Essays on the Intellectual Migration from Germany to America,* 28–61. New York: Columbia University Press, 1985.

———. *Permanent Exiles: Essays on the Intellectual Migration from Germany to America.* New York: Columbia University Press, 1985.

Jenemann, David. "The Hole Is the True: Deleuze-Cinema-Utopia-Adorno." *Polygraph* 14 (2003): 77–101.

———. Review of *Stations of the Cross: Adorno and Christian Right Radio. Cultural Critique* 50 (Winter 2002): 223–29.

Jenemann, David, and Andrew Knighton. "Time, Transmission, Autonomy: What Praxis Means in the Novels of Kenneth Fearing." In *The Novel and the American Left,* ed. Janet Galligani Casey, 172–94. Iowa City: University of Iowa Press, 2004.

Joyce, James. *Ulysses.* New York: Vintage, 1986.

Kant, Immanuel. *Critique of Judgment.* Translated by Werner S. Pluhar. Indianapolis, Ind.: Hackett, 1987.

Kavina, Lydia. "My Experience with the Theremin." *Leonardo Music Journal* 6 (1996): 51–56.

Kittler, Friedrich A. *Gramophone, Film, Typewriter.* Translated by Geoffrey Winthrop-Young and Michael Wutz. Stanford, Calif.: Stanford University Press, 1999.

Kluge, Alexander. "On New German Cinema, Art, Enlightenment, and the Public Sphere: An Interview with Alexander Kluge." By Stuart Liebman. *October* 46 (Fall 1988): 23–59.

Koch, Gertrud. "Mimesis and *Bilderverbot.*" *Screen* 34, no. 3 (Autumn 1993): 211–22.

Kracauer, Siegfried. *From Caligari to Hitler: A Psychological History of the German Film.* Princeton, N.J.: Princeton University Press, 1947.

———. *Theory of Film: The Redemption of Physical Reality.* Princeton, N.J.: Princeton University Press, 1997.

Krane, Jim. "FCC's Powell Declares TiVo 'God's Machine.'" *SFGate.com*, January 10, 2003. http://www.sfgate.com/ (accessed January 31, 2003).

Lazarsfeld, Paul F. "An Episode in the History of Social Research: A Memoir." In *The Intellectual Migration: Europe and America, 1930–1960,* ed. Donald Fleming and Bernard Bailyn, 270–337. Cambridge, Mass.: Belknap Press of Harvard University Press, 1969.

———. "Introduction by the Guest Editor." *Journal of Applied Psychology* 24, no. 6 (December 1940): 661–64.

———. *Radio and the Printed Page.* New York: Duell, Sloan and Pearce, 1940.

———. "Remarks on Administrative and Critical Communications Research." *Studies in Philosophy and Social Science* 9, no. 3 (Spring 1941): 2–16.

———. "Some Remarks on the Typological Procedures in Social Research." *Zeitschrift für Sozialforschung* 6, no. 1 (1937): 119–39.

Legman, Gershon. *Love and Death: A Study in Censorship.* New York: Breaking Point, 1949.

———. *Oragenitalism: Oral Techniques in Genital Excitation.* New York: Julian Press, 1969.

Levin, Thomas Y. With Michael von der Linn. "Elements of a Radio Theory: Adorno and the Princeton Radio Research Project." *Musical Quarterly* 78, no. 2 (Summer 1994): 316–24.

Levinas, Emmanuel. "The Trace of the Other." Translated by A. Lingis. In *Deconstruction in Context,* ed. Mark Taylor, 345–59. Chicago: University of Chicago Press, 1986.

Levy, Mark R. "The Lazarsfeld-Stanton Program Analyzer: An Historical Note." *Journal of Communication* 32, no. 4 (Autumn 1982): 30–38.

Lichtblau, Eric. "Large Volume of F.B.I. Files Alarms Activist Groups." *New York Times,* July 18, 2005.

Lukács, Georg. "The Tragedy of Modern Art." In *Essays on Thomas Mann,* trans. Stanley Mitchell. London: Merlin Press, 1964.

Lyotard, Jean-François. "Adorno as the Devil." *Telos* 19 (Spring 1974): 128–37.

MacRae, D. G. "Frankfurters." *New Society,* March 28, 1974, 786.

Mann, Thomas. *The Black Swan.* Translated by Willard R. Trask. New York: Harcourt Brace Jovanovich, 1980.

———. *Doctor Faustus.* Translated by H. T. Lowe Porter. New York: Vintage International, 1992.

———. *Letters of Thomas Mann, 1889–1955.* Vol. 2, *1942–1955.* Translated by Richard and Clara Winston. London: Secker and Warburg, 1970.

———. *The Story of a Novel.* Translated by Richard and Clara Winston. New York: Alfred A. Knopf, 1961.

Marx, Karl. *Capital.* 3 vols. Trans. Samuel Moore and Edward Aveling. New York: International Publishers, 1967.

———. *The Portable Karl Marx.* Edited by Eugene Kamenka. London: Penguin, 1983.

McClary, Susan. "The Blasphemy of Talking Politics during Bach Year." In *Music and Society: The Politics of Composition, Performance, and Reception,* ed. Richard Leppert and Susan McClary, 13–62. Cambridge: Cambridge University Press, 1987.

Merleau-Ponty, Maurice. *Phenomenology of Perception.* Translated by Colin Smith. London: Routledge, 2002.

Montague, Stephen. "Rediscovering Leon Theremin." *Tempo* 177 (June 1991): 18–23.

Morrison, David E. "*Kultur* and Culture: The Case of Theodor W. Adorno and Paul F. Lazarsfeld." *Social Research* 45, no. 2 (Summer 1978): 331–55.

———. *The Search for a Method: Focus Groups and the Development of Mass Communication Research.* London: University of Luton Press, 1998.

Müller-Doohm, Stefan. *Adorno: A Biography.* Translated by Rodney Livingstone. Cambridge: Polity, 2005.

Mulvey, Laura. "Visual Pleasure and the Narrative Cinema." *Screen* 16, no. 3 (Autumn 1975): 6–18.

National Broadcasting Company. *Alice in Sponsor-Land: A Chronicle of the Adventures of Alice, the Hatter, the March Hare, and the Dormouse in That Twentieth Century Wonderland on the Other Side of Your Radio Loudspeaker.* Illustrated by Bernard Tobey. New York: National Broadcasting Company, 1941.

———. *Broadcast Advertising: A Study of the Radio Medium—the Fourth Dimension of Advertising.* Vol. 1. New York: National Broadcasting Company, 1929.

———. *Broadcasting in the Public Interest.* New York: National Broadcasting Company, 1939.

———. *It's Not Done with Mirrors.* New York: National Broadcasting Company, 1940.

———. *"Music Appreciation Hour" Instructor's Manual.* New York: National Broadcasting Company, 1931.

———. [*Musical Leadership Maintained by NBC.*] New York: National Broadcasting Company, 1938.

———. *The Place of Radio in Education.* New York: National Broadcasting Company, 1939.

———. *What Goes On behind Your Radio Dial?* New York: National Broadcasting Company, 1943.

———. *The Word of God: Fifteen Years of Religious Broadcasts. The National Broadcasting Company, 1926–1941.* New York: National Broadcasting Company, 1941.

National Public Radio. "Music Testing." *On the Media,* NPR, April 20, 2002.

Nielsen, Arthur C. *How You Can Get the Ideal Radio Research Service.* N.p.: A. C. Nielsen Company, 1946.

Newman, Kathy M. *Radio Active: Advertising and Consumer Activism, 1935–1947.* Berkeley and Los Angeles: University of California Press, 2004.

Nicholsen, Shierry Weber. *Exact Imagination, Late Work: On Adorno's Aesthetics.* Cambridge: MIT Press, 1997.

Nietszche, Friedrich. *Beyond Good and Evil.* Translated by Walter Kaufman. New York: Vintage, 1989.

Oja, Carol J. "Women Patrons and Activists for Modernist Music: New York in the 1920s." *Modernism/Modernity* 4, no. 1 (1997): 129–55.

Orton, Richard, and Hugh Davies. "Theremin." In *The New Grove Dictionary of Music and Musicians,* 25:386–87. London: Macmillan, 2001.

Pensky, Max. "Beyond the Message in the Bottle: The Other Critical Theory." *Constellations* 10, no. 1 (2003): 135–44.

———. "Editor's Introduction: Adorno's Actuality." In *The Actuality of Adorno,* ed. Max Pensky, 1–21. Albany: SUNY Press, 1997.

Pepper, Thomas Adam. *Singularities: Extremes of Theory in the Twentieth Century.* Cambridge: Cambridge University Press, 1997.

Popper, Karl. "The Logic of the Social Sciences." In Theodor Adorno, Hans Albert, Ralf Dahrendorf, Jürgen Habermas, Harald Pilot, and Karl Popper, *The Positivist Dispute in German Sociology,* 87–104. New York: Harper and Row, 1976.

Rabinowitz, Paula. *Black and White and Noir: America's Pulp Modernism.* New York: Columbia University Press, 2002.

Radway, Janice A. *A Feeling for Books: The Book-of-the-Month Club, Literary Taste, and Middle-Class Desire.* Chapel Hill: University of North Carolina Press, 1997.

Riesman, David. With Nathan Glazer and Reul Denny. *The Lonely Crowd: A Study of the Changing American Character.* Abridged ed. New Haven, Conn.: Yale University Press, 1961.

Rubin, Andrew N. "The Adorno Files." In *Adorno: Critical Reader,* ed. Nigel Gibson and Andrew Rubin, 172–90. Oxford: Blackwell, 2002.

Rubin, Joan Shelley. *The Making of Middlebrow Culture.* Chapel Hill: University of North Carolina Press, 1992.

Said, Edward. "The Future of Criticism." In *"Reflections on Exile" and Other Essays*, 165–72. Cambridge, Mass.: Harvard University Press, 2000.

Schama, Simon. "The Unloved American: Two Centuries of Alienating Europe." *New Yorker*, March 3, 2003. http://www.newyorker.com/fact/content/articles/030310fa_fact.

Schmidt, James. "Mephistopheles in Hollywood: Adorno, Mann, and Schoenberg." In *The Cambridge Companion to Adorno*, ed. Tom Huhn, 148–80. Cambridge: Cambridge University Press, 2004.

Shils, Edward. "Daydreams and Nightmares: Reflections on the Criticism of Mass Culture." *Sewanee Review* 65, no. 4 (October–December 1957): 587–608.

———. "Mass Society and Its Culture." In *Culture for the Millions? Mass Media in Modern Society*, ed. Norman Jacobs, 28–42. Boston: Beacon Press, 1961.

Shirer, William. *The Rise and Fall of the Third Reich*. New York: Fawcett Crest, 1950.

Simonet, Thomas. "Industry." *Film Comment* 14, no. 1 (January–February 1978): 72–73.

Stemmrich, Gregor. "Dan Graham's 'Cinema' and Film Theory." *Media Art Net*. http://www.medienkunstnetz.de/themes/art_and_cinematography/graham/.

Stephan, Alexander. *Communazis: FBI Surveillance of German Émigré Writers*. Translated by John van Huerck. New Haven, Conn.: Yale University Press, 2000.

Stern, Guenter. "Spuk und Radio." *Anbruch* 12, no. 2 (February 1930): 65–66.

Theremin, Leon S. "The Design of a Musical Instrument Based on Cathode Relays." Translated by Oleg Petrishev. *Leonardo Music Journal* 6 (1996): 49–50.

Tocqueville, Alexis de. *Democracy in America*. 2 vols. Translated by Henry Reve. Revised by Francis Bowen. Edited by Phillips Bradley. New York: Vintage, 1945.

Turner, Catherine. *Marketing Modernism between the Two World Wars*. Amherst: University of Massachusetts Press, 2003.

Variety. Review of *Syncopation*, May 6, 1942.

Virno, Paolo. "The Ambivalence of Disenchantment." In *Radical Thought in Italy: A Potential Politics*, ed. Paolo Virno and Michael Hardt, 13–34. Minneapolis: University of Minnesota Press, 1996.

Wakeman, Frederic. *The Hucksters*. New York: Rinehart, 1946.

Waugh, Evelyn. "The American Epoch in the Catholic Church." *Life*, September 19, 1949, 134ff.

Werz, Michael. "Anti-Americanism and Ambivalence: Remarks on an Ideology in Historical Transformation." *Telos* 129 (Fall–Winter 2004): 75–95.

West, Nathanael. *The Day of the Locust*. New York: New Directions, 1933.

Wiggershaus, Rolf. *The Frankfurt School: Its History, Theories, and Political Significance*. Translated by Michael Robertson. Cambridge: MIT Press, 1995.

Witkin, Robert W. *Adorno on Popular Culture*. London: Routledge, 2004.

INDEX

David Jenemann teaches English as well as film and television studies at the University of Vermont. He has published essays on Theodor Adorno, Gilles Deleuze, and the novels of Kenneth Fearing. He is researching a book on anti-intellectualism in the United States.